Arabian Oasis City
The Transformation of 'Unayzah

MODERN MIDDLE EAST SERIES, NO. 15
SPONSORED BY THE CENTER FOR
MIDDLE EASTERN STUDIES
THE UNIVERSITY OF TEXAS AT AUSTIN

ARABIAN OASIS CITY

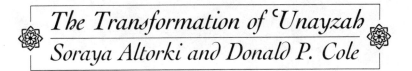

The Transformation of 'Unayzah
Soraya Altorki and Donald P. Cole

UNIVERSITY OF TEXAS PRESS, AUSTIN

First Edition, 1989

Requests for permission to reproduce material from this work should
be sent to Permissions, University of Texas Press, Box 7819, Austin,
Texas 78713-7819.

∞   The paper used in this publication meets the minimum
requirements of American National Standard for Information
Sciences—Permanence of Paper for Printed Library Materials,
ANSI Z39.48-1984.

Altorki, Soraya.
    Arabian oasis city : the transformation of ʿUnayzah / Soraya
Altorki and Donald P. Cole.—1st ed.
        p.   cm.—(Modern Middle East series ; no. 15)
    Bibliography: p.
    Includes index.
    ISBN 0-292-78517-8 (alk. paper)   ISBN 0-292-78518-6 (pbk)
    1. ʿUnayzah (Saudi Arabia)—Economic conditions—Case
studies.   2. ʿUnayzah (Saudi Arabia)—Social conditions—Case
studies.   I. Cole, Donald Powell.   II. Title.   III. Series:
Modern Middle East series (Austin, Tex.) ; no. 15.
HC415.33.Z7U533   1989
330.953'8—DC19   88-38115
                                                         CIP

CONTENTS

PREFACE

The collaboration between the two authors, without which this study would have been impossible, began some twenty years ago when we were both graduate students in anthropology at the University of California, Berkeley. Cole was planning to do his dissertation field research in ʿUnayzah, the hometown of Altorki's father. Although she had been born and raised in Jiddah, where her father had migrated early in this century, and had never been to ʿUnayzah, she had often heard her father and other relatives speak of the city. Also, as a Saudi Arabian, she knew a great deal about the culture and society of the Arabian Peninsula. As a result, we spent many hours together discussing Arabia and the Middle East in general and ʿUnayzah in particular.

Equally, if not more important, Altorki encouraged Cole to persist in his efforts to obtain a visa to go to Saudi Arabia and provided the personal contacts which eventually made it possible for him to go there, for the first time, in 1968. Without her support and that of members of her family (in particular, her brother Ahmad Muhammad Sulayman Altorki and her cousin ʿAbd al-ʿAziz ʿAbd Allah Altorki), Cole's ability as a foreigner to conduct academic anthropological research in Saudi Arabia would have been difficult, if not impossible. For this personal trust and support over two decades and for their undying belief in the value of social science field research in Saudi Arabia, Cole would like to express his deepest gratitude.

As friends and as colleagues at the American University in Cairo, we have continued our discussions of Saudi Arabian culture and society, and when it happened that both were eligible for sabbatical leaves at the same time, we decided to jointly design and conduct a research project together in Saudi Arabia. Cole had originally planned to do his dissertation research in ʿUnayzah but had changed his research topic and conducted fieldwork among the Al Murrah Bedouin, completing the first academic anthropological study of a tribe in Saudi Arabia (Cole 1971, 1973, 1975, 1981, 1982, 1984). Altorki had conducted the first anthropological fieldwork among urban elite families in Jiddah (Altorki 1973, 1977, 1980, 1982, 1986). Our research experiences, as it were, had been at two extremes of Saudi Arabian society—a remote and highly dispersed Bedouin tribe and a group of elite families in the cosmopolitan city of Jiddah. Also, our most intensive fieldwork had been done before the economic boom of the late 1970s and early 1980s induced many changes in the standards and patterns of living for the vast majority of Saudi Arabians.

More importantly, we both recognized the limitations that gender placed on the work of the single anthropologist in Saudi Arabia, where a high degree of gender segregation is maintained. Cole was aware that his previous research was partially biased by his inability, as a male, to formally interview female members of the community he had studied. While Altorki had been able to interview some males in very formal and restricted settings, she knew there was much of the world of males that, being female, she could not observe or have direct access to.

The present research was designed as a case study of change in a small urban community in central Saudi Arabia. Although, as shown in the introduction, no claim is made that this community is typical or in any way representative of similar communities in Saudi Arabia, ʿUnayzah was chosen because it was neither at the remote Bedouin nor cosmopolitan elite extremes of Saudi Arabian society. It was also chosen because we both had long been interested in the city and knew many people from it and because Altorki had relatives there who—given the cultural norms of Saudi Arabian society—would provide an appropriate setting for her to reside and conduct fieldwork in.

In conducting the fieldwork for this study, we lived in ʿUnayzah between October 1986 and January 1987. Each lived and worked independently of the other—Cole resided in a hotel in the new part of town, while Altorki resided in the home of a relative in the old part of town. Although each worked independently of the other, we maintained regular contact and jointly agreed on all aspects of the strategies of conducting the research.

We conducted interviews with a wide range of officials, merchants, farmers, craftspeople, and teachers and other state employees. Although many interviews were conducted with individuals, both researchers conducted group interviews with people of different generations to check the effect of generational differences on certain issues. Observational visits were made to farms, the market, and various institutions in the community. Case studies were made of farms, farmers, craftspeople, traders, agricultural engineers, teachers, and private voluntary organizations. After a general examination of the range of variation, cases were selected in consultation with key informants. Participant observation was also conducted in a wide range of social settings in the community. Throughout, interviews on a given subject were checked with others until patterns were uncovered and information became repetitive. Statistical data were gathered, where appropriate, from various official institutions.

Some areas were easier to explore than others. For example, men were eager to describe their business enterprises or the work they were engaged in but they did not talk about the female members of their families or their own family life with the male anthropologist. Women sellers were unwilling, at first, to divulge information on their current business dealings to the female anthropologist but were not reluctant to discuss past dealings or their previous involvement in agricultural work. It took a long period of contact before a measure of trust was established, but the crucial break came as a result of Altorki asserting previous relationships in the community; after that, the women were willing to discuss their current business activities. Also, in contrast to the men, who did not discuss their relationships with female members of their families, the women were quite open in discussing their relationships with male family members with the female researcher.

All of the work by Cole was conducted with males. He systematically visited the total range of production sites in ʿUnayzah, where he made observations and conducted interviews with owners, managers, and workers. He made observations in the market and interviewed male merchants. He conducted interviews with state officials and employees, with men engaged in private voluntary organizations, and with other key male informants who were introduced to him as being especially knowledgeable on a particular topic. He also regularly attended a wide range of male social gatherings as a participant observer. The men he interviewed and those with whom he socialized as a participant observer were from different socioeconomic levels and ranged in age from about twenty-five to ninety-five. Depending on the subject, topics of discussion dealt with the present, the past, or both.

Throughout his research in ʿUnayzah, Cole was accompanied and assisted by Salih ʿAbd al-Karim al-Marzuqi, a young man in his early thirties who has always resided in the city and who has an extremely wide range of connections with the various components of the community. Not only was he an excellent sociological guide but he took a keen interest in the study (because it was of his own community) and often went out of his way to help the anthropologist in his quest to obtain some needed information. His important contribution to this study is gratefully acknowledged. Cole also expresses his thanks to ʿAbd Allah al-Hatlani, who often accompanied him and introduced him to key informants, and to his friends from a visit to ʿUnayzah eighteen years earlier, ʿAbd ar-Rahman al-Buthi and ʿAli Altorki, both of whom received him as a brother and with whom he had lengthy and stimulating discussions on numerous occasions.

Altorki's work was primarily with females, although, being veiled, she conducted interviews with a few male informants, most of whom were introduced to her by relatives. She systematically observed the women's market and interviewed women sellers there. She also conducted interviews with women who formerly worked in agriculture and with the total range of women engaged in different types of employment today. She interviewed key informants and conducted participant observation in a wide range of women's social gatherings, with relatives, and in women's places of work. Her informants ranged in age from about twenty to ninety and included women from all socioeconomic levels. Topics of discussion dealt with the past, the present, or both.

Almost all her informants were friendly and cooperative. However, three women in particular were invaluable to the continuation of her research. Their insight into their own culture and their assistance contributed greatly to the realization of this project. Although they must remain anonymous, Altorki expresses her deepest gratitude to them.

In the presentation and analysis of the data, many quotations from interviews are presented. In all cases, pseudonyms are used instead of the actual names of informants. In accordance with usage in ʿUnayzah, informants are usually referred to as either *Abu*, "Father," or *Umm*,

"Mother," of his/her son's name. Even when the informant had not yet had a son, a son's name is given, as it is assumed by everyone in 'Unayzah that he/she will eventually, *inshallah,* have a son. The pseudonyms given are typical of names used in 'Unayzah and throughout Najd.

Throughout the book, amounts of money are quoted in Saudi Arabian riyals. At the time of fieldwork, one U.S. dollar was equivalent to approximately 3.65 riyals. The transliteration of Arabic words is based on the system of transliteration used by the Library of Congress. However, all diacritical marks have been omitted with the exception of the hamza (') and the 'ayn ('). Long and short vowels are also not differentiated.

This book involves equal contributions from both authors. Both collaborated equally in the design and formulation of the research project. Both spent similar amounts of time in the field, and the contributions of each are of similar and complementary significance. The body of the text was written jointly, with almost every sentence— whether from Cole's or Altorki's data—being jointly formulated. Cole worked on producing the first main revision while Altorki researched relevant Arabic language studies and analyses. Although the final revision was equally the responsibility of both, Cole did most of the work of preparing the manuscript for publication.

ACKNOWLEDGMENTS

The authors gratefully acknowledge the American University in Cairo, which provided them with sabbatical leaves and grants for the academic year 1986–87. We also express our appreciation to the Population Council for a Middle East Research Award, which covered part of the expenses of the field research, and to the Ford Foundation for individual grants that contributed to the expenses of data analysis and writing the book.

We also express our gratitude to the Center for Middle Eastern Studies and the Department of Anthropology at the University of Texas at Austin, especially Professors Robert A. Fernea and Richard N. Adams, for making arrangements for the authors to be Visiting Scholars and providing office space during the analysis and write-up phase of this project. We thank both of them and Elizabeth Warnock Fernea for reading the manuscript and for their many helpful comments. We also appreciate the support and expert editorial assistance provided by Annes McCann-Baker of the Center for Middle Eastern Studies. James Hitselberger was most helpful in the transliteration of Arabic words.

In addition, we thank Professor Galal Amin of the American University in Cairo for his useful comments on part of the manuscript. A special debt of gratitude is owed to Professor Mark C. Kennedy of the American University in Cairo for his careful and critical reading of the manuscript and for the many suggestions he made for changes.

Within Saudi Arabia, grateful acknowledgment is made to Prince Ahmad Ibn ʿAbd al-ʿAziz Al Saʿud and, especially, Dr. Hamad ʿAbd al-Karim al-Marzuqi, both of the Ministry of Interior, who made the necessary official arrangements for Cole's participation in the study. Thanks are also due to Prince Muhammad Ibn Sa'd Ibn 'Abd al-'Aziz al Sa'ud, the deputy amir of the Qasim, for his cooperation and support.

Those to whom we are indebted in 'Unayzah are too numerous to mention by name. We can mention the amir, Muhammad Al Hamad Al Sulaym, and the mayor, 'Abd Allah Al 'Abd al-'Aziz Ibrahim Al Bassam. To all of the others, young and old, male and female, who gave us so much of their time and who shared so much of their knowledge with us, we can only say that we are deeply grateful and that we hope that this book faithfully reflects the information they so generously and good-heartedly provided us with.

The authors bear full responsibility for the presentation and inter-pretation of the data.

Cairo, 1988

Arabian Oasis City
The Transformation of ʿUnayzah

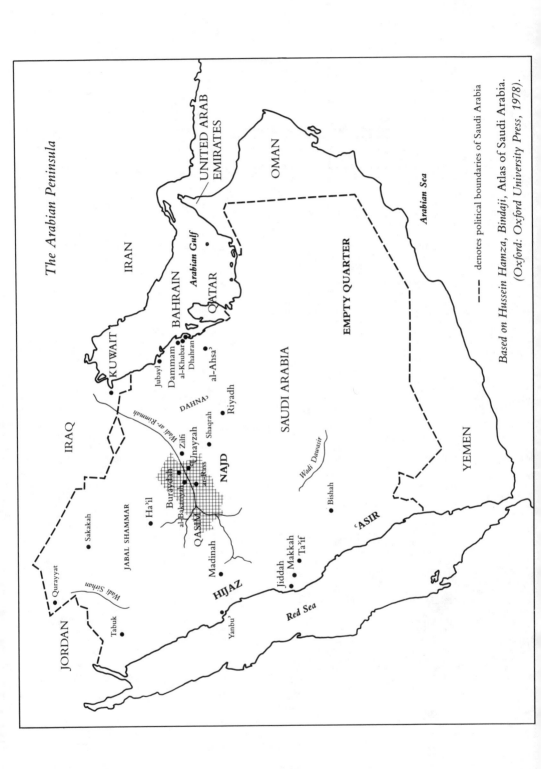

The Arabian Peninsula

JORDAN

Tabuk

Qurayyat

Wadi Sirhan

Sakakah

JABAL SHAMMAR

Ha'il

IRAQ

KUWAIT

IRAN

Wadi ar-Rimmah

Zilfi

DAHNA'

Jubayl

Dammam
al-Khubar
Dhahran

BAHRAIN

Arabian Gulf

QATAR

UNITED ARAB
EMIRATES

OMAN

al-Ahsa'

Shaqrah

Unayzah

Buraydah

al-Bakayrah al-Rass

QASIM

NAJD

Riyadh

SAUDI ARABIA

EMPTY QUARTER

Arabian Sea

Madinah

Wadi Dawasir

Bishah

'ASIR

YEMEN

HIJAZ

Jiddah

Makkah
Ta'if

Yanbu'

Red Sea

Based on Hussein Hamza, Bindaji, *Atlas of Saudi Arabia.*
(Oxford: Oxford University Press, 1978).

- - - denotes political boundaries of Saudi Arabia

INTRODUCTION

The Study and Its Setting

Two types of societal change, transformation and development, provide the framework within which data for this study were collected and are analyzed in this book. By "transformation" we refer to a change in the structure of the society that implies a fundamental change in the society's economic basis, in the forms and compositions of its groupings, and in the rules and mechanisms which regulate the interaction of its individuals, statuses, and groups. By "development" we refer to a process of change which is both incremental and purposive. In the present-day context, development involves an increase in the capabilities of a country to provide a sustainable improvement in the standard of living of its citizens or subjects in areas such as nutrition, health care, shelter, and education. As currently practiced in most countries, development also has the goal of enhancing the power of the country vis-à-vis other countries to achieve and guarantee a significant degree of economic and political independence. Empirically, most efforts undertaken in the name of development are oriented toward the physical aspects of the standard of living. Ideally, in our opinion, these efforts should also be directed toward achieving political freedom for individuals and the guarantee of basic human rights to social and psychological well-being however culturally defined.

If the goals of developmental change are achieved, a change of transformational proportions is likely to occur even if the entity which initiates developmental change does not wish to bring about the transformation of the society. This is particularly the case when developmental change involves a fundamental change in the eco-

nomic basis of the society. Transformation may and does occur outside the context of development. It may be triggered by purposive
change undertaken in the name of development or by a multitude of
other variables, including, among many others, war, pestilence, the
discovery of a new energy source, or the diffusion of ideas, a religion,
or technology.

The present study is not directly concerned with presenting a theoretical discussion of development and transformation, although the
data do provide a rich source of material for such a discussion. Rather,
we use these concepts to present and analyze change that has occurred
in a single community, ʿUnayzah, which is located in the north-
central part of the Arabian Peninsula about 270 kilometers from
Riyadh, the capital of the Kingdom of Saudi Arabia. This framework
is largely derived from theoretical discussions of modes of production
(e.g., Sahlins 1972; Meillassoux 1981; Khan and Llobera 1981; Palerm
1976) and of energy and society (Adams 1975, 1982, 1988) and assumes
that the way a society organizes itself to produce its needed requirements ultimately determines other more social and cultural aspects of
behavior in that society, and that the reproduction (or survival) of
that society depends on its ability to produce those requirements. Following from this perspective, the focus of the study throughout is on
work and the distribution of that which is produced and how these
have changed. To do this, we consider what is done and who does
what and how both production and distribution are organized in
three different phases of ʿUnayzah's existence.

Overview of the Study

ʿUnayzah formerly was the nucleus of a politically autonomous amirate, or principality, that based its livelihood on agriculture, crafts, and
local, regional, and long-distance trade. Work in agriculture and
crafts was predominantly organized along domestic lines, while the
distribution of the products of this work was organized by both domestic and mercantile formations. The domestic organization of
work and distribution was clearly present since the establishment of
settlements in the area some thirteen hundred years ago. We do not
know when the mercantile element developed, but it was clearly
present and long established at the time of Charles M. Doughty's visit
to ʿUnayzah in 1878 (Doughty 1979 [1888]). This political economy
continued until 1904, when political autonomy of the amirate was ter-

minated. However, domestic and mercantile organization of the economy continued to predominate until roughly the time of World War
II. This phase is described and analyzed in Part One of this study.

Part Two presents a discussion of developmental change that included the establishment of the present Saudi Arabian state, which
incorporated ʿUnayzah into its structure as a provincial city and administrative district. This developmental change also included the
emergence in ʿUnayzah of capitalist social formations (mainly between the mid 1920s and the mid 1970s), with the market becoming
prevalent and indispensable in the organization of the economy. Wage
labor, salaried employment, and entrepreneurship became predominant during this period following the establishment and growth, at
the national level, of the bureaucracy and the oil industry, the full
monetization of the economy, and the spread of private firms. During
this phase, Saudi Arabia became integrated into the capitalist world
system.

Part Three of the study focuses on changes introduced into ʿUnayzah by the economic boom that occurred between 1975 and 1982 as a
result of sharp increases in the world market price of crude oil. During this period, crafts disappeared, agricultural production was transformed, and agribusinesses were introduced. The local population
became almost fully engaged in salaried employment and/or managerial entrepreneurship. Vast numbers of expatriates were imported
as wage laborers or salaried employees in almost all sectors other than
security.

In documenting the changes which occurred during the boom, we
indicate the societal transformation that occurred and evaluate whether
it is consistent with development. Although development is a country-
wide phenomenon, we demonstrate that, in the case of ʿUnayzah,
development was truncated even though a high standard of living was
achieved. Instead of increased capabilities at the local level to provide
a sustainable improvement in the standard of living, the community
became highly dependent on state loans, subsidies, and salaries, on a
large expatriate labor force, and on the import of almost all consumer
durables and technology.

This book represents the first anthropological field study of the
transformation of a local community in Saudi Arabia since the boom.
With the exception of the work of Robert A. Fernea (Fernea and
Fernea 1985; Fernea 1987), other published studies (e.g., Vidal 1955;
Cole 1975; Katakura 1977; Sowayan 1985; Altorki 1986) either predate

the boom and the changes it brought or do not concern themselves primarily with those changes.

This study, in the main, is ethnographic. Indeed, many of the data are presented in the actual words—translated, of course—of informants. This strategy was chosen for two main reasons. First, we had little specific information about 'Unayzah or similar communities in the region before we went there. Almost all works on this area (with the notable exception of Rosenfeld 1965) have singled out the nomadic Bedouin and have, at best, only recognized the presence of sedentary communities based on agriculture and trade without further consideration. Aside from the writings of Doughty (1979 [1888]), Philby (1928), and Rihani (1976 [1924]), nothing else was available to us; and we did not know how much we could rely on their accounts or, if essentially correct, how long the formations they described had continued.

If our knowledge about 'Unayzah in the past was limited, we knew even less about the present other than the fact that a great deal of change had taken place. Of course, anthropological and sociological studies have been published about sedentary communities and societies in other parts of the Arabian Peninsula and Gulf (e.g., Barth 1983; Wikan 1982; Eickelman 1984; Gerholm 1977; Mynthi 1979; Khouri 1980; Rumaihi 1975), but because of the sociocultural specificity of Najd, we felt we should not rely too heavily on them in designing the study. Because the basic ethnography had yet to be done, we decided that it would be inappropriate to impose a strictly theoretical framework on our research.

The other main reason for making this a primarily descriptive study, and for letting the people tell much of the story in their own words, derives from our reaction to much of the literature that has been published on Saudi Arabia in recent years. Quite a lot has been written about society in Saudi Arabia by foreigners who happened to live there but who were not social scientists. Much of this has been anecdotal at best and often inflammatory and misleading. More serious are the writings of social scientists who have either never been to the country or have only briefly visited some of its main cities. They have based their studies mainly on statistical data but have nonetheless been emboldened to draw basic conclusions about the nature of the society in general. Most of these studies were conducted during the period of the boom. Significantly, they totally ignore the development that occurred between the 1950s and the beginning of the boom in the mid 1970s. Their limited focus has led them to deny the actual and potential contributions of the local population to development. Consequently, they overemphasize the role of expatriate manpower and expertise. An example is provided by an Arab social scientist who erroneously argues that "migrant labor [in] Saudi Arabia . . . is virtually shaping the host country's new institutions and forging its modern infrastructure from scratch" (Ibrahim 1982:104). Much of this literature is also flawed because of the application of methods and theories that have resulted from studies of very different kinds of societies.

Because our anthropological study was conducted in a single community, we are able to record only what has happened in that single community. But as will become obvious, many of the changes which the people of ʿUnayzah have experienced are the result of decisions taken elsewhere—in the national capital and, indeed, in other countries far removed from this desert oasis. That changes are largely the result of decisions taken outside the community is related to the nature of Saudi Arabia's national economy, which depends so heavily on the sale of a single, nonrenewable, primary product—oil—mainly to countries which, in the terminology of dependency and world system theorists (e.g., Amin 1973, 1982; Cardoso and Faletto 1969; Frank 1979; Wallerstein 1974; Wolf 1982), are at the so-called center of the present world system.

Stereotypes Challenged

In *Orientalism*, Edward Said (1978) has clearly shown how stereotypes have distorted the views of Westerners and even some local scholars of Arab society. Tidrick (1981) has also demonstrated how nineteenth- and early twentieth-century English travelers and political/military agents particularly misrepresented the social realities of the Arabian Peninsula and romanticized the Bedouin and their way of life. This study—based as it is on empirical field research—explodes numerous misconceptions and stereotypic views about Saudi Arabian society in general and Najd in particular.

One of the most pervasive stereotypes about Saudi Arabia is that its historic and geographic core, Najd, was a "Bedouin zone" in which camel breeding was the main source of livelihood (e.g., Sweet 1965, 1971). This stereotype is promoted by numerous Arab scholars from outside the Arabian Peninsula who also stress that the area never achieved any form of sociopolitical organization higher than that of the tribe (e.g., Ibrahim 1982:151). However, the most extreme statement of this unfounded belief is perhaps that of Safran, who claims that

> the difficulties of earning a livelihood, the dearth of surplus resources, the vast distances of the peninsula, and nomadism and tribalism combined to place Arabia in a kind of Hobbesian state of nature in which each tribe was permanently at war with all the others, except for short and temporary alliances. Hostility between the settled and bedouin tribes was particularly profound, assuming an added "cultural" dimension of contempt for each other's occupation and way of life. Yet contrary to Hobbesian theory, this state of affairs was not deemed to be an unbearable evil to be escaped at all costs. On the contrary, the bedouin tribes especially regarded war, mutual raiding, and looting not as deplorable necessities from which they would escape if they could, but rather considered them to be exciting features of a desirable way of life, providing occasions for the display of various kinds of virtuosity to be immortalized in heroic verse and song. (Safran 1985:21)

This study does not deny the importance of the Bedouin nomads in this region. On the contrary, it shows that they were a highly productive element in the regional economy and provided important inputs into the development of both regional and long-distance trade. However, they were only one element in the regional economy and society. Also existing were agriculture and craft production, sedentary villages and cities, and highly developed trade and transport networks, as al-Hamad (1986) also shows. In addition, urban-based amirates, of which ʿUnayzah is but one example, have existed for centuries. These communities transcended the limits of kin-based tribal chiefdoms. It is true no continuous centralized state authority governed in this area before the establishment and consolidation of the present Kingdom of Saudi Arabia. However, long periods of centralized authority existed under the Bani Khalid from the last quarter of the seventeenth century until the last decades of the eighteenth and under the Al Saʿud during the first Saʿudi kingdom, which lasted from 1744 until it was destroyed by a foreign invasion in 1818.

That Najd was an area fit only for the breeding of camels is belied by Philby's description of a meal he had in ʿUnayzah in the late summer of 1918 in which he was served "rice, mutton, chicken, stuffed chicken, fried eggs, tomatoes stuffed with mince, lady's fingers, figs, peaches, dates, cow's buttermilk, and pomegranates" (Philby 1928: 167). With the exception of the rice, all of this was locally grown.

We do not deny that Najd consists of vast stretches of desert range-lands which are mainly conducive to the nomadic herding of camels, sheep, and goats. However, rich agricultural oases have long existed in Najd and, in the past, they produced enough to meet the needs of their own local inhabitants, most of the dates and grains consumed by the Bedouin, and a surplus for export to the holy cities of the Hijaz. Furthermore, by tapping deep underground sources of water, parts of this area have within the past five years contributed significantly to the agricultural "miracle" that has made Saudi Arabia one of the few Arab countries which is self-sufficient in wheat, the traditional staple carbohydrate consumed in the region.

Another area of misconceptions and stereotypes has to do with the organization of work in the prestate, preoil society and, in particular, the role of women in work outside the household in both the past and contemporary periods. Generalizations based on the stereotype of the Bedouin tribe as the predominant form of social organization in the past suggest that work was mainly organized by the domestic unit or kinship group or was performed by client groups of subservient tribes or slaves. This study shows that although work in 'Unayzah was predominantly organized within the context of family and kin networks, neighborhood ties were also important and, in addition, there was a not insignificant amount of wage labor. Women, though segregated and veiled, worked outside the household in a wide range of agricultural activities—sometimes within the context of domestic and kin units but also as neighbors and as hired workers on the farms of nonkindred. They also bought and sold in the market, some of them on a full-time and regular basis.

At the present time, and in contrast to the widespread notion that women in Saudi Arabia today are mainly confined to the home, this study shows that many women have careers outside the family—as sellers in the market and in a number of modern salaried occupations, especially teaching. Furthermore, it shows that having a career out-side the home is positively valued not only by many educated women but also by their fathers, who, in numerous cases, have included a stipulation in the marriage contracts of their daughters affirming their right to work if they should so desire.

This study contradicts numerous other stereotypes. It is hoped that these cases will become obvious as the reader proceeds. Saudi Arabia is often treated, both in the mass media and, unfortunately, sometimes in scholarly works, as a unique and special case. To the Westerner, it is all too often a mysterious land of Bedouin and archaic customs that has suddenly obtained vast riches which it can wield for good but more likely for ill in the wider world economy. To many Arabs, it is a land of primitive Bedouin who have become nouveaux riches, some of whom hypocritically combine adherence to an austere and puritanical version of reformist Islam at home with hedonism in the fleshpots of other Arab countries and in Europe, America, and Asia.

This study probes beyond the stereotypes and shows that, while the country has its own specificity and unique characteristics, it has experienced a process of development similar to that which has occurred throughout the Third World. Its recent revenue from the sale of crude oil created an economic boom that interrupted the developmental process; but many features of the boom are shared with other oil-producing countries and areas and, indeed, with many other economies which have been dominated by income from the sale of a single, highly valued primary product in the world market.

The Setting: ʿUnayzah Today

Located in the Qasim region in the heart of Najd, ʿUnayzah is on the south bank of the Wadi ar-Rimmah. ʿUnayzah is the name of an amirate of some 3,500 square kilometers (Sharif 1970:185) and of a city with a population currently estimated by local officials to be about 70,000. According to the 1974 governmental census, the total population of the ʿUnayzah amirate was 42,337, while the city itself had a population of 26,990 (al-Wasil 1986:108–109). In 1962, a governmental census reported that the population of the city was 23,455 (Sharif 1970:185). The current estimate of 70,000 for the city is undoubtedly high; but there has been rapid growth since the time of the last census (in 1974) as large numbers of Bedouin and villagers have migrated into the city, as a large expatriate labor force has been recruited, and as a result of rapid natural increase among the old local population and the migrant Bedouin and villagers. Based on figures for employment and for school enrollments, which we present in chapter 7, our "guestimate" is that the population of the city is presently about 50,000.

The amirate of ʿUnayzah includes the towns of Midhnib and al-Bakariyah and a number of small villages. However, this study is mainly concerned with the city of ʿUnayzah, which serves as the administrative capital of the amirate. Within the context of the contemporary Kingdom of Saudi Arabia, ʿUnayzah can be characterized as a medium-size provincial city. In many ways it is similar to other large provincial communities in the country—its people deal with the same national bureaucracy and have been the beneficiaries of many state-sponsored development programs and projects. Outside the community, their primary sphere of activity is within Saudi Arabia, mainly in the large cities of Riyadh, Jiddah, Makkah, and the urban complex of Dammam, al-Khubar, and Dhahran in the Eastern Province. These cities have become the major focuses for people throughout the country seeking such things as higher education, specialized health care, or employment or other income-generating opportunities. Yet, strictly on the basis of this study, we cannot conclude that ʿUnayzah is typical or in any way representative of other communities in the country.

Although our observations suggest that ʿUnayzah is increasingly similar to other large provincial communities in Saudi Arabia, many differences between it and other communities remain. For example, its old rival, Buraydah, located some twenty kilometers away on the north bank of the Wadi ar-Rimmah, has surpassed it in size and become the capital of the administrative district of the Qasim, of which ʿUnayzah is a part. While all the other local amirates in the Qasim report directly to Buraydah for administrative purposes, ʿUnayzah maintains a special status, reporting to the amirate of the Qasim for some matters but also having its own directorates of various national ministries that report directly to Riyadh.

ʿUnayzah has not been the site of exceptionally large-scale state or state-sponsored projects in the last decade or so, as has been the case in many other small to medium-size urban centers. No large military bases have been established there, as in the cases of Khamis Mushayt and Tabuk. It is not the site of major industrial development projects, as at Yanbuʿ and Jubayl. Unlike al-Ahsaʾ, it has not seen massive irrigation works built, nor is it the site of the development of very large scale agribusinesses, although it has been a major site for the development of new agriculture by individual entrepreneurs and farmers. It has not become a center of state administration at the regional level, as in the cases, for example, of Buraydah, Abha, Haʾil, and Tabuk. It has not attracted a significant migration of people originally from other parts of the country, as has been the case for all the cities mentioned above. Although it has attracted a number of Bedouin and villagers from its own nearby region, the population of 'Unayzah (excluding expatriates) remains more homogeneous than is the case for other Saudi Arabian cities.

Arriving in the near vicinity of 'Unayzah from the modern Qasim airport or on one of the major paved roads which link it to Riyadh and the other cities of the country, one will be struck by large patches of agricultural land that are interspersed with the desert environment. Most of these have large central pivot irrigation systems and have recently been developed mainly to grow wheat. Approaching the outskirts of the city (depending on the road taken), one will see either thick groves of date palm trees with lush green fields of alfalfa or new, well-laid-out small farms that grow fruit trees, some date palms, and vegetables.

Much of the city is newly constructed and is now spread out over a large area. The central part of the city is focused around a main mosque and the market, both of which have been newly constructed, although they are located in the same places as they were in the old city. The mosque itself is of gleaming white marble, but the mud-brick minaret of the old mosque remains in front of it. Behind the mosque and in areas adjacent to the market are the remains of old mud-brick houses, many of which are in a state of decay and uninhabited. However, a few local people continue to live in this old part of town, either in mud-brick houses built twenty to thirty years ago or, more likely, in new houses constructed of concrete. Most of the people who live in this area and in old houses are expatriate males. The market consists of several large open spaces which are filled with buyers and sellers on Thursdays and Fridays and of numerous small shops located either in one-story buildings that have been constructed by the municipality or in privately owned buildings of one or two stories. Within this central part of town, there are large areas that are still devoted to farming—mainly old date palms along with alfalfa.

Moving out from the central market area, there are several neighborhoods composed of two-story modern houses that are quite close together along relatively narrow streets. Most of these neighborhoods were developed in the late 1960s and early 1970s, often on land that had previously been in cultivation. The city is roughly bisected by the Riyadh to Buraydah road, which passes along what used to be one side of the wall of the old city. Along this road are several buildings that have five or six stories and include several banks and one of the city's two hotels. There are other buildings of one to three stories that are occupied by a variety of agencies of agricultural supply companies, contracting firms, furniture stores, and the like. Across this road and on a hill in an area that was formerly desert are located most of the new homes that people have recently acquired, mainly with loans from the Saudi Arabian Real Estate Development Fund. The majority of local people live in this area today. The streets are wide and straight, and almost all the houses are "villas" of two to three stories in height surrounded by high walls.

'Unayzah has few apartment buildings, mainly occupied by expatriates. The vast majority of local people live in new air-conditioned houses made of concrete or fired bricks and sometimes faced with imported marble. Each house usually has separate entrances for men and women. On the ground floor, each house invariably has at least one reception room, a dining area, and washrooms for men, as well as a kitchen. Separate from these areas there may be reception and dining rooms for women. Alternatively, these rooms for women are located on the second floor along with bedrooms, which may also be on a third floor if one exists. Many of the houses are furnished with Western-style chairs, sofas, and dining tables and all of them have Western-style beds, kitchens, and bathrooms. However, many of them also have traditional Arab-style reception and dining areas where people sit on carpets on the floor with pillows for backrests. Quite a few of the new houses also have swimming pools.

As mentioned, almost all the new houses are enclosed by high walls that separate them from the street and from other houses. However, not all the areas within new neighborhoods are fully developed. Large vacant lots and areas often lie between houses and other built-up areas. Moreover, some neighborhoods are at quite some distance from the town and are more like satellites of the city. These remote neighborhoods are usually for people of "limited incomes" and are mainly Bedouin settlements. Within all the newly built-up areas, mosques have been constructed, small grocery stores have been established, and most of these areas have bakeries and other shops as well. All these areas have been built with the automobile in mind. The streets are well paved and the distances that one has to travel, sometimes even to go to the mosque, are great enough to require the use of a car. Therefore, it is rare to find anyone walking in the streets of the new part of town, with the occasional exception of expatriate males or local women going to visit a nearby neighbor. Local males almost always go by car or pickup truck.

Present-day 'Unayzah is clean and well served by electrical, water, sewerage, and telephone networks. The main streets are wide and pleasant thoroughfares, many of which are lined with trees and shrubs. Fountains adorn the main squares and intersections. Several parks have been built, and these, along with the farms in the old central part of the city and on its outskirts, provide a sense of openness, quiet beauty, and relaxation. No shantytowns or settlements exist in or around 'Unayzah; but, as mentioned earlier, many expatriates live, sometimes in crowded conditions, in the old part of town in houses which have decayed with neglect. Many expatriate farm laborers also live in isolated and often primitive conditions on farms owned by local people.

'Unayzah is thus not unlike most other small cities and even many villages in contemporary Saudi Arabia. People live in new housing that is basically Western in style, although decorative motifs are sometimes Arab in origin. The automobile has become ubiquitous, as has the sight of expatriates on the streets, in restaurants, or in the market. 'Unayzah is a small city, quiet and peaceful, and most of the local people know each other and their families well. It is not at all like the huge, sprawling, bustling cities of Riyadh or Jiddah or those of the Eastern Province with their gleaming skyscrapers, luxury hotels, and cosmopolitan élan. However, if it is a more-or-less ordinary town today, people who visited it in the past considered 'Unayzah to be a very special community and one of the greatest of Arabian cities.

PART ONE

Political Autonomy, Domestically Organized Production, and Mercantile Trade

CHAPTER I

The Autonomous Amirate

This chapter presents the historical background and regional contexts which are necessary for understanding the political and economic structure of ʿUnayzah in the past and, to an extent, even in the present. It describes the main characteristics of ʿUnayzah as an autonomous amirate until 1904. It also describes and analyzes the division of labor and organization of production which predominated until the 1920s and which continued to exist until about 1950.

Historical Background

An ʿUnayzah is mentioned in pre-Islamic poetry, but it is uncertain that the place referred to is the same as the present-day ʿUnayzah. Although settlements were established in the area during the Roman period, the present city is considered to be the result of a number of small agricultural settlements joining together to form a city by the middle of the thirteenth century (Sharif 1970:271). These settlements date from the first century of Islam (latter part of the seventh or early part of the eighth century A.D.). The first of these was al-Jannah, which was settled by members of the Bani Khalid tribe. This settlement was followed by the establishment of al-Dhabat, al-ʿUqayliyah, al-Milayhah, and al-Khurayzah. Each was originally enclosed by its own wall but later on became a neighborhood of ʿUnayzah and, as such, continues to exist today. Some of these small settlements were mainly of the Bani Khalid while others were of the Subayʿ tribe (al-Wasil 1986:198–201).

The early history of these settlements is obscure. However, they based their livelihood primarily on agriculture, although evidence indicates that some of the settlers continued for a while to lead a semi-nomadic pastoralist existence. Each settlement was composed primarily of members of a single clan and was physically separated from the others by large open spaces. The settlers eventually erected a mosque in an open space between the settlements and developed a market nearby. Nonetheless, competition often existed between the settlements and within each of them. This competition occasionally led to open conflict and warfare, with alignments generally following the main tribal division between the Bani Khalid and the Subay'. During periods of conflict, agricultural production tended to decline seriously, and on several occasions people were forced to migrate—to Buraydah or other already existing settlements or to new settlements which they founded (including al-Khubrah, al-'Awshwaziyah, and al-Bakariyah).

During periods of relative quiet, agriculture flourished and the population of each settlement grew, both from natural increase and from new settlers moving in. As this occurred, housing would sometimes be built on agricultural land within the settlement, forcing people to take up farming outside the settlement walls. Eventually, this process of expansion led to the linking of all the settlements beyond their own walls and the building of a single wall to include them all. Enough land to support all the population during a time of siege was included within the wall. However, the process of growth continued, and on at least two different occasions new walls were erected to enclose larger areas (al-Wasil 1986:205–208).

At least by the end of the eighteenth century, 'Unayzah was united as an amirate under the leadership of men of tribal descent from the Subay'. Conflicts between descendants of the Subay' and the Bani Khalid for the control of the city and its dependent villages had come to an end. Soon afterward, 'Unayzah had its own *qadi,* or religious judge. In 1818, 'Unayzah, which was described as a large city at that time, submitted to the forces led by Ibrahim, son of Muhammad 'Ali, the pasha of Egypt. These forces had invaded Najd to destroy the first Sa'udi state. However, they did not remain for long, and 'Unayzah became free of their domination. During the remainder of the nineteenth century, 'Unayzah was caught in the middle of the rivalry between the Al Sa'ud and the Al Rashid for the domination of Najd. At certain periods, it was autonomous and free from any outside control. At one point, it became the capital of the Qasim when Jiluwi Ibn

Turki Al Saʿud established himself there as ruler. While some factions within the city sided with the Al Rashid, others sided with the Al Saʿud. Eventually, in 1904, ʿUnayzah joined with the forces of ʿAbd al-ʿAziz Ibn Saʿud on the basis of an agreement that the amir of ʿUnayzah would always be from within the community—in particular, from the Al Sulaym lineage of the Subayʿ (al-Wasil 1986:204–206).

Regional Contexts

Any discussion of ʿUnayzah must take into consideration the physical, social, economic, and political characteristics of the regions within which it is located and with which it shares general commonalities. The larger region is that of Najd, while the more immediate one is the Qasim.

Najd is the central region of what is today the Kingdom of Saudi Arabia. It is a vast arid territory which stretches from Jabal Shammar in the north to beyond the Wadi Dawasir in the south and from the inland side of the mountains of the Hijaz to the Dahnaʾ sands in the east. Najd is the home of sedentary communities of farmers, craftspeople, and merchants and of nomadic Bedouin tribes. Most of the great tribal descent groups of the Arabian Peninsula, outside of Yemen and Oman, are based in this region. These include the Qahtan, Dawasir, ʿUtaybah, Mutayr, Shammar, Subayʿ, and ʿAnazah, as well as the ʿAjman, Bani Khalid, and Al Murrah, which, however, are more on the fringes of Najd to the east. Najd is also the homeland of the Al Saʿud and of the Al ash-Shaykh, the families which together headed the religiopolitical movement that culminated in the establishment of the present Kingdom of Saudi Arabia.

Throughout much of history, Najd was an area characterized by a high degree of autonomy from central state control. Within the area, communities such as Haʾil, Buraydah, and ʿUnayzah were urban places with their own amirs under whose leadership the citizens provided for their own defense. These cities (and the villages attached to them) were like islands in that they were surrounded by vast stretches of desert that were controlled by autonomous Bedouin tribes. The basic bifurcation within the area was between the *badiyah*, "nomads," and the *hadar*, "sedentary folk," but symbiotic ties linked many of the *hadar* to the *badiyah* through ties of kinship and tribal origin. A rich trade also flourished between the sedentary communities, which provided agricultural products and crafts, and the Bedouin nomads, who produced animals (mainly camels and horses) and animal products.

In this setting of numerous autonomous cities and tribes, competition often led to raids. Periods of relative stability existed when agriculture and commerce flourished, but periods of conflict led to decline in production, as shown in the case of ʿUnayzah. Cultural as well as political diversity occurred within the region, as evidenced in different dialects between tribes and between different cities and subregions. However, in comparison with other regions of the peninsula, such as Yemen, Oman, or the Hijaz, the inhabitants of Najd all shared a common repertoire of cultural and social knowledge.

We recognize the bifurcation of the society on the basis of the nomadic and the sedentary; however, frequent interaction between them led to the sharing of many cultural values and norms. The bifurcation itself does not establish rigid boundaries between the two groups. Each category can, in fact, be extended at times to include members of the other category. For example, a city dweller may refer to someone in a village as a member of the *badiyah*. However, when in the village, *badiyah* refers to the nomadic Bedouin. Conversely, the nomads use the term *hadar*, "sedentary," in a flexible way. Therefore, these categories must be understood within specific historic periods and not as absolute categories that apply throughout history, segmenting society into two polar opposites. Also, while all the nomadic population was organized on the basis of tribes, the sedentary population included large numbers of people who were themselves descendants of those same tribes. Few of the sedentary people of tribal origin were effective members of a tribal social organization, and such membership was largely irrelevant to their settled life. However, they did, and do, draw on tribal ideology to establish an identity and to obtain status in the community.

An example of this phenomenon is the use of descent as one basis for social stratification. The use of descent status (tribal versus nontribal) by both settled and nomadic communities is now limited to establishing marriage boundaries between groups. In the past, differences in descent status translated into occupational differentiation and differential political power, as will be shown later in the case of ʿUnayzah.

Because of its location and because of the internal conditions of competition and the prevalence of numerous small and autonomous units, Najd remained relatively isolated, not only from the wider

Arab world but from influences from other regions of the peninsula. Najd was involved in caravan trade with Yemen, Hijaz, Hadramawt, Oman, Iraq, Syria, and Egypt, but this trade was conducted by men who left the area and went to those places and did not result in out-siders moving into Najd. The area has never been directly ruled by outsiders. At some times central states based outside of Najd claimed the allegiance of the region or parts of it, but they never established permanent settlements and had little cultural impact.

Thus Najd maintained its specificity despite its involvement in long-distance trade. The nomadic groups in Najd, as well as the townspeople and villagers, differ significantly from those of the moun-tainous and coastal regions of the peninsula, the documentation of which is beyond the scope of this book. However, as the result of the religiopolitical movement led by the Al Saʿud and the Al ash-Shaykh, men from Najd conquered the other regions of the Hijaz, the ʿAsir, and the eastern coastal areas during the first decades of the twentieth century, leading to their inclusion in the contemporary Kingdom of Saudi Arabia. This feat is described in Part Two.

The Qasim is a subregion of Najd. Doughty, who had spent most of his time in Najd among the Bedouin or in the Bedouin-dominated city of Haʾil, marveled at the sight of cows, strongly associated with sedentary folk in Arabia, instead of camels grazing on grass and bushes in the desert sands when he first entered this region in 1878. His Bedouin companion told him that the region had many towns and villages. Doughty himself observed that

> the inhabitants are become as townsmen: their deep sand country, in the midst of high Arabia, is hardly less settled than Syria. The Kusman [people of Qasim] are prudent and adventurious. . . . Almost a third of the people are caravaners, to foreign provinces, to Medina and Mecca, to Kuweyt, Bosra, Bagdad, to the Wahaby country, to J. Shammar. And many of them leave home in their youth to seek fortune abroad; where some (we have seen) serve the Ottoman government in arms: they are still lately the Ageyl at Bagdad, Damascus, and Medina. . . . In those borderlands are most of the emigrated from el-Kasim,—hus-bandmen and small salesmen; and a few of them there become wealthy merchants. . . . The poor of Kasim . . . wander in their own country; young field laborers seek service from town to town, where they hear that *el-urruk,* the sweat of their brow, is likely to be well paid. (Doughty 1979 [1888], 2:337–338)

Although Najd, in general, is strongly flavored by the nomadic Bedouin, the Qasim is mainly the land of their sedentary cousins. Nomadic pastoralists graze their herds in the great sand areas of the Qasim, but that which gives the Qasim its specificity are numerous villages and several large towns and cities. Thanks to the Wadi ar-Rimmah, which runs through this area, water has always been close to the surface, and agriculture for centuries has provided an important source of livelihood. But the economy was not based exclusively on agriculture. Trade, crafts, and labor migration were important elements as well. Both trade and labor migration brought this region, perhaps more so than other regions of Najd, into touch with the wider world. This exposure served to stimulate education and the quest for secular knowledge among many of the Qasim's inhabitants earlier than was the case with the Bedouin nomads, who remained more isolated. It is commonly said in the Qasim today that their early involvement with modern education is due to their travels abroad. This is no doubt in part true, but we would stress that these were sedentary communities in which literacy, particularly in the form of Holy Qur'anic studies, had always been valued and engaged in.

The Old ʿUnayzah

ʿUnayzah was, and is, an integral part of the Qasim, but as people from the town proudly point out, ʿUnayzah was Umm al-Qasim, the "Mother of Qasim." It may be a rather ordinary town in Saudi Arabia today, but ʿUnayzah clearly demonstrated many unique and special characteristics in the past when compared with other communities in the area, whether sedentary or nomadic. Doughty, who visited ʿUnayzah in 1878 after having been expelled from Buraydah and abandoned along the way, described the city, which one of his friends there reckoned to have 15,000 souls, as a "free township . . . [with] the people living in unity." During his sojourn in the city, he found many who were educated, well read, highly aware of the outside world, and of a liberal and hospitable countenance, and he said that the "one good day" he spent in Arabia was a day in ʿUnayzah (Doughty 1979 [1888], 2:357–485).

In the summer of 1918, British explorer and political agent H. St. John Philby traveled by camel from the then small mud-brick town of Riyadh to ʿUnayzah, which he called "one of the great cities of Arabia." He commented:

And, much as I had already heard of the difference between 'Anaiza and the rest of Najd, of the open-handed hospitality of its people and of its complete freedom from any kind of religious or sectarian bigotry, I must admit that my actual experiences astonished and bewildered me. It seemed to me that I had stepped suddenly out of barbarism into a highly civilized and even cultured society, where the stranger within the gates, far from being an object of aversion and suspicion, was regarded as the common guest of the community to be entertained—somewhat mercilessly and regardless of his own feelings—by every household that claimed to count in the local scheme of things. I was fortunate to have seen and experienced almost every province of Najd before coming to the Qasim and to have tasted the bitter in full measure before the sweet—doubly fortunate in that, though Buraida was yet to remind me that its sister-city was altogether exceptional, my last memories of Central Arabia are intimately associated with the days of my sojourn in this gem among Arabian cities. (Philby 1928:160–162)

When 'Abd al-'Aziz Ibn Sa'ud, later to become the first king of Saudi Arabia, entered the city in 1904, he passed through the market and reportedly said he hoped his own capital of Riyadh might one day develop and become like 'Unayzah (al-Wasil 1986:112). In the 1920s, Amin Rihani, the Lebanese writer and advisor to 'Abd al-'Aziz, visited 'Unayzah and called it the "Paris of Najd" (Rihani 1976 [1924]). This epithet continues to be known and used by numerous Saudi Arabians today.

Like its present counterpart, the old city had as its focus the main mosque and the area of the market. The old mosque was built of mud brick and, with its great minaret, was of a style that was distinctive to 'Unayzah. The market, one of the largest in Najd, consisted of large open and covered areas and is described in detail later below. The inhabited parts of the old city were characterized by very narrow and crooked streets, which were usually always in shade. On either side of the streets, houses of two to four stories had been constructed immediately adjacent to each other, with extensions sometimes being built out from the second story of a house across the narrow street, leaving a passageway underneath. All the houses were of mud brick, using the trunks of *'athal,* "tamarisk," trees as beams. Like the materials of which they were constructed, all the builders and their helpers were local, forming one of the old craft occupations of the city. This architecture was sophisticated; engineering and architecture students whose families used to live in such buildings now come back to ʿUnayzah to study the old architecture for term papers and projects as part of their university training.

Each house usually had three entrances, one each for men, women, and animals. The men's entrance led directly to the men's *majlis,* "reception room," which was a long rectangular room with cushions around the sides. At the opposite end of the room from which one entered there was a hearth where coffee and tea were prepared over a fire, the smoke of which escaped through small windows at the top of the room. The walls of many of these rooms were blackened with smoke, which was a sign that the man was a generous host and had many social relations. Indeed, men often comment that, unlike today, the doors to their reception areas were always left open and that any man passing by was welcome to come in and drink coffee, even if the host was not present.

The women's entrance led directly into the interior of the house, which was usually a covered courtyard with rooms leading off it. The kitchen was located on the second floor, as were rooms used for sleeping. Many of the old houses had about ten different rooms, as well as a roof where people slept during the hot summer months. Houses with wells of their own had special places for washing and performing the ablutions, as well as an area for bathing. Each house had areas for storing firewood, dates, wheat, and other foods. The food storage areas were locked and strictly controlled by the senior woman in the house. Almost every house had a number of animals that were kept on the ground floor, and many had several palm trees that grew within an open court at the back of the house.

Unlike today, people lived very close together, and more than one nuclear family usually lived within a single dwelling. Houses were grouped closely together in named neighborhoods (of which there were about twenty-five) that were often separated from one another by palm gardens and farms. Each area had its own mosque or mosques. Rich and poor were mixed within any neighborhood, and people in the neighborhood were of mixed origins, seldom coming from the same kinship group. The ties of neighborliness were highly valued, with a high degree of socializing taking place among men and among women.

Women particularly met around an area known as the *hasu,* which was the area around the well used for washing, bathing, and ablutions. While the homes of wealthier people all had these, as did mosques, the houses of poorer people often did not. The poorer women of the neighborhood would share a single *hasu,* which would be built in the home of one of them, with a special entrance on a back street. Nearby would be a place to pray. These areas were strictly reserved for women and became centers of socializing for women who were not busy working.

The old city, which was like a densely knit web of both physical and social structures, lasted until the 1950s and 1960s, when it began to be transformed or abandoned. At the time of fieldwork, most of it was already destroyed or in ruins. By then, the old city was mainly a memory—disdained as backward by a few, but cherished by many who commented with pride about its distinctive architectural qualities and the strong ties of neighborliness that it fostered.

The Division and Organization of Labor

Within the sedentary urban population of the autonomous amirate several major occupational categories existed, and within each of these categories were numerous specializations. The major categories were *ʿulamaʾ* (sg. *ʿalim*), "the learned" (in religion); *umaraʾ* (sg. *amir*), "rulers"; *fallalih* (sg. *fallah*), "tillers of the soil" or "peasants"; *tujjar* (sg. *tajir*), "merchants"; *jammamil* (sg. *jammal*), "cameleers"/ "caravanners"; and *sunnaʿ* (sg. *saniʿ*), "artisans"/"craftspeople."

While occupational specializations tended to be inherited, these categories were not mutually exclusive. Although not common, an individual would sometimes change his occupation during the course of his lifetime, and a son did not always follow his father's occupation. Likewise, a daughter did not always follow the occupation of her mother. Also, an individual could hold more than one occupation at a time, though tending to be identified with only one of them.

Occupational mobility was possible, but the system was not completely open, and some occupations were governed by considerations of descent and gender. Within ʿUnayzah, the three descent categories were those of the *qabili,* "tribal"; the *khadiri,* "nontribal"; and the *ʿabd,* "slave." Those of *qabili* status were males and females who were recognized as being of unquestionable descent from a tribe—in the case of ʿUnayzah, mainly the Bani Khalid, Subayʿ, or Bani Tamim. Those of *khadiri* status were males and females who were freeborn but who, for a variety of reasons, could not claim recognized tribal origins. Those of *'abd* status were mainly people of African origin who themselves, or more likely their ancestors, had been imported into Arabia as slaves. Apparently, relatively few were of slave status in the past, and at present their descendants form only a small minority in the city.

The occupation of amir was always limited to a man of *qabili* status. Certain craft specializations such as leather working, silversmithing, goldsmithing, blacksmithing, and butchering were confined to people of *khadiri* status. On the other hand, other craft specializations as well as the other main occupational categories were in practice open to all without regard to descent.

Aside from descent, gender played a role in determining access to certain occupations. With the exception of a few craft specializations, all the major occupational categories and their subspecializations were open to males. Females, on the other hand, were more restricted in the occupations they could follow. They could not become either *'ulama'* or *umara'*, which were two of the most important occupations. Women were also barred from occupations that would require them to travel long distances alone. However, they were actively engaged in the occupations of farming and some craft specializations (such as leather processing and those not followed by males) and they were also engaged in commerce, although on a smaller scale than males. Of course, they also performed a wide range of household work, which males did not engage in.

The complex division of labor in the economy of autonomous 'Unayzah extended beyond the boundaries of the sedentary urban community to include villages in the region and, of particular importance, the nomadic Bedouin. The Bedouin specialized in raising camels, horses, sheep, and goats and also produced large quantities of *samn*, "ghee," and other milk products (such as dried goat's cheese). They sold these in the markets of 'Unayzah or to merchants from the city who traveled out to their camps. In return, they bought locally produced agricultural products (such as dates and wheat) and items imported by local merchants (such as coffee, cardamom, tea, sugar, rice, and cloth). In addition, they purchased almost all the tools and implements used in their herding activities (such as leather buckets, well wheels, and ropes) and household utensils from among locally produced items that were available for sale in the market in 'Unayzah.

Thus the economy of 'Unayzah in the past produced almost all the items needed to meet its own needs along with a surplus, which was used to meet many of the needs of the nomadic Bedouin in the region. In turn, the camels, horses, and ghee obtained from the Bedouin provided items which led to the development of long-distance trade to other urban centers in the Arabian Peninsula and especially to Syria, Egypt, Iraq, and eventually even as far away as Bombay, India. In return for products produced by the Bedouin, 'Unayzah merchants both imported and transported items from abroad to sell in their hometown.

Political Organization and Authority

Doughty reports that after arriving in 'Unayzah in 1878 he was taken the following morning to the amir. In his words,

> Aly led me over the open market-square: and by happy adventure the Emir was now sitting in his place; that is made under a small porch upon the Mejlis, at the street corner which leads to his own (clay) house, and in face of the clothier's suq. In the Emir's porch are two clay banks; upon one, bespread with a Persian carpet, sat Zamil [the amir], and his sword lay by him. (Doughty 1979 [1888], 2:364)

A member of a collateral branch of the family from which the amir of Doughty's day was descended described the administration of political authority in the past. According to Abu Yahya, who is about fifty years of age,

> in the past, the government here was the *umara'* and the *qadi*. But the amirs knew *fiqh* ["jurisprudence"] quite well. People would come to the amir who, until about thirty years ago, sat every day in the Majlis on a raised platform where there were three seats—one for the amir, one for his *wakil* ["deputy"], and one for any person who had a complaint or an issue to discuss. Below them sat the *akhawi* ["tribal retainers"/"companions"] and slaves of the amir. It was here that justice was dealt out and problems solved.
>
> If a person brought a complaint against another, that person would be immediately sent for and brought in by the *akhawi* or slaves. The amir would listen to what the other person had to say about the issue at

hand. The amir would always try to bring about a reconciliation between the parties and thus come to a mediated settlement between
them. If they could not agree, he would send the case on to the *qadi,*
who would be present in the great mosque which also fronted the
Majlis.

Most conflicts between people in the past were of a minor nature—
someone's cow had strayed and destroyed part of someone else's field,
and the latter sought payment for damages done, for example. Those
who crossed the *hudud* [literally, "limits"; i.e., committed a serious
crime] were few. The people of ʿUnayzah have always liked *al-hudu'*
["quietness"]. But the few who committed serious crimes were punished according to the prescribed Shariʿah punishments. Yet, the physical punishment was nothing compared to the social shame, as everyone
knew everybody else; and to have one's name mentioned at the time of
punishment in the Majlis in front of the mosque was something terrible
to a person who was a *muwatan* ["citizen"] of ʿUnayzah. There were no
jails here in the past.

Doughty describes a similar picture of little serious crime in ʿUnayzah in the past. According to him,

> persons accused of crime at Aneyza (where is no prison), are bound
> until the next sitting of the Emir. Kenneyny told me there had been in
> his time but one capital punishment; this was fifteen years ago. The
> offender was a woman. . . . She had enticed to her yard a little maiden,
> the only daughter of a wealthy family, her neighbors; and there she
> smothered the child for the (golden) ornaments of her pretty head, and
> buried the innocent body. . . . Common misdoers and thieves are
> beaten with palm-leaf rods that are to be green and not in the dry,
> which (they say) would break fell and bones. There is no cutting off the
> hand at Aneyza; but any hardened felon is cast out of the township.
> (Doughty 1979 [1888], 2:395)

According to Doughty, the amir collected considerable revenue
from the local population in the form of annual dues. No tax was
levied on houses, shops, or animals, but wheat was taxed in some
cases at 2.5 percent and in other cases at 5 percent of the produce. The
amir also collected 7.5 percent of the date harvest. Important merchants with ties to commercial trading houses abroad were, according

to Doughty, richer than the amir and paid him a modest contribution in money. Most of these revenues "which were full of envy—[came] not to [the amir's] purse: there are expenses of the public service, and especially for the mothif ['guest house']" (Doughty 1979 [1888], 2:474).

Aside from mediating conflicts and maintaining law and order, the amir was responsible for the military defense of the community and for leading it in warfare. According to Doughty,

> the Emir writes the names of those who are to ride in a ghrazzu ["raid"]; they are mostly the younger men of households able to maintain a thelul ["riding camel"]. Military service falls upon the substantial citizens. . . . The popular sort that remain at home, mind their daily labor; and they are a guard for the town. . . . Two men ride upon a warfaring thelul; the radhif is commonly a brother, a cousin, or client (often a Beduwy) or servant of the owner.—If one who was called be hindered, he may send another upon his dromedary with a backrider. If he be not found in the muster with the Emir, and have sent none in his room, it may be overlooked in a principal person; but, in such case, any of the lesser citizens might be compelled. . . . The townsmen rode in three troops, with the ensigns of the three great wards of Aneyza; but the town banners are five or six, when there is warfare at home. (Doughty 1979 [1888], 2:474–475)

The amir, although he had substantial power, did not monopolize power in all community decisions, as can be gleaned from the above statements. Similar to shaykhs ruling before the contemporary period in the Arabian Gulf (Rumaihi 1984), in Haʾil (Rosenfeld 1965), and in Buraydah (Doughty 1979 [1888]; Helms 1981), his power was backed by a militia of the townsmen which he called into existence at times of warfare to defend the community. He also had an entourage of armed slaves and Bedouin companions who served as a law-enforcing agency within the community. However, he shared authority with the *qadi* and with some of the families in the community, especially those who were tied to him by descent and affinal bonds. He also typically consulted with prominent figures, many of whom were merchants, and learned men in the community. In his *majlis,* he dialogued with various members of the community, and decisions were usually based on consensus. Sometimes it was not possible to maintain this delicate sharing of power. ʿUnayzah's history testifies to the existence of periods of internal strife and competition between families of different tribal descent groups to obtain power.

Periods of internal conflict were sporadic. More permanent was the threat of violence constituted by the independent and warlike tribes of Bedouin who controlled the deserts surrounding the city. However, the Bedouin never invaded the city. Travel and the movement of trade outside the community were negotiated according to established procedures and payments which guaranteed safe passage through territory controlled by Bedouin tribes. Alliances were established with numerous Bedouin groups, but these were never permanent and were always subject to abrupt changes. Alliances had to be renegotiated often in response to volatile and ever-changing relationships among the Bedouin themselves.

The potential for conflict with the Bedouin, however, was muted by the dependence of the Bedouin on essential products produced by the city and for their need to sell animals and animal products to city-based merchants. Indeed, what held this system together was trade. Significantly, the amir's *majlis* was located in the very center of the market. According to Doughty, aside from warfare against the Al Saʿud, the main reason that men from ʿUnayzah embarked upon military expeditions at the time of his visit was to punish those who had attacked and robbed caravans or citizens of the community.

Disparities and Tensions

Both disparities and tensions existed within the old ʿUnayzah. Aside from differences derived from descent status, there was marked inequality in the distribution of wealth. At the top of the scale were well-to-do merchants, who usually had ties with external trading houses and who also tended to be landlords and moneylenders, and the amirs, who had political power and who often had trading interests but not at the same level as those of the major merchants. There were medium-scale merchants, who often came to own land but were not moneylenders. Less well-to-do were small-scale merchants, craftspeople who owned their own means of production, and small-scale *fallalih* who owned their own land. Beneath these were sharecroppers. At the bottom of society were those who worked as hired laborers on farms, menial workers who fetched such things as firewood and water, and some of the craftspeople.

As elsewhere in Najd and in the Arabian Gulf (cf. Rumaihi 1975), indebtedness to merchants and moneylenders was pervasive in the old ʿUnayzah and provides clues to areas of potential conflict between the different parties involved in these relations. On one side were merchants who extended credit and lent money and who were able to become the owners of the means of production through dispossessions as a result of people being unable to repay loans. On the other side were *fallalih* who owned and worked small family farms, sharecroppers, hired laborers, some of the craftspeople, and menial workers. The potential for conflict between these was probably muted by several different factors, which include the ability of the debtor to borrow from others when pressed to pay; the interest of landlords to keep workers on their lands to insure future revenue from the land; an ideology which includes doing good deeds, being compassionate to the meek, and fearing Allah; and a community ethic that would be seriously violated by dispossessing a person from all means of survival. Both Rumaihi (1975) and al-Najjar (1985) indicate that indebtedness in the Arabian Gulf shaykhdoms often led to slavelike relations; however, no evidence indicates that this was the case for ʿUnayzah.

The more serious tension that sometimes erupted into violence was competition for political power and authority within the community. There were also the Bedouin. One cannot deny the existence of political rivalries and violent conflicts, but one must be careful not to overstate this aspect. Raids and warfare figure prominently in the local folklore, mainly in the form of poetry (cf. Sowayan 1985). Conflict and violence are the things that capture the popular imagination, as can be seen by reference to almost any newspaper in the Western world today. But they may well exaggerate the actual situation.

What is perhaps more significant is that agriculture and craft production, as shown in the case of ʿUnayzah, continued even during most periods of conflict. As Doughty noted, "the popular sort" (that is, the workers) remained at home and did their work while the more "substantial" citizens were those who went off on raids. Moreover, conflict among tribes and the potential of "highway" robbery never seriously interrupted ʿUnayzah's caravans and long-distance trade. Significantly, one of the city's intellectuals today considers that Doughty's statement that "Aneyza can never be taken by famine" was his most perceptive. Indeed, a more serious threat than warfare were probably the *jarad*, "locusts," which were considered to be a great delicacy but which often caused major damage to crops. Also, epidemic diseases occasionally spread through the community, killing many.

In conclusion, we would argue that 'Unayzah in the past had its specificity but was not unique within the peninsula. It shared many features with Ha'il, as described by Rosenfeld (1965), although unlike Ha'il it was not strongly associated with a single, powerful Bedouin tribe and never attempted to establish a centralized state to control the region at large or the trade routes which passed through it. Like Huraydah in the Hadramawt described by Bujra (1971), 'Unayzah had a significant degree of stratification, although its elite did not base its claim to such status on descent from religious personages but more on wealth and power, which never completely solidified along descent lines. Moreover, all the people of 'Unayzah, rich and poor, considered themselves people of the community, unlike the case in Huraydah, where only the poorer elements of the population were considered such. Also, many parallels exist with Daghara in southern Iraq as described by Fernea (1970), but farming was not limited to people of tribal status, and many merchants in 'Unayzah, unlike those in Daghara, invested in agricultural land, although like the merchants in Daghara those in 'Unayzah provided credit and loans to farmers.

The old 'Unayzah is not easily classified according to current social science categories. Although some consider tribal identity and organization to be foremost in Najd among both the nomadic and sedentary populations (cf. al-Hamad 1986), this was not the case in 'Unayzah. Identity with the community as a whole—over and above family, kin, and, for some, the tribe—was strong. 'Unayzah was not a closed corporate community but one which engaged in a wide range of activities within the local region and beyond. In some ways, 'Unayzah was like a city-state, but this comparison cannot be pushed too far because people identified and interacted with others outside their community—on the basis of tribal connections, trade networks, and the universalistic religiopolitical structures of Islam.

'Unayzah, as an autonomous amirate, was a complex community in which elements of different modes of production coexisted. Elements of what Amin (1973) and Wolf (1982) call a tributary mode of production existed but did not dominate the system. As the next two chapters will show, agriculture and craft production were primarily organized by domestic social formations that bring to mind the domestic mode of production as described by Sahlins (1972),

Meillassoux (1981), and others; but nonkin and nondomestic reciprocal labor was present along with some wage labor. Also, trade and
transport were predominantly organized by mercantile structures in
which elements of capitalism—the extraction of surplus value, risk
taking, and the profit motive, for example—were present. Moreover,
all this complexity was clearly the result of indigenous evolution.
Neither autonomous ʿUnayzah nor its region was ever colonialized or
penetrated by foreign representatives of capitalist economies and
societies.

CHAPTER 2

The Old Agriculture

The settlements that eventually evolved to form the city of 'Unayzah based their livelihood on agriculture. Throughout the centuries, agriculture continued to provide the productive basis of the economy. The occupational category of *fallah* until about twenty years ago was one of the city's most important—in terms of numbers of people involved and in terms of the contributions of this sector to the overall output of the community.

In 'Unayzah today, people speak of *az-zira'ah at-taqilidiyah*, "traditional agriculture," or simply *az-zira'ah al-qadimah*, "old agriculture," to refer to the ancient farms that continue to dot many parts of what is now the old section of town. While only a few continue to work in this type of agriculture, many of the older generation of men and women worked in it and were able to provide us with detailed descriptions of what they did and of how their work was organized. Most of their descriptions specifically refer to a period between the late 1930s and the 1960s. Important changes were introduced during that period, but much of what they told us closely conforms to what Doughty described for the time of his visit in 1878.

The old agriculture was located within the confines of the city wall and often between neighborhoods. There were also farms on the outskirts of the city and along the sides of the Wadi ar-Rimmah. According to Sharif (1970:119) and al-Wasil (1986:68), the total amount of agricultural land in 1961 was 64,383 dunums (6,438.3 hectares), not including land in dependent villages or towns within the amirate. Although new agricultural expansion had occurred by 1961, much of 'Unayzah's agricultural output still came from old farms.

Located in the middle of a vast desert, ʿUnayzah is what Westerners would call an oasis. The local inhabitants, however, do not use the Arabic term *al-wahah,* which is usually translated as "oasis," to refer to ʿUnayzah. To them, an *al-wahah* is nothing more than a small place where agriculture is practiced around a small well or two in the desert. ʿUnayzah is not such, for to them it is, and was, a *madinah,* "city." Its urban classification derived not only from its size but from its functions as the center for the political administration of the whole amirate and as a market center, in addition to having a Friday mosque. In what have been called "preindustrial" cities of this type, it was not uncommon that a large proportion of the population worked in agriculture (cf. Sjoberg 1960; Abu-Lughod 1971). That agriculture can be the occupation of urbanites is not uncommon in the Middle East, as, for example, in the case of Damascus, which had rich agricultural lands within the bounds of the city. Indeed, London in the past had large agricultural and grazing lands within its boundaries; many of these are now parks.

All agriculture in ʿUnayzah depends on irrigation. Rains in the area are not regular. In some years, there are heavy rains that lead to floods that inundate the farms, especially those in the wadi but also occasionally other farms. In other years, almost no rain will fall. The average rainfall, according to al-Wasil (1986:43), is 124.3 millimeters per year. When the wadi flows, it may flow between two and sixty days, and water also collects in low areas, where it may stay after the wadi stops flowing. In addition, subterranean water that is near the surface of the land is used. This water is supplied from the rain and the flow of the wadi and is thus replenished. This is the water that supplied the irrigation for the old agriculture. While some of the wells have sweet water, much of the water has a high salt content.

Within the confines of the city of ʿUnayzah, the soils are generally characterized as being very hard and difficult to turn because they have a high content of gypsum and silt. The topsoil is deep here because of sedimentation from the wadi. This land is good mainly for palm trees and alfalfa. In the wadi, the soils are varied and there are various mixtures of sand, clay, pebbles, and silt. Despite the relatively high content of salt, this area does not suffer from the problem of being alkaline. Parts of the wadi are surrounded by sand dunes and are thus difficult to irrigate, and some of the soils have deteriorated due to drainage problems. To the south of ʿUnayzah, the soils are more sandy and retain water well but they are on the way to becoming more alkaline. With their high calcium and low sodium, these soils are good for dates, as well as for citrus and grapes (al-Wasil 1986:58–63).

In the summer months of June through August, the average daytime high is 41.5° Celsius, with the highest recorded temperature being 47°. In the winter, the average daytime high is 23°, with an average low of 9° at night. The lowest is 0°. Winter temperatures can drop suddenly due to cold northerly and northwesterly winds. Temperatures also sometimes rise suddenly in both spring and autumn, when the hot *simum* winds blow from the southwest (al-Wasil 1986:39).

Land Tenure and the Acquisition of Land

A relatively complex system of land tenure developed in ʿUnayzah. To understand this system and its evolution, it is useful to begin with a discussion of the desert areas surrounding ʿUnayzah. These areas are referred to as *al-barr*, "wilderness," or *'ard baydah*, "white land" or undeveloped land. In these areas, a wide variety of both perennial and annual plants were and still are grazed by the herds and flocks of the Bedouin. In the past, these areas provided ʿUnayzah with important sources of both firewood and *ʿushb*, a wild desert grass, which was gathered, stored, and later used as fodder, with much of it being taken to the market, where it was either bartered or sold for cash. In addition, these areas were used for grazing animals that belonged to people in the community.

Until 1953, when a state decree abolished the *hima*, "preserve," system throughout the country (Hajrah 1982:23–24), ʿUnayzah had an area in the desert which was reserved for the grazing of its own herds of animals and to which others were not allowed access. This *hima* was communal property and belonged to the people of ʿUnayzah. Grazing was controlled on a seasonal basis and, during certain periods of the year or sometimes even during whole years, grazing was forbidden in an effort to allow the area to recuperate and replenish itself. Furthermore, it was forbidden to cut down any trees or bushes, to collect firewood, or to cut grass from within the *hima*. Regulation of the use of this area was strictly enforced by the amir. In recent years, the *hima* system has been revived to a certain degree. The area has been marked off by concrete pillars and can be used only as a communal grazing area, with the cutting of trees or bushes or the development of private agricultural land being once again forbidden.

Undeveloped land outside the *hima* or even within the confines of the walls of the city was considered the territory of the community as a whole. However, individuals could and did obtain private ownership of such land through the Islamic principle of *ihya'*, which means "to endow with life." This is based on a Tradition of the Prophet Muhammad accepted as authentic by all four legal schools of Sunni Islam. This Tradition states, in translation, "He who endows barren land with life, it becomes his." In order to obtain legal ownership of such land, the person developing it had to prove that it had in fact been barren and did not belong to someone else. Ownership of land obtained in this fashion is known as *mulk hurr*, "freehold." Such land could be bought and sold without any limitations and could also be passed on from one generation to the next through inheritance.

However, it is unlikely that the people who developed barren land in the past in and around 'Unayzah did so with the primary intention of establishing private ownership rights to the land. For most, the purpose of such activity was to provide livelihood through farming, and that which was of value was the produce of the land. Only a few—mainly merchants—invested in the development of land primarily for the exchange value of its produce. That land was owned as private property implies that it was a commodity; however, as such it had little value, as there was almost no market for the buying and selling of land. Much land remained in the area that could have been developed for agriculture; the only limiting factors were those of technology and the lack of labor.

An example of how private ownership of land came about essentially as a by-product of an activity to obtain a product from the land is the planting of *'athal* trees. This story is particularly cherished by the people of 'Unayzah. Any adult will tell you how in the past some men would carry young *'athal* trees on their backs for several kilometers into the outskirts of the city, where they would plant them in the sand. Men or women would then regularly carry water to them for a period of six months to a year. After that, they did not have to be watered and would grow on their own. When the trees were fully grown, they would then be cut and brought back into town, where they were used in the building of houses, for doors, and in a number of tools and implements.

As people today point out, the planting of *'athal* trees had a number of unintended consequences. One of these was that they controlled the shifting of sand dunes and protected the city and its farms from being inundated by sand. Also, they provided shade and served as windbreaks. More importantly, for those who planted them they provided the means for obtaining private ownership of the land on which they were grown. This was acquired through the process of *ihya*. As the city has expanded within the past two decades, much of this land greatly increased in value and thus, for some, what had originally been a way to supplement a meager livelihood provided an avenue to great wealth. These considerations are widely appreciated in the community to such a degree that several men insisted that the anthropologist take a picture of the trees, as they felt the trees were highly symbolic of both the old and the new ways of life and of their struggle to eke an existence out of an essentially volatile and difficult environment.

Ownership of most of the old agricultural land occurred in much the same way as has recently happened in the case of the *'athal* trees. Many did not document the ownership of agricultural land until two or three decades ago, when land increased in value as a commodity and when official documentation became institutionalized.

Another way of obtaining land was through what is referred to in 'Unayzah as an *'iqta'*, "grant," from the amir of 'Unayzah. If a person wished to develop a piece of unused land that was within the territory of the amirate, he presented a request to the amir, who, if he had no objections, would then send one of his assistants to measure the land, record its location, and verify that it was in fact barren and not owned or claimed by others. When this was done, the amir would either verbally grant the land to the individual or, as has been the case more recently, give the individual a written document with his seal affixed to it. Land obtained in this fashion was considered to be freehold and, like that obtained through *ihya*, could be sold or passed on through inheritance.

A third way of obtaining land was through repossession of land which had been put up as collateral against debts. This was mainly done by merchants and moneylenders. In the words of Abu Talal, a man about fifty years old and a descendant of one of 'Unayzah's most prominent land-owning merchant families,

> our family came to 'Unayzah over two centuries ago from another town in Najd. We have always been merchants and we have always

helped the many poor *fallalih* here in ʿUnayzah by giving them loans. If they could not repay them, as was often the case, we would take possession of their lands, and the *fallalih* would work on them as sharecroppers. Although we are landowners, we have never farmed the land ourselves. We were not the only ones, however, who gave loans to farmers. There were other merchant families who did this as well.

The *fallah* by no means lost his land every time he took a loan from a merchant, and we are unable to specify how much agricultural land exchanged hands in that manner. However, all our informants agreed that many farms were owned by merchants and that much of their land was obtained through repossession, although few recalled specific incidents of such repossession.

In ʿUnayzah, people who had freehold ownership of agricultural land were reluctant to sell it outright to others. However, they did lease it to others for various periods of time that ranged from about fifty to one thousand years. Possession of land in this fashion is referred to as *subrah*. When land was obtained in this way, a contract was drawn up between the owner of the land and the person leasing it. The period of time of the lease was stated, as was the amount of annual fees to be paid. The amount to be paid was usually in the form of a certain amount of wheat or dates or, more rarely, a certain amount of money. In such cases, the lessee and his descendants have the right to use the land but do not own it. The lease on the land may also be sold to others. Much of the old agricultural land in ʿUnayzah is said to have *subrah* on it.

Some of the agricultural land in ʿUnayzah was, and is, held as *waqf*, "trust." At one point this was freehold land which was bequeathed as a trust for the support of a religious institution or the owner's descendants. Like freehold land, such land was often leased to others, although the lease arrangements were somewhat different. The beneficiaries would lease it for a season or more for money or a percentage of the produce of up to 10 percent. Other arrangements could be made for longer periods, in which case the beneficiaries would receive up to half the produce of the dates and enough animal fodder to meet the needs of their animals. Such lease arrangements could also be made for non-*waqf* land, although this was uncommon.

When inheritance of land over many generations is added to the various forms of land ownership and leasing arrangements, it is not surprising that any given piece of land is likely to have a complicated and often confusing history. It is not uncommon for a piece of land to be owned by the descendants of someone who leased it as *subrah* to someone some five hundred years ago. The original lessee may have passed it on to his descendants, who then sold the lease to someone else, who may also have sold it. The descendants of the original owner may have moved to another place and are no longer in 'Unayzah. Yet they own the land and the lessee must pay them their dues or they may reclaim the land. At the same time, palm trees that have been planted by the lessee belong to him rather than to the landowner, as do any buildings that the lessee has erected on the land. People in 'Unayzah recognize that *subrah* land is particularly complicated, and there are specialized brokers in the community who collect the fees (now usually calculated in cash) from lessees and pass them on to the owners, who may be unknown to the present lessee.

Most farms were small. Of 293 landholdings which Sharif identified as existing in the 'Unayzah area in 1961, 45 percent were 2.5 hectares or less in size, while 20 percent were half a hectare or less in size. On the other hand, 35 percent had between 2.5 and 10 hectares, while 20 percent had more than 10 hectares (Sharif 1970: 118–121). Most of the larger farms had been recently established and thus do not belong to the old agriculture. Also, by 1961 numerous farms had been abandoned or were being converted to urban land use. However, the pattern of many small farms with a few larger ones existed at the time of Doughty's visit in 1878 and can be considered a characteristic of the old agricultural system—at least since the nineteenth century.

Sharecropping

Although Sharif (1970: 120) and al-Wasil (1986: 71) indicate that most of the old agricultural land was farmed by its owners, our data indicate that this was not the case. Although we did not conduct an agricultural census, all the people we talked with said that the most common way for land to be farmed was through sharecropping arrangements. While some of the people referred to as *fallalih* did work on their own land, most of it is said to have been owned by merchants and farmed by *fallalih* sharecroppers.

Various types of sharecropping arrangements were made. The most common was an arrangement in which the sharecropper provided seeds, animals, fertilizers, labor, and the costs of irrigation. The landlord provided developed land, including a well. He would receive one-third of the produce of the palm trees or one-third of the wheat (or a combination of these two). The sharecropper would receive the remaining two-thirds of this produce plus all the other crops that he grew on the land.

Another type of arrangement existed for undeveloped land or land that had fallen into disuse. The owner would enter into an arrangement with a sharecropper to develop it on the basis of a splitting of the produce on a one-fourth/three-fourths basis, with three-fourths of the produce going to the person (i.e., the sharecropper) who developed it.

The following case illustrates a rental agreement in which a family farmed land as sharecroppers, paying a proportion of the produce of the date trees as rent to the landlord. They rented this farm for twenty-eight years, which was longer than most sharecropping arrangements we heard about. The case also shows the leasing of land as part of a *subrah* relationship, in which the amount to be paid is set forth as an absolute amount of wheat and barley. Umm Nasr, a woman about fifty, described the situation:

> When I was thirteen, I got married and moved with my husband to live on his father's farm. We lived with my husband's younger brother and his wife and my husband's parents. My husband's father had rented that farm for a period of twenty-eight years. The arrangement was to pay one-quarter of the dates to the owner and nothing else. We grew dates, wheat, alfalfa, and vegetables. We had nine camels and we hired a family to attend to the *sawani* ["irrigation mechanism/system"].
>
> At the end of that rental agreement, my husband and his brother took a lease on a farm for five hundred years, paying annually 190 *sagh* ["bushels"] of wheat and 18 *sagh* of barley. When we took this farm, it was not in good condition. We have greatly improved it, and my husband and his brother are devoted to farming. We now grow grapes and citrus fruits, as well as the traditional crops.

Sharecropping agreements were formally agreed upon between the landowner and the *fallah* and, at least in relatively recent times, have been written down. The usual agreement was for a period of about six years. The arrangement could be renewed, although it was not at all uncommon for sharecroppers to move from farm to farm during the course of their lifetime. Numerous old *fallalih* men, most of whom have now become landowners of newly developed farms, reported that they had formerly been sharecroppers and had worked on as many as five or six different farms with different owners.

Irrigation

The old agriculture depended on irrigation from wells that were dug by specialists from within the community. Digging the wells involved work that is perceived by people in ʿUnayzah today as having been both difficult and dangerous, although well paid. The wells varied in depth between about five and fifteen meters. They were approximately three meters in diameter and the upper parts of them were lined with stones or with the trunks of palm trees.

Water was drawn from the wells by a mechanism known as the *sawani*. This consisted of up to five pulleys which were made of wood and attached to the trunks of ʾathal trees. Ropes made of palm fiber or of camel leather were used to pull leather buckets filled with water which were emptied into basins for distribution through runnels to the farm. Although human beings sometimes drew water from wells, this was normally done by camels, which were guided back and forth by women who sang to them and who also fed them a combination of alfalfa and *shawk,* a thorny plant. People today say this was a "sandwich," since the alfalfa was put on the outside and the *shawk* in the middle "to fool the camel." Up to twenty camels in four shifts of five were used. They started in the evening and continued throughout the night and into the morning until around noon, when a break would be taken until late afternoon or early evening and the process would start over again.

People today often speak with nostalgia of the old *sawani*. They particularly remember the women singing and speak of the wonderful sound of "wishshsh" the water made as it emptied into the basins. However, irrigation required a heavy input of human labor, and the camels that were used were both expensive to buy and to feed. In larger and medium-size farms, the usual arrangement was for the *fallah* to hire a family to carry out this work.

An example of a case in which the *fallah* hired a family to carry out the work related to irrigation is provided by Umm Fahad, who is about sixty years old. When she was recently married, her husband had a sharecropping arrangement with a landlord named Abu Ibrahim. She and her husband, together with their children and his unmarried sister, lived and worked together on this farm. This was about forty years ago. According to Umm Fahad,

> although my husband distributed the water to the fields, he hired a family to work the *sawani*. We owned twenty camels, which were used to draw the water out of the well. The family my husband hired consisted of a man, his mother, and his wife and their children, and they lived on the farm. They worked throughout the night and into the morning the next day. The man and his wife and mother would rotate in guiding the camels back and forth as they brought up the water. The camels were used in four shifts of five at a time. They had to be harnessed and this was usually done by the man. The women prepared a mixture of alfalfa and of straw or thorn, which was like a sandwich, and fed this to them. It normally required two people to feed the camels—the woman and one of her children or her mother-in-law. Occasionally, they also had to level the ground where the camels walked back and forth, and this was mainly done by the women. One person also supervised the pouring of the water from the buckets into the *birkah* ["basin"], where it was collected for later distribution to the fields.
>
> The man of this family received 30 riyals per month, although this was not always paid monthly. We also gave them some of the produce of the farm such as vegetables in season, dates, and pomegranates. They provided the rest of their food, although we occasionally gave them some milk and eggs.

According to informants, the use of as many as twenty camels in the *sawani* was the maximum ever used to water land from a single well. On small farms where there was less land to irrigate, the *fallah*, whether sharecropper or freeholder, had a smaller *sawani* and often used as few as two camels. As his farm was small and his income thus limited, he could not afford to hire labor to operate the *sawani*. Therefore, he and his family provided all the work needed for irrigation. In cases when the camels became too weak to work or died and could not be replaced, both the men and the women had to do the hard work of drawing water out of the well.

Crops and Labor

The main traditional crops were dates, pomegranates, figs, wheat, millet, barley, alfalfa, pumpkin, squash, peppers, eggplant, okra, black-eyed peas, watercress, onions, leeks, coriander, cumin, fenugreek, melons, and watermelons. All the traditional crops are still grown, along with a number of new crops that have been introduced since the 1950s. The *fallalih* also had cows, sheep, goats, camels, donkeys, and chickens. Almost all agricultural work is now done by expatriate males, as will be shown in Part Three. However, all agricultural work was done by local men and women in the past.

The two most important crops were dates and wheat. These were not only important for subsistence but were used for a number of transactions within the community. They were also the main products sold to people from outside ʿUnayzah—mainly to the Bedouin and, in the case of dates, to people in the cities of the Hijaz. Within the community, dates and wheat were important items used to pay off debts, to pay leases on land, and often as payments to craftspeople for any services performed.

Dates had and still have a very important place in the local culture of the people of ʿUnayzah. They were, and are, regularly served both with coffee and as part of almost every meal. People talk a great deal about them and are very proud of them, especially two varieties, the *barhi* and the *sukkari,* which are of very fine quality. They often made a point of telling both anthropologists of the many products that, aside from the fruit itself, were derived from the date palm and that played central parts in their material culture in the past. These products included numerous items made from the fiber of the tree and from the wood of its trunk. However, what is most significant is that the date was the most important staple in their diet in the past. The seeds were also boiled and fed to animals as fodder, although as one woman said, "The animals have become too modernized and now refuse to eat them!"

All the work related to palm trees was done by males except in very rare cases when poverty made it necessary for females to do some of the work. The planting and care of the saplings during the first three to four months of their existence requires expert knowledge, and a specialist was and still is sometimes brought in to do this work. Both young trees and old ones have to be watered regularly—

twice a day in the hot months if planted in sandy soil and once a day if in clay. After they have grown for about five years, fertilizer has to be applied. Depending on the variety, the young palm tree is ready to bear fruit after three to ten years. However, before bearing fruit, all the trees—whether young or old—must first be pruned and then inseminated. This work was done by the *fallah* if he had the expert knowledge and ability to do so. Otherwise, he brought in an expert. As in the past, this work takes between ten days and one month on an average-size farm and is done in April.

A month and a half after they have been inseminated, the branches bearing the fruit have to be disentangled from each other. They are then supported with sticks, and about ten days later a number of branches are tied together with rope. The tree is then left alone for about a month until the dates begin to be harvested. The time of the harvesting depends on the variety of the palm tree and continues throughout the summer and into the early fall. Altogether, there are at least thirty kinds of dates in 'Unayzah that differ according to color, size, sugar content, moisture, flavor, potential for storage and processing, and time of maturity.

All the work of watering the trees, preparing them to bear fruit, and harvesting them was the work of local males. With the exception of watering the trees, all tasks required the men to climb up the tree, which was quite dangerous, especially as the old trees were very high and the men often did not have strong enough ropes to support themselves. Indeed, it sometimes happened that the man would fall to his death. Given the difficulty of this work, it is remarkable that blind men sometimes did it and became experts in this type of work, as is the case with two blind brothers and two others who were known to the anthropologists.

The processing of dates after the harvest was predominantly a female activity. First, the dates were sorted by hand according to quality. The women processed good quality dates by mixing them with a bit of syrup that had been saved from previous seasons. They were then put into closed containers and pressed. Another way of processing them was to wash the dates with water and then place them in containers that allowed the water to drain. They were then placed in big containers and four or five days later were pressed by hand. Finally, heavy weights were placed on the dates and they were left until winter. Slightly different techniques were used to process dates of medium and low quality. The medium quality dates were placed into special storage containers built into every house, and these were the dates that were consumed on a regular basis throughout the year. The poor quality dates were often fed to animals.

While dates are the crop that people most often talk about, wheat was equally important in their diet and was also used as a form of payment in a number of transactions. Wheat was used in making bread and as the main ingredient in a number of dough-based dishes which are native to 'Unayzah and the Qasim. Wheat is also important because it brought into being collective work groups that transcended the boundaries of the extended family and because it illustrates an important aspect of the sexual division of labor in the society.

Preparing the soil for the planting of wheat was a reciprocal collective activity that was performed by groups of men who were usually neighbors and who might or might not be related by kinship. These men turned the soil with a hoe, working as a group and singing as they proceeded. The soil was then left for a few days to dry and then animal manure was applied by a man (if possible, hired for this purpose) who rode a donkey and distributed the manure on the soil. Then the group of men turned the soil again to mix the soil and the manure together. After this was done, the seeds (which had been saved from the previous year's crop) were planted by the *fallah,* usually assisted by a child or a woman. The soil was then leveled by the *fallah* and divided into basins which were then flooded with irrigation water.

As the wheat grew, the only work required was that of irrigation and occasional weeding. At the time of the harvest, the role of women became more important. They cut the wheat with a sickle, sometimes assisted by men. They piled it in the fields, and it was then transported to a central location on the farm for threshing. If there was a large quantity of wheat, it was carried by men; otherwise, women carried it.

Threshing brought into existence another reciprocal collective work party. Neighbors came with their animals (usually cows), which were driven around on the wheat to separate the husk from the grain. A number of men raked the wheat back into the circle when necessary.

When the wheat had been threshed, women took charge of the processes of winnowing and sifting. They first threw the wheat into the air to separate the straw from the grain. They then passed it through a sieve. If the wheat needed further threshing, this was done by the women by pounding it with a special gavellike implement. They then sifted it several more times. Some of the sieves were small and could be managed by one woman, while others were larger and required two people, either two women, two men, or a man and a woman. Finally, the grain was put into sacks by women. The sacks were then weighed by men "to be exact." The grain was stored at home for consumption, but if any was to be sold, the men took it to the market.

Alfalfa, locally called *tzat,* was and still is extremely important as the main fodder crop. It has to be planted only once every three to five or more years depending on the quality of the soil, whether it is under shade or in the open, and the presence or absence of insects and pests. It is harvested throughout the year by cutting it with a sickle and is usually fed to animals fresh. Machines now often perform the work of harvesting, but some people jokingly say, "The animals do not like it when it has been cut by the machine!" However, many farmers continue to prefer harvesting alfalfa by hand because the machine cuts it too close to the ground and thus may damage it. Once it has been harvested, it quickly grows again and must be cut every two to three weeks before the seeds develop. Consequently, and unlike dates and wheat, alfalfa requires regular work throughout the year.

In the past, women worked almost every day of the week cutting alfalfa, which was then fed to their animals or wrapped into bundles and taken to the market for sale either by the woman or, more commonly, by a man. As was the case with wheat, the preparation of the soil and the planting of the seeds was men's work and was done by reciprocal collective work parties. Also, whenever alfalfa was to be replanted, women harvested it after the seeds had developed and then threshed, winnowed, and sifted it in a process similar to that for wheat, although animals were not used.

The growing of vegetables in the past involved the work of both men and women. The fields were prepared by men and then seeds were planted by either men or women. Irrigation was also done by members of either sex, but weeding and taking care of the plants as they grew was done by women. The harvesting of the crops likewise was the work of women.

The above discussion of both irrigation and the patterns of work related to the cultivation of different crops is basically that which was done on small and medium-size farms. The basic production unit was the extended family, which either owned the land on which they worked or were sharecroppers. Throughout the year, the family provided the labor that was needed for the everyday work of the farm. If they could afford it and the farm was relatively large, they might hire a family to do the work of irrigation, but in most instances this was done by family members.

The sexual division of labor was such that males did the work related to date palms, the turning of the soil and the preparation of the fields and basins for all crops, the distribution of irrigation water, and the threshing of wheat. Females did the work of weeding, harvesting, winnowing, and sifting. Both sexes could do the work normally done by the other sex if necessary. At certain periods in the agricultural cycle, a work force larger than that which could be provided by the extended family was needed. This was achieved through reciprocal collective work groups of neighbors. These were usually men, although women might participate in such groups at the time of the wheat harvest. People who worked together in these groups were not paid, although they were given a meal, and each person had the obligation to work on the farm of others when needed.

On larger farms, the extended family was not big enough to provide the labor required. Almost always a man with his wife and children were engaged to operate the *sawani* and, sometimes, to distribute the water to the fields. Both men and women would be hired on a seasonal basis to work in the preparation of the fields and basins and at the time of the wheat and date harvests. These workers were paid on a daily basis. Some farmers also hired laborers to work throughout the year in weeding and for harvesting crops like alfalfa, and these laborers were paid monthly. Payment for both types of laborers was commonly both in kind and in cash.

A case illustrating a small, rather poor farm is provided by Umm ʿAli, who is in her fifties and was born in Makkah. Her father was from ʿUnayzah. He divorced her mother shortly after her birth and she and her mother returned to ʿUnayzah and lived with her mother's father, who owned a farm which had a well, four or five cows, three donkeys, and a few goats. There were about one hundred date palms. They also grew wheat and alfalfa, as well as vegetables. According to Umm ʿAli,

> I was raised with my grandmother and grandfather and my maternal uncles and aunts. Over the years, my uncles married. One of them moved away, while the other brought his wife to live with us.

I was very young then but I can remember that my mother and her brother daily went out to collect firewood and *'ushb*. My grandfather looked after the palm trees and my grandmother attended to the *sawani*. Sometimes, the men and the women on that farm drew water from the well themselves because there were not enough animals. Early in the morning, my grandmother would work on the *sawani* with one of the other women helping her. If another woman was free, she would help with feeding the animals as they drew up the water. My grandfather and one of my uncles looked after the palm trees and distributed the water for irrigation.

At lunchtime, which in those days was before the noon prayer, the men took a break and the women turned to grinding wheat, weaving straw mats, and attending to household duties. Everybody returned to work on the farm from mid-afternoon until around sunset. The women then prepared the main meal, and when that was over attended to the animals and milked the cows, prepared the fodder to feed the animals the next day, and also did a lot of work to process the wheat for the next day's meal. They would also work on making a number of different straw products which they would later on take to the market to sell. After sunset, the men would eat their meal and then relax and go to sleep.

I remember that when the land had to be prepared for planting the wheat, men from the neighboring farms would come to help my grandfather and uncle. Also, at the time of the harvest, my grandfather and uncle both worked helping the women, who were joined by other women from the neighboring farms. In those days, everybody helped everybody else. We helped our relatives and neighbors and they helped us. Nobody paid [money] in those days.

When the wheat harvest was over, my grandfather loaded his donkeys and took the wheat to the market, where he gave it to a merchant who had given us credit throughout the year for buying food or animals or whatever we needed.

Although we usually had enough to eat, I remember a time when there was absolutely nothing to eat in the house. I was crying because I wanted some food. My mother felt pity for me and so she went out to a neighbor's around noon and took some leeks from them. She took these to the house of Abu Hamad, whose family was rich. She took the leeks to them as a gift, hoping that they would give her some dates. She came back very late in the afternoon with some dates, and we all jumped on them and ate them all up.

As this case illustrates, when extra help was needed beyond the extended family, neighbors worked together on a reciprocal basis and without pay. This case also shows that owning a farm did not guarantee that one would never be hungry. This was due to a combination of factors that include the small size of many farms and the pattern of indebtedness to merchants which in its extreme form led to the alienation of the property itself.

Another case was provided by Umm Mansur, who is over sixty years of age. This case illustrates occupational change in the old ʿUnayzah, work within the domestic setting, and lease arrangements paid for in kind. Umm Mansur's father worked as a pearl diver in the Arabian Gulf and then returned to ʿUnayzah to become a sharecropper. He rented various farms, sometimes for up to ten years at a time. He mainly grew dates, melons, vegetables, and wheat. As she recalls,

it was basically the family who did the work and took care of the animals. My mother and father worked on the *sawani,* and my father usually distributed the water to the land. We all helped when it came to preparing the land, but it was basically my father and his nephew and paternal cousin who came and helped him to turn the soil with the hoe. They would stay for dinner and this was the only "pay" they received.

My mother and other women took care of the animals and other tasks on the farm. They were particularly busy at harvest time when, together with the men, they would thresh, winnow, and sift the wheat. They put the wheat in sacks, which they bought from Bedouin women.

When I was about fifteen, I married a man who worked cutting firewood and had a camel on which he transported items for people in ʿUnayzah. My husband's brother had rented a farm, and we all lived together, and I helped him and his wife in all the work on the farm. I did all sorts of work. I worked on the *sawani.* I cut alfalfa. I sifted wheat and alfalfa. I even helped turn the soil for planting and I even climbed palm trees. On the side, I made straw mats. I was not very clever, so it took me one month to produce one mat. Others could do this in ten days. I sold the mats in the market and bought things for us all. My husband's brother had rented the land for one-quarter of the dates produced on the farm, which were given to the landowner, who was a merchant.

My husband gave up working in transport with his camel, and we both took up agriculture together. We leased [in a *subrah*-type arrangement] five different farms over a period of sixteen years. For one farm, we paid fifty *waznah* [a measure] of dates per year and nothing else. For another one, we paid fifty *sagh* of wheat. For the others, we paid thirty *waznah* of dates and thirty *sagh* of wheat. I remember a time when we could not pay all that produce to the owner and we had to buy from the market to make up the difference. All the other crops we produced on the farm belonged to us, including the animals, although we had to borrow to buy them.

I worked on these farms with my husband, our sons, their wives when they later married, and our unmarried daughters. My brother and his wife would also help us for free when we needed extra labor, and we would help them when they needed us. When my husband got too old, he gave up agriculture and only worked as a *mu²adhdhin* ["prayer caller in a mosque"]. We gave up the leases.

Distribution of Agricultural Production and Indebtedness

Part of the production of the *fallah* family, whether freeholder or sharecropper, remained with the family and provided the main source for their own sustenance and for the reproduction of their crops. Dates and wheat were stored for use throughout the year. Seeds were saved and used for planting the next season's crops.

In addition, all producers paid a proportion of their date and wheat production as taxes to the amir (and later to Ibn Sa'ud). Sharecroppers paid up to one-third of their date and wheat production to the landlord. What remained was placed on the market, used as payment in kind to obtain animals (especially for the *sawani*) and the services and/or products of craftspeople, or used for the payment of debts to merchants and moneylenders.

Fallalih producers often supplemented their own agricultural production by the collection of *'ushb* from the *barr* and by craft production of various straw and palm tree products. These items were mainly placed on the market, although some were used by the producers. On occasion, they also worked as day laborers on large farms.

The *fallalih* had to obtain animals from others, as well as all the tools and implements used in irrigation and in tilling the soil and processing crops. Some of them had to pay families to operate the *sawani* and, occasionally, day laborers. On occasion, *fallalih* also had to pay to have a house built or a well dug, and those household utensils they themselves did not make were also obtained from others. As was often the case, they did not have the means to pay for these items when they needed them and, therefore, they took them on credit against payment, usually in the form of part of their produce at the time of the harvest.

Since there was a general shortage of cash among the majority of inhabitants, a person who wanted to obtain something belonging to others went to a merchant he knew (who might or might not be a sharecropper's landlord). The merchant would provide him with the item, if he had it in stock, or obtain it from someone else. If the merchant had the desired item in stock, he would give it to the person on credit and, in the case of *fallalih,* quote a certain amount of dates, wheat, and/or other produce as the price to be paid at the time of the harvest. The price quoted by the merchant was always higher than what it would have been if the purchaser had paid for it at the time of the transaction. If the merchant did not have the desired item, he would obtain it from someone who did, pay for it, and charge the purchaser on credit. In such cases, the purchaser did not know the price the merchant had actually paid. Furthermore, the debtor was usually illiterate and did not keep records of the debts he had incurred.

Since the *fallah* paid off his debts in the form of agricultural produce at the time of the harvest, he often did not have enough provisions to last him and his family throughout the year. He therefore had to take food on credit from merchants, especially during the winter months. As his debts increased, his creditors were also likely to increase in number as he borrowed from some to pay off others. Indeed, share-croppers sometimes had to borrow to meet payments to their land-lords, a phenomenon that became a problem after several years of bad crops as a result of plagues of locusts or especially cold winters. As debts proliferated and if he had experienced a series of bad seasons, the *fallah* began to confront a crisis situation which could lead to mortgaging his land or all his dates. The mortgaging of land in ex-treme cases led to the eventual loss of the land to creditors. It should be stressed that creditors seldom, if ever, insisted on immediate pay-ment of debts. The pattern of debt relationships between *fallalih* and merchants in ʿUnayzah is strikingly similar to the situation described by Fernea (1970) for Daghara in southern Iraq. As we were told by ʿUnayzah people who had themselves incurred debts, "some people *yikhafu Allah* ['feared Allah'] and were considerate of the conditions that led to the *fallah* not being able to pay, and they would extend the debts without additional charges."

Frequently, creditors were patient in the collection of debts, as the following case shows. Abu Muhammad is in his late sixties. His father owned a farm on which they grew palm trees, wheat, and vegetables. He recalls,

When I was a boy, none of us had any money, and although we had a farm, we only had a few dates for breakfast and ate one simple meal after sunset. Sometimes we had a cow and drank buttermilk, but this was not always. As a child I remember being very hungry.

I used to go with my father to the market where we would meet Abu Salim, who was a merchant. He gave us cloth, coffee, tea, sugar, and, sometimes in the winter, he would give us dates and wheat. I remember that once we needed to buy a cow. My father went to Abu Salim, who sent him to another man, who gave him a cow.

In the summer when we had harvested all our crops, my father and my older brother took a lot of the dates and wheat to Abu Salim. There were two years in which my father could not pay even small amounts of his debts to Abu Salim. He got upset, and my father became very depressed and was embarrassed. He knew that he could not face Abu Salim and so he went to another merchant whom I did not know. He borrowed from this merchant and paid back part of his debts to Abu Salim. He also brought back some other things that he had taken on credit from this merchant. Later I heard him tell my mother that he had mortgaged the palm trees to this man. Thus, when the next summer came, we looked at all of our dates when they were harvested but we could not eat even one of them and we had to take other dates from the market.

In another similar case, the creditor was very impatient. After a number of years in which the debtor was unable to pay anything, the creditor sent a couple of his men to press the *fallah* to pay. These men had been instructed by the creditor to collect all the dates that were in the *jusah*, the private storage compartment for dates located inside the house. This was the family's main source of food for the winter months. A well-known and respectable member of the neighborhood came to the house and stopped the men from taking the dates away and swore on the name of Allah that he would not allow them to take dates from the home of this man to pay off debts. The indignation expressed by this intervention shows that such behavior was extreme on the part of the creditor and was not accepted by the community. Another case which shows how people sometimes changed from being sharecroppers to being hired laborers as a result of incurring many debts, which they eventually could not pay off, was described by Umm Hamad, who is over fifty-five years old:

> My father used to be a sharecropper on land that belonged to Abu Khalifah. We all worked on the farm growing alfalfa, cumin, coriander, squash, eggplant, onions, millet, wheat, and dates. I remember always that we had a problem paying the rent of the land to the landlord and the debts to the creditors. While we did not talk about it much, it was a constant worry for both my father and mother. Several times we could not pay. Things became so bad that my father decided not to try to renew the arrangement with the landlord when its time came up. Probably it would not have been renewed even if he had asked. It was at this time that I got married and went to live with my husband's father. My father and the rest of my family went to live on another farm where they worked on the *sawani*, receiving a monthly pay. This was somewhat better because each month they got a bit of money and they were also given some food from the farm to eat.

Another case is provided by Umm Khalid, who is about sixty years old. Her father married altogether fourteen different wives at different times. She was raised by her paternal uncle and lived with him and his wife and their three children. Her uncle was an *'uqayli*, "long-distance trader," and used to go to Syria to bring back merchandise, which he sold wholesale in 'Unayzah. This case is an extreme one in that it shows a man who took advantage of his relatives who had trusted him because he was a kinsman. It also shows how a sharecropper could be deprived of access to the use of land as a result of debts, as well as the dangers of not keeping records of debts and repayments, which is something that the *fallalih* seldom did as they were often illiterate and left the record keeping to the creditor. In Umm Khalid's words:

> I got married when I was quite young, but my husband died soon after we were married. I married again, and we lived with my husband's father and his family. They owned a small farm but they also rented a farm as sharecroppers from my husband's maternal uncle. He also gave us things we needed on credit. I remember that this went on for eight years, and we paid him back both in crops and sometimes in money. Because he was a relative, we never wrote down our payments to him.

One day he came and said that we were very much in debt and threw us out. He sold our animals and took back the land. It hurt us very much because we trusted him as a kinsman and did not bother to record what we paid him. Years later, when they looked at the accounts, they showed that we actually had money owing to us.

Fallalih were often in debt to a merchant who gave them credit or to a moneylender. If they were sharecroppers, they also owed part of their dates and wheat to the landlord. The landlord, the merchant, and the moneylender could be the same person, although this was not always the case. Although some people in ʿUnayzah say that *fallalih* got into debt mainly due to mismanagement, it should be clear from the above analysis that *fallalih* seldom had any choice and were easily drawn into a vicious cycle that in its extreme form could lead to the loss of the farm and their animals, which were the main sources of their livelihood. Although the *fallah,* whether freeholder or sharecropper, was often in a difficult situation because of his debts, people perceive that his situation was better than that of the day worker, who had nothing but his labor to rely on and who was more vulnerable to fluctuations in the agricultural cycle. Having access to land and its produce, even if burdened with debts, provided people with a sense of security, because they could usually find something to eat and most likely even borrow more against it.

Although individual *fallalih* sometimes had to supplement their own agricultural production with other work and often became indebted, the total agricultural production of ʿUnayzah was sufficient to meet the basic food needs of the total population of the city, which included large numbers of people who did not engage in agricultural production. In addition, ʿUnayzah's agricultural production contributed to meeting the needs of the Bedouin in the region, while parts of it were "exported" to the Hijaz and other parts of Najd. This surplus agricultural production thus provided the basis for the development of craft production and of local, regional, and long-distance trade controlled by ʿUnayzah merchants.

CHAPTER 3

Craft Production and the Old Market

The agricultural productive base of ʿUnayzah's economy in the past was supplemented by local craft production and by the pastoral production of the Bedouin. The articulation of these three bases was organized by the local market. Together, the three productive bases provided the surplus which allowed for the development of long-distance trade, which made ʿUnayzah famous and some of its merchants and traders relatively wealthy.

Socially and politically, the Bedouin existed separate from ʿUnayzah, although some ʿUnayzah people shared tribal descent with some of them. Economically, Bedouin were linked to ʿUnayzah as consumers of the city's agriculture and craft production and as purveyors of animals and animal products, which ʿUnayzah traders marketed locally and abroad. Profits obtained by the traders from the sale of animals and their products stimulated the import of mainly luxury items into ʿUnayzah, where they were sold and whence traders further distributed them to other cities, towns, villages, and Bedouin camps. The transport of both imported and locally produced items was accomplished by camel caravans based in ʿUnayzah.

Craft Production

Although the Bedouin existed outside the bounds of ʿUnayzah as different social communities, craft producers were an integral part of the local society. More than one hundred years ago, Doughty noted that handicraftsmen here in a Middle Nejd town (of the sanies' caste), are armourers, tinkers, coppersmiths, goldsmiths; and the workers in wood are turners of bowls, wooden locksmiths, makers of camel saddleframes, well-wheel-wrights, and (very unhandsome) carpenters [for they are nearly without tools]; the stone-workers are hewers, well-steyners and sinkers, besides marble-wrights, makers of coffee mortars and the like; and house-builders and pargeters. We may go on to reckon those that work with the needle, seamsters and seamstresses, embroiderers, sandle makers. The sewing men and women are, so far as I have known them, of the libertine blood. The gold and silver smiths of Aneyza are excellent artificers in filigrane or threadwork; and certain of them established at Mecca are said to excel all in the sacred town. (Doughty 1979 [1888], 2:429)

With the exception of a few older individuals, no one does this work in ʿUnayzah today. However, when asked to list all the specialized occupations other than those of *ʿulamaʾ, umaraʾ, tujjar,* and *fallalih* that he could remember, Abu ʿAliʾs eyes sparkled as he thought for a while before responding. He is seventy-two years old and of slave ancestry.

As a child, when I was about ten years old, I used to work with my mother and father, who gathered firewood in the *barr* to sell in the market. Later on, I worked in the transportation of firewood, first by donkey and then by camel. Then I worked in the repair and sale of weapons and later on became a driver for the Ministry of ———. I am now a farmer. I have bought some land in the wadi and have my own farm now. Three of my sons are *ʿasakir* ["policemen"; "soldiers"], while one is an employee at the bank and another is a teacher. I have not educated my daughters beyond primary school because there is no need for them to be educated or to have jobs. Their work is to serve their husbands. This is good for them and I do not want them to have to work like my mother did, gathering firewood.

The most difficult and dangerous specialized occupation that used to exist here was that of well digger. This was done by men who were very strong and was not necessarily passed on from father to son. Anybody, whether *qabili, khadiri,* or *ʿabd,* who had a strong body could choose to do this work. It brought in good money, more than any other special occupation, but the men who did it died young. This was because of the smoke [dust] of the clay of the wells. They always had bad coughs. There were not many who did this work and they could work in other things as well.

The next most difficult work was that of cutting stone from a quarry that is nearby. These stones were used in the foundations of houses and above doors, and they were also used in the wells. These men had strong bodies, and this was the only kind of work they did.

There were also special camel men who transported the stones from the quarry to the town. This was all that they did, and this was because the camel man had to know how to load the camels with the big, heavy stones. Other camel men specialized in carrying *'athal* trees to be used in the construction of houses, and others brought firewood. These camel men all had only one camel and always worked here within the *dirah* ["territory"]. They were different from the *jammamil,* who had forty or more camels and brought goods which had been shipped from Bahrain to ʿUqayr or Kuwait, and after Ibn Saʿud, to Jubayl.

There were the *sawani* workers, who worked as a family—men, women, and children—and would go and live on a farm for six months at a time. This was very hard work and they spent many hours at it, especially at night.

There were women who carried sweet water in jars on their heads from one of the four main sweet wells. They worked within the town and carried the water to the houses of many people who did not have sweet water in their houses. These women were paid on a monthly basis and they brought the water to the houses every day without fail.

There were also those who worked in leather. These included the *dabbabir* ["tanners"], who processed the skins in their houses, which were all located in a special quarter of the town because of the bad smell, which people did not like. The whole family worked together in this—men, women, and children—and it was passed on from generation to generation. They usually married from among themselves. Aside from these, there were those who bought the leather which had been processed and made many things out of it. They made leather ropes, which were used by the farmers for climbing palm trees and also in the drawing of water from the wells. They made buckets, milk containers, babies' cradles, belts, sandals, and many other things. There were some women who did this work, but they were usually men who worked in their *dakakin* ["shops"] in the *suq* ["market"] whence they sold the product to the buyer.

As for the metalworkers, there were those who worked in copper and made coffeepots and so forth and there were those who worked in iron and made all kinds of tools. There were men who repaired weapons, but there were none who made swords or daggers. This was all done in Najran, in Yemen, or in India. There were also gold- and silversmiths who made jewelry.

There were carpenters who made beautiful doors out of *ʾathal* wood and from other types of wood as well. They also made large and small windows, which they decorated with colors. They made saddles as well as many other things, including bowls and other utensils that were used in the houses. They even made wooden keys and locks. They were really clever and some of them were very skilled and became famous. They not only made things for people here in ʿUnayzah but for people in villages and for the Bedouin.

Speaking of skilled workers, there were also those who worked in the building of houses. These included those who made mud bricks and others who built the house. The builders worked under the direction of an *ustadh* ["master craftsman"].

Finally, there were the *hammarah* ["donkey boys"], who hung around the *suq* and transported items home for the buyers.

Generally, in these occupations the sons followed the work of their fathers. They were usually paid in kind, but the price was quoted in money—in the *riyal fransi* [Maria Theresa dollars]. Only since about 1330 [A.D. 1910] have people normally been paid in money. The sons of the poor almost never had any chance to do anything except help their fathers and mothers. The only other opportunity the sons of the poor had in the past was to go to the gulf—to Kuwait or Bahrain—to work as pearl divers there. But now things are better. All the sons of people who worked in these occupations have become educated and they are teachers or government employees now. Some of them have also become very rich businessmen—even richer than some of the old merchants. There are only a few old men who do this kind of work now. There are still some sandal makers, but they import the leather from Pakistan and India and only put on some decorations.

Thus, craft work occupied a significant proportion of the population, and ʿUnayzah was more than self-sufficient in most craft production. Some of this work was associated with considerations of descent status. Important to note is that Doughty speaks of the "sanies' caste" (from *sunnaʿ* [pl.] or *saniʿ* [sg.], meaning crafts worker) and mentions that some of the craftspeople were "of the libertine blood."

Abu ʿAli also made a point of saying that any man "whether *qabili,
khadiri,* or *ʿabd*" could be a well digger and said that those who processed skins were relegated to a special section of town. He also
stressed that the work of some of the crafts was very hard and suggests that those who followed these occupations were poor and had
few if any opportunities for improvement within the community.
Such evidence indicates that many of those who followed craft occupations were of low social and economic standing in the community.
That this was generally the case was confirmed by other informants.

According to Abu Salah, who is about forty-five years old and one
of the town's intellectuals and who is also of *khadiri* background,

> the population of Najd is composed of three distinct social categories,
> the *qabili,* the *khadiri,* and the *ʿabd.* The *qabili* are those who are of pure
> Arab descent, which means that they are of tribal descent. They in-
> clude most of the Bedouin and many settled people. In the past, they
> considered that the most proper occupation for a man to follow was
> that of a military fighter. They could also be herders, farmers, or mer-
> chants; but they considered some other occupations, such as working
> in leather or with metal or being a butcher or a barber, as *mub halal*
> ["impure"] and thus improper for themselves.
>
> Those of *khadiri* status come from many different backgrounds and
> include people whose ancestors came into the area from other non-
> Arab places in the Middle East, whose ancestors were expelled from
> tribes or decided to leave the tribe, whose ancestors were forced to take
> up "impure" occupations out of economic necessity, and so forth.
> They are people who may or may not be of Arab origin, but what is
> important in classifying them is that they are not recognized as being of
> pure descent through both males and females from Arab tribes. In-
> cluded in their ranks are some of the greatest leaders in the history of
> the Arab world (such as Salah ad-Din al-ʾAyubi, who was of Kurdish
> descent) and many of the great philosophers and teachers of the past
> (such as Ibn Sina). However, in Najd those of tribal background have
> always been the political leaders and they have dominated the society.
> People of *khadiri* status have been farmers, merchants, *ʿulamaʾ,* and im-
> portant state administrators. Yet, in the past, many worked in craft
> occupations.
>
> Those of *ʿabd* status are mainly descendants of African slaves. Like
> those of *khadiri* status, they have worked as farmers and they could be-

come merchants and *'ulama'*, but they have also done the jobs that people of *qabili* status refused to do.

This is changing now and has already changed a lot. Modern technical work is now accepted by all—even by the Bedouin, who used to consider farming and trade to be acceptable but not really appropriate for a person of pure tribal descent. But the predominance of tribal values here had a negative impact on development in the past because those at the top of the society scorned a number of essential occupations.

Despite the disdain people of tribal status had for some craft occupations, it is important to note that not all such work was considered improper for those of high-ranking tribal descent. Moreover, men of both *khadiri* and *'abd* status could, and did, become *'ulama'* and worked in government, farming, trade, and transport.

As throughout the peninsula, some crafts were organized by domestic units (cf. Rumaihi 1975:40). In 'Unayzah, domestic organization clearly existed in the case of the tanners. Although not technically a craft activity, *sawani* work often engaged a domestic unit on a full-time basis as an occupation. Well digging, on the other hand, recruited men as individuals. Other craft work tended to be passed on from father to son and, in some cases, from mother to daughter. In crafts such as carpentry and smithery, males of a domestic unit or nondomestic kin unit often worked together. The same occurred in the case of females who worked as water carriers. Work related to making mud bricks for housing sometimes involved both males and females of a domestic or kin unit. Training and recruitment into most craft occupations involved apprenticeship. However, the *subiyan,* "apprentices," could be either relatives or nonrelatives in most cases.

Some craft production was performed at home. This was especially the case among women who worked in the production of straw products and in sewing and baking. Other crafts, such as well digging and house building, were obviously performed wherever the work was required. Much of the craft production, however, was performed in shops in the *suq*. No matter where the work was done, their products and services were marketed. Although some had small gardens near their houses and some may have had a cow or two which provided milk, all full-time craftspeople relied on the marketing of their products and services for their livelihood. They were sometimes paid for their work in kind, but they also received cash. In some cases, they sold directly to the consumer. However, much of 'Unayzah's craft production reached the consumer via merchants and traders who also provided craftspeople with most of the food they consumed. That this was the case leads to a discussion of the market.

The Market

The old *suq* was one of the great bazaars typical of Middle Eastern cities. There were many narrow winding streets and alleys, large areas covered by mud-brick vaults, and large open areas as well. Most sellers and craftspeople worked out of shops, but others spread their wares on the streets or in the great open spaces or walked up and down hawking their wares, which they carried with them.

The *suq* of 'Unayzah was established hundreds of years ago in an open space between the original settlements and was one of the elements that led to the development of 'Unayzah as a city, as noted in chapter 1. Aside from being the commercial center of the city, the *suq* was the social center for men in the community. Informants say that men used to put on their cloaks and go to the *suq* every afternoon, whether they had business to conduct or not. They met friends, neighbors, and relatives and came into contact with men from all segments of the community. The *suq* thus played a major social role in the community by providing a place where men could maintain ties of a social nature with a wide range of community members. At the same time, it was a major communication center, as it was here that the men heard the news from each other and discussed events of interest in the community. Furthermore, the *suq* provided the main locale from which political authority was administered, as shown in chapter 1.

In 1878, Doughty observed that "the tradesmen's shops are well furnished" and that "the streets are thronged on Fridays; when all the townsmen, even the field labourers, come in at midday, to pray in the great mesjid, and hear the koran reading and preaching: it is as well their market day" (1979 [1888], 2:375). He also recorded that

> the salesmen are clothiers in the suk, sellers of small wares [in which are raw drugs and camel medicines, sugar-loaves, spices, Syrian soap from Medina, coffee of the Mecca Caravans], and sellers of victual. In the outlying quarters are small general shops—some of them held

by women, where are sold onions, eggs, iron nails, salt, (German) matches, girdle bread [and certain of these poor wives will sell thee a little milk, if they have any]. On Fridays, you shall see veiled women sitting in the mejlis to sell chickens, and milk skins and girbies that they have tanned and prepared. (Doughty 1979 [1888], 2:429)

Forty years later, in 1918, Philby, who was generally a careful observer not given to exaggeration, estimated that there were "not fewer than 1000 shops all told in the main and various subsidiary *Suqs*" (1928:174). He also estimated the population at that time as being at least 15,000. If the average nuclear family size at that time was, say, five, that would mean that about one-third of the nuclear families in ʿUnayzah had shops in the *suq*, as it was not common for them to have more than one shop at a time. In addition, there were many others who were involved in market activities who did not have shops. While we can only speculate about the exact number of shops and the proportion of people who worked in the old *suq*, all our sources indicate that it was very large and engaged a large proportion of the population. As already noted, ʿAbd al-ʿAziz Ibn Saʿud was very impressed with it when he visited it for the first time in 1904. Also, people from ʿUnayzah today fondly recount the story of a man who went to Riyadh many years ago and complained to a companion about not being able to buy anything in the then very small market at ʿAbd al-ʿAziz's capital. His companion, they say, answered him thus: "Where do you think you are—in ʿUnayzah?"

According to descriptions provided by older informants who remembered it well, the focus of the old market was an area known as the Majlis. This was a large open place directly in front of the main mosque of the city. Around its sides were more than one hundred large shops and a number of houses. There were numerous small entrances that were like alleyways or paths. In the shops and in the open space men sold all the items that were related to camel caravans and all the items that were needed by the Bedouin in their herding activities. These included leather buckets, ropes, saddles, weapons, leather bags for carrying coffee and cardamom, and numerous other products, most of which were produced by craftspeople in ʿUnayzah. There was also cheap clothing that the Bedouin bought, as well as dates and wheat and imported rice, coffee, cardamom, tea, and sugar. It was to this area that the Bedouin brought their products for sale—ghee, dried goat's cheese, wool, camels, sheep, and goats. On Fridays an auction was held here, and the area would be thronged with Bedouin and people from outlying farms, many of whom would be both buying and selling.

Another larger open area called the Hiyalah was near the Majlis. It was surrounded by shops and houses, and in this area men sold meats, fruits, vegetables, alfalfa, charcoal, and firewood. Between the Majlis and the Hiyalah, but off to one side, there was an area called al-Musuwkaf, where men held auctions all day long every day of the week. Also near the Hiyalah was an area where barbers practiced and where straw baskets, ropes, and wool yarn were sold.

Leading off from the Hiyalah was another main *suq* called al-Qaʿ, which was a wide street with many shops and numerous small alleys and entrances. It extended for quite some way and had a covered area. Here, either from shops or from the pavement, many women sold cloth, cooking utensils, spices, cakes made at home, date seeds as fodder for animals, straw products, pumpkins, leeks, henna, and occasionally silver and gold. In another covered area nearby were more shops for women sellers and public facilities for women. Nearby was another *suq* where men both made and sold various metal products—iron, copper, silver, and gold. In another area, called Umm al-ʿAsafir, women sold their wares.

The *suq* was the center in which a wide variety of specialists exchanged their products, sometimes for barter and sometimes for cash. It was to the *suq* that farmers daily brought vegetables in season, alfalfa, and straw products for sale to people with other specializations in the city or to Bedouin. The major products of the farms, dates and wheat, were marketed here by merchants. The dates and wheat were sold to Bedouin and nonfarming specialists in the community and, in many cases, were sold back to farmers during the period before harvests, when they would have exhausted their own supplies which they had stored the previous year.

The *suq* was also the center for the sale of locally produced crafts. The products of the Bedouin nomads of the region were brought here either by the Bedouin themselves or by local merchants or their agents, who went to the Bedouin camps to purchase them, either for cash, for barter against items which they brought to the camps, or against credit for the purchase of items from the *suq* later on. While some of the Bedouin's animals and animal products were sold in the market of ʿUnayzah, much of their produce was first collected in the *suq* and then exported by traders who specialized in this activity. Finally, the *suq* was the center to which items from abroad were imported by local merchants who maintained ties with trading houses (many of which were established by migrants from ʿUnayzah) in distant cities and ports. Much of what was imported was sold locally, but a not insignificant amount of imported goods was redistributed from ʿUnayzah for sale in the markets of other cities in the region, such as Buraydah and Haʾil.

Many transactions in the *suq* took place in shops or with sellers who sat on the pavement to sell their goods. Another major way of selling in the market was through auctions. As mentioned earlier, a weekly auction was held in the Majlis and every day auctions were held in the area known as al-Musuwkaf. Also, men walked up and down the narrow streets and alleys of the *suqs* auctioning articles. According to one of the old merchants of ʿUnayzah, a man who is eighty-eight years old,

> everything except meat was sold by auction. Merchants bought from each other, but they also bought from auctions. One used the auction if one needed to get money quickly or if one wanted to sell goods that had been around for a long time. Also, if we had new items that were not well known in the *suq,* we used the auction. This was also the case for merchandise that arrived from abroad in bulk. There were many *dallalil* who did this work.

The *dallal* [pl. *dallalin*), "broker, auctioneer," was and still is a central figure in market transactions in ʿUnayzah. He is usually both an auctioneer and an intermediary who not only sells items for others but arranges other aspects of the transfer of goods and produce from one party to another. An example of the work of a *dallal* and of an auction is described below. While this description is for the contemporary period, informants say that the process was the same in the past. According to Abu ʿAbd Allah, who is about thirty-five and an employee in an office of the Ministry of Agriculture and Water,

> dates in ʿUnayzah are marketed mainly by auctions that are held at the farms. This is unique to ʿUnayzah and is not done even in Buraydah. What happens is that, during the date season but before they are harvested, auctions are held by five or six very well known *dallalin* who know all the people here. They have to know the people well because

later on they are the ones that collect the money and arrange the transfer of the dates from the farm to the buyer.

When there is going to be an auction, the *dallal* walks through the market shouting in a loud voice that there will be an auction at such and such a place on such and such a date. Some of them nowadays even print out flyers, which they pass out in the market, and some have even advertised in newspapers, if the auction is to be at a very large farm.

Each *dallal* specializes in a certain area of ʿUnayzah, and most buyers go to the areas that are near them. People buy dates for their own household use throughout the year, and there are also merchants who buy dates at the auctions and then sell them later in the market. The *dallal* has a *katib* ["clerk"] who works with him. The *dallal* and the *katib* arrive at the farm at around seven in the morning. The owner serves coffee and tea, and when enough people have arrived the auction starts. They go to each tree, and the produce of that tree is auctioned off to the highest bidder. The *katib* records in his register the amount of the bid, the name of the bidder, and the tree.

Later on, when the harvest is completed, the *dallal* and the *katib* go to the house or shop of the bidder to collect the money from him. If the produce has been damaged or part of it destroyed, an appropriate amount is deducted from what the bidder pays. The *dallal* and the *katib* together take two and a half to three percent of the sale price as their fee. They arrange the transfer of the dates from the farm and give the farmer the money they have collected from the buyer.

As this case and the earlier reference to buying and selling in Bedouin camps indicate, not all transactions of buying and selling took place within the marketplace itself. In addition, a lively trade was conducted by women who worked out of their own households, either selling to other women who came to their houses or through taking goods to sell in the houses of other women whom they visited, a phenomenon which is discussed in greater detail within the context of women's visiting patterns in chapter 11.

Credit, Moneylending, and Indebtedness

The discussion of agriculture has already shown that *fallalih* often incurred debts that were difficult, and sometimes impossible, to pay back. The accumulation of debts sometimes led to occupational change and to the loss of land put up as collateral. Craftspeople and the Bedouin were also often in debt to a merchant who gave them credit or to a moneylender who gave them "cloth." Moreover, merchants, traders, and caravanners often incurred debts with merchants and moneylenders.

The incurrence of debt as a result of buying goods on credit was, and is, straightforward in ʿUnayzah and needs no special explanation. However, the mention of moneylenders giving people cloth requires a discussion of the ways in which credit was extended and money lent out in a Muslim community such as ʿUnayzah. Islam clearly prohibits *riba*, "usury." However, there were people who were said to have lent money for interest (a practice which is also said to continue at present). The interest, referred to by people as *al-ghaʾibah*, "that which is not mentioned," varies from one moneylender to another. However, the average quoted by most informants is 10 percent annually. If a person borrowed 100 riyals, he would have to pay back 110 after a year or 120 after two years, and so on. In this manner, people say *yiglib ʿalayh ad-dayn*, "the debt turns on him," meaning that with time the debtor owes more and more money and often can, at best, only afford to pay the interest. People say that this could also occur with debts that were to be repaid in kind.

More commonly, merchants lent money by providing the borrower with *budaʿah*, "merchandise," to be sold in the market. The person who takes the merchandise to the *suq* takes a risk and may sell it for either more or less than what he originally "paid." All informants say that this is not usury and therefore is an acceptable business practice, since risk is involved. Some recall men walking in the market calling out, "Min yishtari mal ad-dayan?" (Who will buy the property of the lender?). A more subtle way which was and is practiced is, as some put it, "to sell you money by giving you merchandise." This complex process involves the "sale" of an item, usually cloth, which the moneylender has with the intention of buying it back at a lower price. The merchant would then give the borrower that lower sum. The borrower then has to pay back the original price with which he "bought" the merchandise, in addition to an increase in the price due to the delay in payment. For example, a man wants to borrow 1,000 riyals. He goes to a merchant, who offers to sell him cloth for 1,000 riyals. The borrower is free to take the cloth to the *suq* and try to sell it and take a risk; but the merchant says that he himself is willing to buy it back at a lower price, say 950 riyals. The borrower agrees and takes 950 riyals, and the cloth stays in the shop. A year later, when he goes to pay back the merchant, he owes 1,000 riyals, which is the amount for which the merchant sold him the cloth, plus an amount that might be as much as 20 percent of the cost of the cloth because his payment was delayed for a year. Thus a person would actually get 950 riyals but have to pay 1,200 riyals after a year.

According to informants, this practice, called *at-tawarruq,* is accepted by some of the legal schools in Sunni Islam in case of need. Others argue that, since the intention is to obtain money and since interest is in fact made on the transaction, it is usury and thus forbidden. Some informants felt that times existed when a person needed money and this was the only way to obtain it, and therefore this practice was tolerated. However, they also felt that the practice had been overused by moneylenders. The moneylenders, on the other hand, see this as a legitimate activity of buying and selling and making a profit.

Almost all informants, and especially the older ones, indicated that indebtedness was pervasive in the old ʿUnayzah. Most see it as having been a harsh burden that particularly fell on the *fallalih* sharecroppers. Others commented that the high cost of obtaining credit and loans was a major barrier against the development of productive enterprises in the past. Nonetheless, credit and loans in the form of *budaʿah* were available and sometimes provided the necessary capital for an individual to establish a successful enterprise, as is shown in a case in the following chapter.

CHAPTER 4

Caravans and Long-Distance Trade

The discussion so far has concentrated on activities that took place in 'Unayzah. However, work often took men from 'Unayzah on long and sometimes dangerous journeys within the peninsula to Bedouin camps, the Yemen, cities of the Hijaz, and ports on the Arabian Gulf. They also went to Iraq, greater Syria, Egypt, Bahrain, and India. Some worked in camel transport, both in caravans and as small-scale carriers. These were called *jammamil,* "cameleers." Others worked as mercenaries, wage laborers, and in trade. These were called *'uqaylat.* Both categories linked 'Unayzah to the regional market and 'Unayzah and the region to the wider external world.

Transport: The Jammamil

At the time of the battle of Sabilah (1929), about forty *jammamil* (sg. *jammal*) in 'Unayzah engaged in the long-distance transport of goods by camel. Each had a "fleet" of between 40 and 140 camels. As late as the 1920s and 1930s, these fleets were still the main links for 'Unayzah with the wider world. They operated between 'Unayzah and the ports of Kuwait and Jubayl. They also went to the cities of Makkah and Madinah in the Hijaz and to Riyadh. *Jammamil* from 'Unayzah also carried goods from al-Ahsa' to Riyadh; others mainly operated back and forth between 'Unayzah and Buraydah.

People say that 'Unayzah merchants used to import merchandise from abroad not only for sale in the market of 'Unayzah but for further distribution to merchants in Buraydah. This transport did not involve as many camels as did the large caravans that connected

'Unayzah with distant cities. Quite often the *jammal* would have only four or five camels or even fewer. One man, Abu Turki, who is about sixty-five years old and now a wealthy gold merchant and owner of real estate, remembered the days when, as a boy, he used to travel back and forth between Buraydah and 'Unayzah.

> My father worked regularly as a *jammal,* moving back and forth be-
> tween 'Unayzah and Buraydah. He worked directly with merchants
> from here and would carry goods that they had imported from Jubayl
> to send to merchants in Buraydah. They would pay him a fee for each
> load that he carried. When I was about sixteen or seventeen, I began to
> take goods from a merchant in 'Unayzah that I would try to sell for
> a higher price in Buraydah. I usually managed to make a little profit,
> but if I could not sell the goods there, I would bring them back. This
> merchant was kind to me because I was a relative of his and because I
> was young.
>
> I would load one camel with the goods and ride another one. I
> would leave 'Unayzah after sunset and travel all night, dozing off to
> sleep as I sat on the camel. By early morning I would reach Buraydah
> and try to sell the merchandise. At night I would begin the trip back to
> 'Unayzah. For a long time, while I was doing this, I never slept lying
> down but always sitting in the saddle of the camel, which instinctively
> knew the way.

The caravans linking 'Unayzah to the Arabian Gulf port of Jubayl mainly brought items such as rice, sugar, coffee, tea, cardamom, and kerosene. From Kuwait they brought the same items, as well as cloth and spices. These caravans usually returned to Kuwait and Jubayl empty from 'Unayzah, although they sometimes carried ghee. The caravans that went to the cities of the Hijaz carried dates, wheat, and ghee and brought back ginger, black pepper, tea, coffee, sugar, and cardamom. Caravans that went to Riyadh carried wheat, millet, barley, dates, and sometimes even vegetables.

The trip to Jubayl took about twenty days one way, and about three round trips a year were made. According to informants, the cost per camel load at the end of the 1920s was between 15 and 20 Maria Theresa dollars. Each camel carried up to two hundred kilograms, the equivalent of two large sacks of sugar. The camels that a *jammal* had were always females or males that were not studs, and because they were working all the time the females never gave birth. Therefore, a *jammal* could not replace his camels with young ones, as is the case among the Bedouin, who raise them. Sometimes he may have obtained them through inheritance, but a major way of obtaining them was through the process known as *buda'ah*. This process was used not only for obtaining camels for transport but was a widespread practice among 'Unayzah merchants who wished to invest in goods but did not have sufficient capital to buy them outright.

In the case of the *jammamil*, a merchant would purchase a camel and entrust it to a *jammal*, who made journeys with it until the money obtained from the transport of goods by it covered its cost. At that point, the merchant and the *jammal* together became owners of the camel on a fifty-fifty basis. If the merchant or the *jammal* no longer wished to continue the relationship, the camel was taken to an auction and sold. The amount of money obtained from the sale was split in half between them. If, on the other hand, both wanted to continue the relationship, the merchant would pay the *jammal* half the market value of the camel. Then the whole process would begin over again as though the camel had been newly purchased. If the *jammal* wanted to buy out the merchant's share, he would pay him half the price of the camel. Under these arrangements, the merchant would, in fact, have regained his capital investment in the camel plus 50 percent of the price of the camel. If the *jammal* did not want the camel, then the merchant would regain the original payment plus the camel. The *jammal*, on the other hand, began to gain only after he had, through its labor, paid for the initial price of the camel. At that point, his gain was tantamount to half the price of the camel.

Most of the *jammamil* transported goods for merchants. Sometimes merchants gave them a paper to submit to an agent in, for example, Jubayl who would provide them with the goods that the merchant wanted. Sometimes, if there was a relationship of trust, the merchant would give money to the *jammal* and ask him to make the purchases on his behalf. This was always formalized on paper, and when trust existed, this way of obtaining goods was more advantageous to the merchant, because the agent charged a commission while the *jammal* provided the service for free.

Each caravan had a number of *subiyan* (sg. *subi*), "youths, apprentices," who accompanied it in addition to the *jammal*. These were either the *jammal*'s own sons or nephews or they were hired by him. The *jammal* himself only rode and directed the caravan, while the *subiyan* were responsible for loading and unloading the camels. Thus, the number of them depended on the number of camels in the caravan. In addition, there was a herdsman, usually a Bedouin, who accompanied the caravan and was responsible for grazing the camels.

Abu Mish'al is about eighty years old. He is frail of body but lucid and clear in his mind. He has a twinkle in his eye but expresses a nostalgia for the days when he traveled back and forth across the desert sands between 'Unayzah and faraway places. His youngest daughter is about twelve. Several merchants used to commission him to go to Jubayl and bring back merchandise. Some of them specified their instructions for their agents to dispense goods to him. Others gave him money to purchase things for them. At one time, he had about 20,000 riyals with him. That was a lot of money.

> Allah protected us from the Bedouin. But we also had weapons with us.
>
> It took twenty days to reach Jubayl. We started out at the time of the dawn prayer and we traveled until the afternoon prayer. If it was hot, we would pray the sunset prayer and then travel throughout the night until after dawn. We carried some food with us and we sometimes slaughtered a goat. We were strong and healthy in those days and we would eat the whole goat—no problem.
>
> About halfway we stopped at a well for the camels to drink and to refill our leather containers with water. We carried eighteen leather water containers with us. There we met other *jammamil* from 'Unayzah who were coming back from Jubayl.
>
> When we arrived in Jubayl, I went to find the agent of the ———. I had a paper for him instructing him to give me things to take back to 'Unayzah. Jubayl was very small in those days—just the port, a few thatched houses, and a couple of buildings. We did not stay long—just long enough to buy the goods with the money Abu Hamad had given me. We loaded rice, sugar, coffee, tea, cardamom, cloth, spices.
>
> The boys were divided into two groups of three each. Each group was responsible for sixty camels and they would race each other to see which group could load and unload the camels faster. We worked very hard. Nobody could do that work today.
>
> It was a big problem whenever a rain came. We had to build a tent as big as this room and then rush to pile all the sacks inside, especially the sugar. That was really a problem. I remember once a merchant took a *jammal* to court because he did not bring back all his sugar. The *jammal* said "the rains took it" and the *qadi* did not pass judgment on the case.

Also, sometimes the wadi would fill up with water and we would have to wait for days to cross. By Allah, those days were hard, but it was also a good time. . . .

When we got back to ʿUnayzah, we delivered the goods to Abu Hamad and he paid me 15 Maria Theresa dollars per load. The camel carried about two hundred kilograms of sugar or rice. Some of this money had to go to a number of men who had camels with me as *budaʿah*. There were four merchants that I usually dealt with in ʿUnayzah. They also worked with other *jammamil*.

ʿUnayzah is Umm al-Qasim ["Mother of the Qasim"]. We sent out from here everything. Riyadh sends us things now, but we used to send things to them. I would carry wheat, millet, barley, dates, ghee, eggplants to Riyadh. Sometimes I would take part of the camels and carry these things to Riyadh and then meet the others in Jubayl.

Before there was Jubayl, we went to Kuwait. We also went to Jiddah and Makkah. When we went there, we took ghee and *sukkari* dates with us. When we went to Kuwait or Jubayl, we took nothing. It took longer to reach Makkah, about one month. Makkah was very large and we would stay there for quite a long time. But it was rough going on the way. It was very dangerous on the way back from Makkah to the Qasim. There was a lot of trouble in those days. We brought back ginger, cardamom, black pepper, tea, coffee, rice, sugar. On occasions, we sometimes took along with us men and boys from ʿUnayzah who went there to look for work. There were a number of people from the Qasim in Makkah and in Jiddah, and they would go to them to help them find some work to do.

As this case indicates, transport was organized as a profit-making enterprise. Although merchants sometimes financed the acquisition of camels, most *jammamil* owned the means of transport and engaged in this activity to obtain cash income. Many also worked as agents of merchants in the procurement of imported merchandise. Sometimes, the *jammamil* also worked as agents or as entrepreneurs in the procurement of Bedouin products for local sale or for export, as explained by Abu Mishʿal.

During the summers, we did not make trips. We usually made three or four trips a year, but in summer we stayed put. Sometimes, however, I would take money from people to go out to the desert to buy things from the Bedouin. That would take most of the summer. I and some of my *subiyan* traveled as far as Bishah looking for the Bedouin who would be camped around wells because it was summer and their camels had to drink. I would buy camels and ghee and dried cheese from them. All this was for the people who gave me the money. It was cheaper to buy from the Bedouin in the desert. Also the Bedouin were afraid to leave their herds to take things to the city because, if they left, other Bedouin would eat [i.e., attack and raid] their herds. The Bedouin were fierce in those days—not like they are now. But they had thousands of camels and they produced lots of ghee.

When we got back toward ʿUnayzah, I would leave the camels I had bought in the Nafud with the *subiyan*. I would go in to ʿUnayzah and look for the wholesale buyers and for the people who had given me the money. I told them about the camels I had bought and I told them when they would arrive. They would then go out to see them, and there would be a *dallal* with them, and the wholesale buyers would buy what they wanted. There were *ʿuqaylat* [explained below] and they would sometimes buy camels from the ones I had bought, and they would take off with them and go west [i.e., to Syria or Egypt to sell them there]. The *ʿuqaylat* would pay on the spot. What was not sold was brought into ʿUnayzah and sold at auction by the *dallal*. Then the *dallal* would collect all the money from the wholesale buyers and from those who bought at the auction. This would take about two weeks.

Then I would invite the people who had given me money and the *dallal* and a *katib,* who wrote things down, to a lunch and we would settle our accounts. The *dallal* was paid a quarter of a riyal per camel. We wrote down all the expenses of the trip. If we bought a rope or a leather bucket, we wrote it down. If the merchants had paid for the expenses of the trip, I took one-third of the profit. If I had paid the expenses, I took half of the profit. And if there was no profit, I took nothing. Also, if there was a loss, I had not lost anything, except for being tired.

This case points to the importance of the *jammamil* as the main source of transport linking ʿUnayzah to at least part of the wider world. It also indicates that the *jammamil* worked independently of one another. However, other *jammamil* told us that at earlier periods the *jammamil* had traveled together in large groups and that their schedules of departure from ʿUnayzah were coordinated by the amir. Also, they paid a fee to Bedouin tribes across whose territories they traveled and either relied on the *wajh*, literally, "face" or "honor," of the tribal shaykh who granted permission to cross or took a *rafiq*, "companion," from the clan or tribe. That they had to do this was at least in part due to raids and warfare; caravans loaded with an abundance of goods and money made an especially attractive prey for booty-hunting armed Bedouin. With the development of the centralized state, the power of the Bedouin tribes was undermined, which in turn facilitated the movement of goods in smaller, more independent groups. However, the payment of a fee for right of passage guaranteed by either *wajh* or the *rafiq* should be seen not only as a tribal custom but as a mechanism which provided for protection and safe passage in the absence of state control.

Long-Distance Traders and Labor Migrants: The ʿUqaylat

While the *jammamil* specialized in transport and occasionally were engaged in the process of buying and selling animals, the *ʿuqaylat* (sg. *ʿuqayli*) were primarily specialists in buying animals in the Arabian Peninsula which they took to sell in other parts of the Arab world and India. They also worked outside the region as mercenaries and as wage laborers.

The term *al-ʿuqaylat* has at least two different referents. On the one hand, it is the name of a large Arab tribe that was one of the branches of the Banu Kaʿb, and it is said that the tribe spread from Syria into Iraq and extended into North Africa and Andalusia in Spain. One of their clans was concentrated in Basrah while another ruled Musul during the time of the Abbasid Caliphate (al-Misallam 1985:18). Although we know of no evidence that would link it to that tribe, al-ʿUqayliyah is the name of one of the early settlements that later became part of ʿUnayzah.

On the other hand, *al-ʿuqaylat* is used to refer to people from the Qasim who were primarily engaged in buying camels and horses in Arabia that they took to sell in the markets of Syria, Iraq, and Egypt. These people were of various tribal origins and had settled in communities in the Qasim. Whether there is any connection between these two uses of the term is unclear. However, people in ʿUnayzah with whom we spoke used the term in its latter meaning. They used the term as if it were an occupational category or identity, saying, "I was an *ʿuqayli* in those days" or "They called us *ʿuqaylat*."

The *ʿuqaylat* formed a network that operated on a wide scale throughout northern Arabia, greater Syria, Iraq, and Egypt, and eventually even extended as far away as Bombay. This network involved men who were settled in various communities in Najd, especially in the Qasim, and others originally from these places who had taken up residence in towns and cities outside the area. The men from Najd traveled in groups along regular routes and took the animals, which they purchased from the nomadic Bedouin, to sell in the markets of greater Syria, Iraq, and Egypt, where they mainly interacted with the *ʿuqaylat* resident there, typically near marketplaces. While in these areas, the men from Najd not only socialized with the *ʿuqaylat* resident abroad but also were involved in trading and labor relationships with them and relied on the network of relationships that existed among them for assistance in any time of need, including any problems that might develop between them and local political authorities. Also, at least some of the *ʿuqaylat* who had taken up residence abroad established important commercial houses which played important roles in the export of merchandise to communities such as ʿUnayzah. Although many of these married from among the local people abroad, they continued to maintain not only commercial but social ties with their home communities, and some occasionally returned for visits that lasted for as long as several years at a time.

The *ʿuqaylat* we are referring to were mainly associated with trade in camels and horses, but there were some who dealt in sheep. Furthermore, there were men from the Qasim who volunteered for service as soldiers in the armies of the Ottoman Empire and, later on, in the army of the sharif of Makkah during World War I. According to Doughty, many had gone as groups from Qasim "to dig for wages in the work of the Suez Canal" (1979 [1888], 2:450). All of these were called *ʿuqaylat*. Thus, while the term is used in the Qasim to refer in a specific way to men who engaged in long-distance movement and trading of animals, its meaning is extended to refer to men from the Qasim working abroad on a temporary basis or in the armies and even more generally to people from the Qasim who permanently settled abroad.

The phenomenon of the *ʿuqaylat,* at least from the perspective of the Qasim, involved a number of different aspects, all of which were interrelated. These include migration; buying and selling operations; long-distance "transport" of animals in caravans, usually across the territories of various autonomous tribes; networks of social, political, and economic relationships; and temporary labor migration.

According to al-Misallam (1985:27–44), who uses the term in both its specific occupational meaning and its more general geographic meaning, as well as to refer to people who worked in long-distance caravans, the *ʿuqaylat* have a long history which is characterized by periods of fluctuation. Until the sixteenth century, the fluctuations in their activities were mainly related to the changing relationships between tribes within the peninsula. However, as Qasimis, they themselves were often of tribal descent and had contacts with nomadic tribes which facilitated the traffic of their commercial caravans and which enabled them to work as guides and caravan leaders. Also, they developed trade in camels, horses, and sheep.

From the sixteenth century on, political changes in the wider Islamic world began to affect them, as did the beginning of the development of centralized political authority in Najd. Changing economic opportunities in the distant regions in which they traded also had their impact. Thus, when the Ottoman sultan Sulayman I (who assumed power in A.D. 1520) initiated a reform in the army by raising the salaries paid to soldiers, Arab tribesmen, including people from the Qasim, joined the army. Also, when Baghdad's economy blossomed during the late eighteenth century, caravan trade increased as did the demand for horses, camels, and sheep. This activity coincided with a period of stability in Najd during the first Saʿudi state.

However, the invasion of Najd by Ibrahim Pasha in 1818 brought an end to stability in Najd and initiated a period of nominal Turkish control. The Turks exiled the amir of the Qasim to Madinah, initiating the exodus of numerous other leaders. Various families began to compete for control of both the pilgrim and commercial caravans and for political control of Najd. The Al Rashid became particularly influential and taxed the caravans, creating dissatisfaction among many in the Qasim. Finally, in a battle that occurred in 1891, many *ʿuqaylat* fought against the Al Rashid, who nonetheless won. It was after that that the Al Saʿud were forced to flee Najd, eventually ending up in Kuwait. They returned in 1901 and recaptured Riyadh from the Al Rashid. According to al-Missalam (1985), up to three thousand *ʿuqaylat* from Syria, Palestine, and Egypt came to Kuwait to support Ibn Saʿud and actually joined up with him at al-Bakariyah in 1904 when he recaptured control of the Qasim. However, while al-

Misallam stresses the support of the ʿuqaylat for the Al Saʿud during this period, it is well known that one of the leading merchant families of ʿUnayzah who were also ʿuqaylat abroad supported the Al Rashid.

The reconquest of Riyadh and then that of the Qasim by the Al Saʿud were among the first steps on the way to the creation of the present centralized state. The ʿuqaylat continued to buy up camels, horses, and sheep and to take them to the markets of Syria, Palestine, Egypt, and Iraq. This activity continued until the early years of World War II, when much of this trade and movement was curtailed. National borders became more established and it became more difficult for the ʿuqaylat to cross into different states. The end of the ʿuqaylat was also brought about by the development of motor transportation and the shifting of the focus of the economy away from the production of animals toward the development of the new economy based on the extraction and export of oil.

It is not possible to establish whether the ʿuqaylat formed professional associations as did the Swasa in Morocco (cf. Waterbury 1972). What is clear is that when abroad the ʿuqaylat offered assistance and support to other ʿuqaylat. They helped each other in business-related matters, providing capital and dealing with the authorities in the guest countries, for example, and built a network of social ties between them that was activated regularly. In fact, they tended to live in the same neighborhoods, frequent the same coffeehouses, and, according to al-Misallam (1985), reportedly formed a political group in Iraq that was involved in local politics.

The following case illustrates the pattern of movement and the network of relationships that the ʿuqaylat used throughout journeys that lasted for more than several months at a time. Abu Talib is eighty-eight years old. He is a spry old man whose mind is alert. He has a shop in the market but is no longer able to attend to it regularly, employing an expatriate to sell in the shop. He says that he has essentially retired but he wants to at least have his name in the market.

> When I was just a baby, my father had climbed up a palm tree to harvest dates, but he fell and was killed. I was raised by my uncle, who was a merchant. When I was about fourteen, we heard that the sharif of Makkah was recruiting soldiers for his army. This was the time of the war between the British and the Turks [World War I]. He paid soldiers 6 sterling pounds, which was a lot of money in those days. I went with

a number of other boys from 'Unayzah. We waited for the first *jammal* heading for the Hijaz and rode with him. This was the first time I had ever been away from 'Unayzah. We took a few dates with us and my mother gave me some *klayjah* [a kind of cake] and that was all I had with me. We were poor and times were hard. In those days, we had only one *thawb* [a man's garment] a year, which we got at the time of the *'id* ["feast"].

We arrived in Madinah, and there we signed up with the army. There were fourteen of us from 'Unayzah and we all stayed together in one tent. There were boys and young men from other parts of the Qasim and people called us *'uqaylat*. When I got there, I heard that they would pay more if you worked with dynamite. They paid 10 pounds sterling for that, and I decided to take my chances. We put dynamite on the railroad to blow it up. There were a lot of us who did this and the Englishman Lawrence worked with us. We went all the way to the north and into Jordan.

When the war was over, I had saved up quite a lot of money. I decided to come back to 'Unayzah and to buy some camels to sell in Syria. On the way back, I passed by Tabuk where a lot of people were dying. People did not know what was happening to make so many people die. But it was cholera, which came about because so many people had been killed in the war and their bodies had been left unburied on the battlefields. I became ill but recovered and came on back to 'Unayzah. There were a lot of people dying here, too, but it was not as bad as in Tabuk. This is the year we call *sanat ar-rahmah* ["the year of the blessing"].

I took some of the money I had saved and bought some camels from the Bedouin. I was about nineteen then and had not yet married. There were others from 'Unayzah who also had bought camels, as well as others from Buraydah. We joined together and traveled to the northwest and reached Sakaka. Then we traveled up the Wadi Sirhan. We stopped at Qurayyat for water and went on into Jordan. There were no border guards in those days and we did not carry passports or anything like that. At Gharb al-Hammad in Jordan we rested for a few days because there was good water there. From there some of the *'uqaylat* went to Amman. I and others went on to Damascus. There we met Abu Fawaz, who is from 'Unayzah, but he had lived for many years in Damascus, where he was a big merchant and was so well respected that he was known as an amir of the *'uqaylat*.

I sold the camels I had and then decided to go to Baghdad with some other *'uqaylat*. I bought two horses there to take to Egypt. Abu Fawaz had an agent in Baghdad and we saw him. He and other *'uqaylat* in Baghdad showed me where to go to buy the horses. On the way to Egypt, we passed by Damascus and then went on toward Palestine. There were only four of us traveling together this time and, after we entered Palestine, we passed near a Jewish settlement. They started shouting at us and we could not understand what they were saying. They called the British soldiers, and they came and arrested us and said that the Jews had said that we were smuggling and that we had stolen the horses from the sharif. We were put in the jail. But there was an *'uqayli* in the town and he came and talked with us. As soon as the soldiers heard that we were *'uqaylat*, they released us and apologized to us.

We went on to Egypt by way of Gaza and al-Arish. In Gaza there were a lot of *'uqaylat*, and there was a big central market there. Merchants from Amman, Damascus, and Egypt had agents there. We crossed the Suez Canal at Qantara. The *karantina* ["quarantine"] was there, in Qantara Sharq, and we had to pay a fee to the Egyptian government to enter. We crossed the canal on a ferry boat and then went to Isma'iliyah. From there we went to Cairo and arrived at Kafr al-Jamus, which was on the outskirts of Heliopolis. That is where people had horses, and there were stables there and a racetrack and trainers. My brother lived in Egypt and he knew a lot about the horse trade. He too was an *'uqayli*, but he had been in Egypt for a long time and had married from there. His children still live there now.

One of my horses was a racehorse. My brother introduced me to an Egyptian who had a lot of racehorses. I showed him my horse, and he offered 140 Egyptian pounds. I said that I wanted 170. He said that 150 was the most he would offer. I said OK; but if the horse won his first race, I wanted 20 more extra. When the horse ran his first race, he won, and the man gave me the 20 extra pounds.

I stayed in Egypt three months that trip. There were many *'uqaylat*, and we were always together. When I went back to 'Unayzah, I did not carry anything with me—just the money that I had earned and which I planned to spend on buying more horses or camels to bring back to sell in Egypt.

I continued to work as an *'uqayli* until 1931 and made many trips to Egypt, but I have not been to Egypt since the last trip I made in

1931. Egypt is a great country, and we saw many things there, and when I see films on television now I recognize all the main squares and important places.

On the other trips that I made to Egypt, I would take both camels and horses which I bought from the Bedouin. They used to raise thousands of camels in those days and they made lots of ghee. They worked very hard then and produced a lot. The price of camels here varied depending on the year. If it was a good year in terms of rain, the camels would be fat and they would demand high prices. But if there was not much rain or no rain, the prices would fall, and they would be cheap to buy.

Also, when we traveled across the territory of a Bedouin tribe with our animals, we had to pay them a fee. We paid this to the shaykh of the tribe, and he would send a *rafiq* to accompany us and to guarantee our safe passage. Or sometimes the shaykh would give us his *wajh* to guarantee that his people would not attack us or rob us. We had to pay the Mutayr, Harb, Shammar, ʿAnazah, and Huwaytat, and each tribe had many smaller tribes; we had to deal with each one of them separately. The Huwaytat always caused a lot of problems, and the Bedouin in Egypt were a real scourge—especially those on the way between Cairo and Suez.

We usually crossed the Suez Canal at Qantara Sharq and there was the *karantina* there. The Egyptians charged 75 piastres for each camel that entered and they kept the camels in the *karantina* for a long time. There was an agent of Abu Fawaz there, and we would pay him 25 piastres, and he would take care of all the work with the Egyptians. He would give them baksheesh, and they would let us cross quickly. In Egypt, we would take the camels to various camel markets. From Ismaʿiliyah, we would cross to Zaqaziq and from there go to the markets at Bilbays, Shabin al-Kom, and finally to Imbaba, which is where the Sudanese bring their camels.

At first, I did not buy things to bring back to sell here. But then I started to buy things in Egypt because they were cheaper there. All the things I bought were made in Europe and were shipped in transit to Suez and I took them in Suez. One always had to pay baksheesh to the Egyptian customs officials. I did not bring back much because I could not carry much as I had sold all but one or two baggage camels. When I got back to ʿUnayzah, I would either sell these items at an auction if I wanted money quickly or I would leave them with a merchant to sell if

I was not in a hurry. However, goods became expensive in Egypt because they put on heavy customs duties. Since I settled down here in 1931, I have been a merchant in the *suq*.

Abu Talib's story illustrates the case of someone who maintained an average-size operation. There were numerous others like him from ʿUnayzah, Buraydah, and the other towns of the Qasim. The basic pattern described by him has been checked with other informants and was confirmed as being the usual way in which the *ʿuqaylat* operated during the period described. However, a number of big merchants was involved in the animal trade and each year sent large numbers of animals from the Qasim to the places mentioned above. What is perhaps the leading merchant family in ʿUnayzah was part of the *ʿuqayli* system or network. One member of this family became established in Damascus over one hundred years ago, while other members of this family opened large trading establishments in Basrah, Bahrain, and Bombay. Several other merchant families from ʿUnayzah were also established in Basrah, Bahrain, and Kuwait. It was the existence of these large-scale merchant enterprises that most impressed both Doughty and Philby and made them think ʿUnayzah distinctive. According to Philby, "The citizens of ʿAnaiza . . . were enterprising business men on a large scale . . . [and were] accustomed to trade with great commercial centers like Baghdad and Basra, ʿAmara and Kuwait, Bahrain and Bombay, [and were] constantly in touch with the great world" (1928:218).

As the reader will recall, Abu Talib, who told us about his work as an *ʿuqayli,* mentioned that "the Englishman Lawrence was with us" when he worked as a dynamiter in the sharif's army during World War I. Lawrence also wrote of the *ʿuqaylat,* for whom he had a high regard: "These Ageyl were Nejd townsmen, the youth of Aneyza, Boreida, or Russ, who had contracted for service as regular camel corps for a term of years. They were young, from sixteen to twenty-five, and nice fellows, large-eyed, cheery, a bit educated, catholic, intelligent, good companions on the road. . . . [They] had the nature of soldiers, and fought with brains and courage" (Lawrence 1935: 147–148).

It is now about thirty-five years since the last *jammamil* loaded and unloaded their camels and almost half a century since the last *ʿuqaylat* departed with their animals for export. It is interesting that few of the younger people in ʿUnayzah are aware of the crucial roles that the *jammamil* and the ʿ*uqaylat* played in the rich and complex network of trade that emanated from ʿUnayzah. When the car replaced the camel, it obliterated a whole way of life of which there is little social memory among the young.

There is, however, an old *jammal*, Abu Salih, who is now very rich from commerce and the buying and selling that came in recent years. He now has a large herd of camels on his *bustan*, "garden," in the area that used to be covered with *'athal* trees to the west of ʿUnayzah. Every afternoon he goes to visit his camels and "talks" to them, and to the anthropologist he said, "My father loved them and they made a life for us and I love them, too."

In other ways as well Abu Salih symbolically expresses the mixture of the past and the present. He is, for example, an avid follower of soccer games on television. Neither television nor soccer teams existed in his youth, and whenever he watches a game he always asks with a chuckle, "Are those the Dawasir and those others the ʿUtaybah?" That he thinks of the two teams as being like the Dawasir and the ʿUtaybah (two famous Bedouin tribes) recognizes the basic competition that existed between tribes. However, Abu Salih knows that the teams participate in a game that has rules—as did the tribes, traders, and transporters of the past. As this and the preceding chapters show, the market provided a structure which transcended the politically autonomous tribes and cities of central Arabia.

We have described this old system with its many specializations not out of antiquarian interest. In order to understand the contemporary development of ʿUnayzah, one must comprehend the foundation on which that development rests. For a very long time and until not too long ago, ʿUnayzah had a complex economic structure and its population had a high degree of occupational specialization. It was a center tied into various networks that operated locally, regionally, and at an international level. There was also a great deal of symbiosis between the various actors who operated within the structure of these networks.

For generations and long before the emergence of the contemporary economy, the people of ʿUnayzah were on the move both into and out of their city. They were at home with the desert and, together with the Bedouin, developed procedures for traveling across it and for going to the camps of Bedouin to buy and sell. They had moved to the distant cities of the Hijaz, Iraq, Syria, Egypt, India. They had worked in trade there and had learned new things. While they were abroad, they did not forget 'Unayzah, and many returned for both short and long visits and brought back with them new ideas and a knowledge of the wider world. 'Unayzah may have been special in many ways, but other communities in Najd were not dissimilar.

The farmer, the craftsperson, the trader, and the caravanner were as indigenous and as essential to the economy as the Bedouin herder. Today, only the Bedouin herder is widely remembered; but the horses he provided were known in India as 'Unayzah horses because they were sold there by 'Unayzah traders (Doughty 1979 [1888], 2:418). Moreover, as Coon shows, many of the *'uqaylat* "could buy out several shaikhs [of Bedouin tribes] many times over" (1965:203).

PART TWO

Provincial City within a New State and the Development of Capitalist Social Formations

CHAPTER 5

Development of the New State and Education

The data presented in Part One specifically refer to that which existed before the present state began to be established and before the economy of the region was transformed during the present century. For hundreds of years this old ʿUnayzah had existed as a complex system in which domestically organized production, mercantile trade, and political autonomy predominated. However, capitalist social formations and the process of central state formation were emergent in the area since at least the latter part of the eighteenth century. The data presented in Part One show the presence of production for exchange value and of wage labor and also indicate that the market had become a major institution for the organization of production.

The presence of sharecropping indicates the presence of production for exchange value. Merchants obtained possession of land, which they used to increase production for subsequent sale in the market. Regional demand, in addition to local demand, stimulated craft production for exchange, which took place via the market. Long-distance trade led to camels and horses becoming valuable for their exchange value in addition to their use value.

Examples of the presence of wage labor are the hiring of a man with his family to operate the *sawani* and the hiring of males and females to work in some agricultural and craft production. Participation in wage labor also occurred through the temporary migration of young men—both within the peninsula and elsewhere—to work in the digging of the Suez Canal and in the shops of merchants from ʿUnayzah or to serve as mercenaries in the army of the sharif.

Evidence for the emergence of the market as a principal institution for both the organization and distribution of production is provided by the presence of credit and debt in the system. Debts spurred higher levels of production in agriculture and crafts and led to changes in land tenure. Creditors also provided capital for the creation of enterprises in agriculture, transport, and trade.

Although capitalist social formations were present in the old ʿUnayzah we have described, these formations became predominant through a process of developmental change that gathered momentum in the 1930s and continued until the mid 1970s, when the oil boom brought about major changes of transformational proportions. The impact of the boom is described and analyzed in Part Three. In this part, however, we show how capitalist social formations became predominant and discuss the related process of ʿUnayzah's incorporation into the new state as a provincial city.

The New State

The Qasim, along with most of Najd, was seldom under effective centralized control in the past. The major importance of the region to the Islamic caliphate was related to the pilgrimage route, which crossed the area from Basrah to Madinah. The administration of the area shifted from Madinah during the time of the Orthodox caliphs to Baghdad under the Abbasids, back to Madinah and Makkah during the time of Fatimid rule, and by the eighteenth century was linked to Istanbul, sometimes through the *wali,* "governor," of Basrah. In general, however, the area remained peripheral to the main external centers of political and economic power, and while *zakat,* "religious tax," and tribute were supposed to be paid to the centers, this was often not done.

Within the area, however, an internal process of state formation was initiated in the last quarter of the seventeenth century with the creation of a state under the Bani Khalid based in al-Ahsaʾ. In the eighteenth century, an alliance between Shaykh Muhammad ibn ʿAbd al-Wahhab, a religious reformer, and Muhammad ibn Saʿud, the amir of Dirʿiyah, led to the creation of a religiopolitical movement that rapidly gained momentum and began to spread throughout much of Najd. This movement was successful in defeating its enemies (including the Bani Khalid) and by the end of the eighteenth century and the beginning of the nineteenth century had become a powerful and centralized state under the leadership of the Al Saʿud that eventually controlled most of Arabia, including parts of the Yemen. The expansion of this new state constituted a threat to the Ottoman Empire, which mounted an invasion of the country and defeated it (cf. Winder 1965).

The Ottoman defeat of the first Saʿudi state led to the breakdown of centralized authority, as the Ottomans were unable to maintain effective control. Decentralization prevailed once again throughout the region, although a new political force under the leadership of the Al Rashid rulers of Haʾil emerged and eventually gained control of much of Najd, including Riyadh, which had become the home of the Al Saʿud after the Ottoman destruction of Dirʿiyah.

Rosenfeld (1965), based on written sources, has analyzed the basic characteristics of the Rashidi state and shown that economically it was based on trade, commerce, and tribute and militarily relied on slaves, mercenaries, and townsmen from Haʾil in both the achievement and maintenance of power. Although the Al Rashid were sedentary descendants of the Shammar Bedouin tribe, he shows that the tribally organized Bedouin were not reliable fighters for the state and, indeed, caused a major problem for it. They dominated the periphery of this state, centered at Haʾil, often refused to pay tribute, and were sometimes quick to change their allegiances to the Al Saʿud or to go their own way. Although Rosenfeld does not mention it, Salamé (1980) shows that the Al Rashid also drew strength from an alliance with an external power, the Ottomans. Perhaps more than anything else, the support of the Ottomans allowed the Al Rashid to dominate Najd and, in 1891, to force the leader of the Al Saʿud, ʿAbd ar-Rahman, along with members of his immediate family, into exile.

In 1902, ʿAbd al-Rahman's son, ʿAbd al-ʿAziz, reconquered Riyadh and then engaged himself in a movement to reestablish Saʿudi control throughout much of Arabia. By the spring of 1904, he had regained control of central Najd, including the areas of Washm, Sudayr, and the Qasim. By 1906, he had consolidated his control of the area by decisively defeating the Turkish-supported Ibn Rashid, who was forced to retreat to his home city of Haʾil. In April 1913, the Turkish garrison at Hufuf in al-Ahsaʾ was attacked and defeated, and the rest of the eastern area quickly came under his control.

By the end of 1921, Haʾil had been retaken, and the Al Rashid were finally defeated. In the same year, the highlands of the ʿAsir were incorporated into ʿAbd al-ʿAziz's territories. In 1924, his armies decisively defeated the troops of the sharifian rulers of the Hijaz at Khurmah. They entered the city of Taʾif, where a serious massacre of the local populace, which had been abandoned by the sharifian troops, took place. In October 1924, the city of Makkah came under ʿAbd al-ʿAziz's control without a fight, and by the end of 1925 all the Hijaz had been brought under his control.

On January 8, 1926, the leading citizens of Makkah offered their allegiance to ʿAbd al-ʿAziz and proclaimed him king of the Hijaz. A year later, he was proclaimed king of the Hijaz and of Najd and its dependencies. On January 22, 1932, the final formal step in the creation of the contemporary state was taken when it was renamed *al-mamlakah al-ʿarabiyah as-saʿudiyah,* literally, the Saudi Arab Kingdom, but officially it is called in English the Kingdom of Saudi Arabia. As Salamé (1980: 35–41) cogently argues, all the Saʿudi attempts at establishing a centralized state were purely indigenous and were in response to local political and economic factors. The present kingdom, unlike many other states in the region, does not have its roots in any Ottoman regional division, and it does not spring from a colonial structure imposed on the area.

One of the major factors which led to the success of the Saʿudi attempt to establish a new centralized state was its religious base, which provided people with a common ideology as well as the legitimacy for authority. A second factor was the creation of a military force in the form of the Ikhwan, the Brotherhood, which involved the recruitment and sedentarization of some segments of the Bedouin in new settlements known as *hujur* (sg. *hujrah*). These settlements were located throughout most of the territory of the new state. According to Kishk (1981), the Ikhwan performed the role of a revolutionary party in the establishment of the new political formation.

One must not overlook the role of the urban community in the creation of the state. In fact, the most persistent and ardent supporters of the new state were people from old sedentary communities—villages and cities—in Najd. Some of them actually fought, particularly at critical times, for the Al Saʿud, who are themselves sedentary people of tribal descent, not unlike many others from Najd.

Although some scholars stress the role of the Ikhwan (e.g., Habib 1978; Kishk 1981), the social bases for the new state came largely from the urban population of Najd. As al-Hamad (1986: 35) explains, the interests of merchants and farmers were threatened by the disorder prevailing in the absence of centralized authority. Along with Helms (1981: 104), he argues that both nomadic and sedentary sectors were responsive to the Wahhabi ideology, which was instrumental in undermining tribal pluralism and local political autonomy in favor of centralized authority.

The old sedentary population of Najd played important roles in the establishment of the state. They sent out preachers to "convert" the Bedouin. They provided loans from wealthy merchants and a core of trusted administrators who had at least some modern education. They also played key military roles in the fighting that accompanied the rise of the state. This was particularly the case at the famous and decisive battle at Sabilah in 1929, when ʿAbd al-ʿAziz was forced to raise an army, mainly from among men from the Qasim, to defeat the increasingly independent-minded forces of the Ikhwan (cf. Habib 1978:138). As many of our informants mentioned, throughout the early period of the development of the new state ʿUnayzah sent fighters to support ʿAbd al-ʿAziz.

The raising of revenue, unfortunately, was a problem that confronted ʿAbd al-ʿAziz throughout most of the time of his campaigns and during much of his reign. Merchants provided significant amounts of money, both in the form of contributions and as loans. Most of these merchants were originally from Najd and included people from ʿUnayzah. According to a member of one of the leading old merchant families in ʿUnayzah, "We used to give loans to ʿAbd al-ʿAziz and we did that without charging any interest." However, these loans and contributions, plus taxes that ʿAbd al-ʿAziz was able to collect, did not meet all the financial requirements of the new state. The British gave funds and, as early as 1915, sent military experts, but ʿAbd al-ʿAziz always confronted the British when they stood in the way of the expansion of his territory. Indeed, to guarantee his independence and to protect his autonomy from the British, ʿAbd al-ʿAziz opened the door to negotiations with the Americans for the exploration for oil (cf. Salamé 1980:38–39).

Saʿudi *sultah,* "authority," historically at least, rose from local indigenous factors and owes its emergence and continuity to its own will rather than to any foreign will or determination. Yet its autonomy was compromised by the need for British financial and technical military support. ʿAbd al-ʿAziz sought to lessen his dependence on the British by granting the Americans concessions to explore for oil in 1933; in the end, however, the autonomy of the country was radically compromised as a result of the discovery and exploitation of vast oil resources by American oil companies.

The establishment of the new state involved not only a religious reform movement, military campaigns, and the securing of financial support but also the creation and development of a bureaucracy. Men from Najd, whether nomadic or sedentary, provided a network of loyal compatriots who lived in many parts of the new country as a result of earlier migration out of the area. Some of these were recruited by ʿAbd al-ʿAziz and came to play important roles in the bureaucracy of the new state. In an area such as the Hijaz, highly qualified local men could have worked in the new bureaucracy, and some did. However, in the early stages of the development of the state, men from Najd were often preferred, not only because they were felt to be more trustworthy, but because they and their families were well known to ʿAbd al-ʿAziz and they all shared a common cultural background and regional identity (cf. Altorki 1987c).

An outstanding example of such a man was ʿAbd Allah Sulayman (his real name), who was from ʿUnayzah. He played a major role in the development of the state and also provides an example of a successful migrant from ʿUnayzah during this period.

Perhaps the most important of the King's advisers was a man who almost never attended the political committee because of his many engagements outside it, Sheikh Abdullah Suleiman, the Finance Minister. Suleiman was from Unayzah in Najd. As a youth he had left Arabia for Bombay, which was about the only avenue open for young Arabs who sought adventure and fortune. He grew up without any formal education as a servant in the house of . . . one of the leading Najdi merchants in Bombay during its heyday as a trading metropolis. . . . Anxious to try his hand in commerce, Suleiman left Bombay for Bahrain, where he started up a small business of his own. It was not a great success and he soon found himself looking round for some more secure employment.

Suleiman's brother occupied a minor position as a finance clerk in His Majesty's Domestic Court. He was somewhat overworked and, having obtained permission to take on an assistant, asked Suleiman to join him. . . . Thus, as a lowly assistant to a clerk, he began his career at Court. . . . Gradually the King's admiration for Suleiman grew . . . and the former assistant clerk [was] appointed Finance Minister wholly responsible for the state treasury. Suleiman remained Finance Minister throughout the King's life. . . .

Suleiman was the ultimate *éminence grise,* always self-effacing and keeping himself in the wings. Nevertheless, his power and influence became so monumental that I often thought of him as the uncrowned king of Arabia. . . . At the height of his power, Suleiman was by far the most important man in the kingdom outside the royal family. (Almana 1980:192–197)

ʿUnayzah Becomes a Provincial City

While the state developed gradually as an institution, ʿUnayzah and other communities like it experienced a reorientation in their relations with the outside world. They had formerly been faced with possible highway robbery if they ventured into the desert beyond the walls of the city and, to avoid that, had sometimes had to pay tribute to the leaders of Bedouin tribes. With the establishment of the state, travel became safe. Indeed, one of ʿAbd al-ʿAziz's first concerns had been to defuse the independent power and autonomy of the tribes, and acts of robbery by Bedouin were severely punished.

At the same time, of course, communities such as ʿUnayzah lost their own autonomy and were incorporated into the administrative structure of the new state. When ʿAbd al-ʿAziz established control over Najd, he divided it into five amirates, of which the Qasim was one. The Qasim was further subdivided into four amirates, including ʿUnayzah. Although ʿUnayzah was geographically a part of the Qasim amirate, it remained administratively separate and kept its own flag.

However, after the unification of the kingdom in 1932, the whole country was divided into four provinces, which were further divided into districts. Najd became a province and the Qasim a district of Najd. The administrative heads of both provinces and districts were, and are, amirs from among the Al Saʿud or their affines. ʿUnayzah became one of four amirates into which the Qasim district was divided. These amirates have now increased in number. All came under the direct administration of the Qasim district except for ʿUnayzah, which remained separate until 1969. At present, ʿUnayzah comes under the administration of the Qasim district, the capital of which is its old rival, Buraydah (al-Wasil 1986:10–13).

A folk explanation volunteered by numerous people in ʿUnayzah to account for Buraydah being chosen as the district capital has to do with the location of the first telegraph and postal office in the region. At some point in the early days of the new state, the government offered to open such an office in ʿUnayzah. The amir of ʿUnayzah refused to accept it because he was afraid it would lead to too much external interference in the affairs of the community. The government, therefore, installed the service in Buraydah, at which time 'Unayzah immediately demanded that one be installed in 'Unayzah as well. Nonetheless, Buraydah was first to receive it and, therefore, became the regional capital since it was the first to be directly linked to the outside. As a result of its being chosen as the Qasim district capital, at least according to local opinion in 'Unayzah, Buraydah has attracted more attention and, for this reason, has surpassed 'Unayzah at least in terms of population size if not in other ways.

According to Sharif (1970:277–278), the authority of an amir of a district was different from that of a governor in other Arab countries. In his person, an amir combined administrative, economic, military, and technical authority and was considered the deputy of the king in the district. He was free and answerable to no one but the king. This changed when the state established ministries and the amir became tied to the Ministry of Interior. Following that, central state offices which had not existed before were established and these took on some of the responsibilities of the amir, who thereby lost some of his local authority.

Sharif sees this as a change from an originally decentralized administration during the early years of the formation of the state to the highly centralized administration which prevails at present. The local amir of 'Unayzah is now appointed by the Ministry of Interior, which provides his budget. Although chosen from among members of the same family which provided the amirs of autonomous 'Unayzah at the end of the nineteenth century, the present amir is an employee of the Ministry of Interior and reports to it through the office of the Qasim district amirate in Buraydah. However, most other state offices report directly to their central ministries in Riyadh, thus preserving at least some aspects of 'Unayzah's former status as a separate, autonomous community within the structure of the present centralized administrative system of the state.

Education

One of the most important institutions introduced by the state is secular education. With its national curriculum, the educational system has contributed to the forging of a new national identity (cf. Altorki 1987c). The system has also provided both males and females with the basic skills necessary for them to become salaried employees, professionals, or business entrepreneurs and has thus contributed to the development of capitalist social formations in the country. Although the state is now responsible for it, education in ʿUnayzah also provides an example of how local people have themselves played major roles in contributing to development. Indeed, that which most characterizes ʿUnayzah and, in the minds of its citizens, gives them their specificity, both in the past and at present, is education.

The open-mindedness of its people, their quest for knowledge, and their high regard for and commitment to education are what have always most impressed those who have visited ʿUnayzah and written about it. Doughty, for example, mentions the libraries that various people had, states that numerous people received a news publication from Beirut, and refers to people who were religious scholars and others who were knowledgeable in philosophy. It is also obvious from Philby's description of ʿUnayzah at the time of his visit there in 1918 that quite a few were literate and maintained libraries that included books on both religious and secular subjects.

At least two sources can be found for the educational achievements of ʿUnayzah people before the advent of the modern educational system introduced by the state in 1936. One was the *katatib* (sg. *kuttab*) schools in the city itself. To our knowledge, the history of these in ʿUnayzah has never been recorded. However, when the first secular school was opened in ʿUnayzah in 1926 by a private citizen, there were at least four *katatib* for males and others for females. Informants did not specify how long these had been in existence, but one can safely assume that they were not new and had a long tradition, and, indeed, Doughty mentions that in 1878 he met a scholar who had not traveled but whose "youth had been fostered in learning, by charitable sheykhs" (1979 [1888], 2:383).

The main activity of *katatib* throughout the Islamic world has been to teach the Holy Qurʾan and to disseminate religious knowledge. While the memorization of the Holy Qurʾan and of certain of the Hadith, or Traditions, was the main goal of these schools, some students learned to read and write and were thus able to pursue further knowledge. Some in ʿUnayzah developed specialized religious knowledge which was greatly respected in the community. Even those who were materially impoverished but who had achieved a degree of knowledge of religious subjects were highly regarded. People of all statuses consulted them and sought their advice and, thus, they influenced the behavior of others. Some of these continued to seek further education by traveling to other cities such as Basrah, Madinah, and Makkah.

The other source that stimulated educational achievement was the contact of people from ʿUnayzah with the outside world. Since at least the early nineteenth century, some of the ʿuqaylat from the city had taken up residence in other cities abroad and had been educated there. These returned to ʿUnayzah from time to time and had a strong influence on the community.

Ten years before the first state school for boys was opened, a private school was established in ʿUnayzah by Ibn Salih (his real name). He had studied in Iraq and Bahrain and then returned to ʿUnayzah, where he opened a school that, according to one who studied there, "marked the beginning of modern education in Najd." This school, known as Madrasat Ibn Salih al-Ahliyah, Ibn Salih's Private School, started in 1926, and Ibn Salih and his brother taught the Holy Qurʾan, dictation, writing, composition, and arithmetic. The boys who came to this school paid 1 riyal, if they could afford it; otherwise they were allowed to study for free. It is said that most of the boys who studied there were from among the better-off families, particularly those of the merchants. The poorer boys from among the *fallalih* had to work on the farms and also had to go to the desert to gather *ʿushb,* which meant that, if they enrolled in the school, they would have to miss classes.

King ʿAbd al-ʿAziz is said to have been very pleased with this school and twice came to its "graduation" parties. He was happy to see that the youth in ʿUnayzah sought education. Furthermore, those who studied in Ibn Salih's school provided the first employees in the *diwan al-malaki,* "royal court," because they were the only local men in Najd who had received a modern education. Some of the students in this school later on in life achieved distinction in education, government service, and business in the kingdom. Among those who first studied in Ibn Salih's school is the first Saudi Arabian to receive a Ph.D. degree, a man who also became the rector of one of Saudi Arabia's most important universities and who has also held two ministerial positions. Another has achieved prominence as the mayor of a major city in the country, while another has become an important ambassador.

In 1936, the state opened the first schools for boys in Najd, including the ʿAziziyah school in ʿUnayzah. This school started by offering grades one, two, and three. Those who had completed Ibn Salih's curriculum were more advanced in some subjects but had not covered some of the items in the state curriculum. They were placed in the third grade. During the second year the school was in operation, the fourth grade was added and so on until the sixth grade was offered. In its first year, the 'Aziziyah school had 150 students and 6 teachers, and as people in 'Unayzah proudly point out, all the teachers were from 'Unayzah, although several were 'Unayzah men who had lived in the Hijaz. In Buraydah, they say, the teachers were all from elsewhere, as was the case in Ha'il, where one of the teachers was from 'Unayzah.

In the years that have followed, many more schools for boys have been opened, and there are now twenty-four primary schools for them. The first intermediate school was opened in 1953, while the first secondary school for boys was opened in 1956. 'Unayzah now has five intermediate schools and two secondary schools for boys. In addition, a number of secondary-level technical and teachers' training schools exist. There are now 6,503 students and 425 teachers in the boys' schools, not including those in technical and teachers' training.

Girls' education was originally begun by a number of women who established *katatib* for girls in their homes. Women who are now over sixty years of age remember that they learned in these when they were young girls and say that their teachers had likewise learned in them. Memorization of the Holy Qur'an was the main goal. Each girl had a small wooden board on which the teacher wrote a verse from the Holy Qur'an by using a dye from a plant that grows in the desert. The girl would take this home and memorize it. When she had committed it to memory, the dye would be washed off and a new verse written.

When she had memorized a certain part of the Holy Qur'an, a *zaffah*, "procession," was held. The girl was dressed up for the occasion in gold and fancy clothes and passed in the *zaffah* from the house of her teacher through the nearby streets accompanied by singing. The procession led to her parents' home, where a reception was held in the women's quarters of the house. Incense was burned and usually a meal was served for her teacher, schoolmates, and other female neighbors and relatives. This was always a joyous occasion and many vividly remember it. The *zaffah* usually coincided with the onset of puberty, at which time veiling and seclusion became mandatory for girls. Since they had to stay at home from this period on, many forgot much of what they had learned, although a few who made special efforts to obtain some reading material were able to develop and maintain their literacy. In the words of one, "My brother owned a book shop [in another city] and he sent me books when I asked him. I read everything I could put my hands on. I told relatives who traveled to get me books and I got books whenever I traveled, which was not often. I particularly enjoyed reading some of the world's classics in translation." For women in her age group, this sort of reading was not common. However, women who became teachers in the *katatib* for girls had to make a special effort to develop the required knowledge. This was usually done through the cooperation of male kin. As one of them said, "My father began to lose his eyesight. At that time, he was engaged in religious studies with a well-known shaykh. I helped him by listening to him recite and then checked to see if he had learned it properly. In doing this, I improved my ability to read, as well as my knowledge of the Holy Qur'an and the Hadith."

Many of the girls who went to the *katatib* were from among the wealthier segments of the population. This was because they had the time to dedicate themselves to such activities. However, some of the poor also sent their daughters to the *katatib*.

My father was poor and did many different kinds of jobs. He had one camel which he used to carry firewood and *'ushb* for others. As the eldest child, I helped my father in looking after the camel when it was not being used and I sometimes spent several months a year gathering *'ushb* in the desert. On days when I had to take the camel to the desert to graze, I would dash to the home of the teacher and ask her to write the verses I was supposed to learn on my board. I would then run to take the camel and would study my lesson while I was following it in the *barr*. On other days, I stayed longer in the school. But I did not learn to read and write, although I know enough of the Holy Qur'an to pray.

This case and others that were reported show that the religious education of girls was positively valued. Girls who had to help their families in their work were, nonetheless, sometimes sent to learn. Also, the teacher had to be paid, whether in money or in the form of dates, tea, sugar, wheat, or other payment in kind.

When the boys' schools began to develop and recruited teachers from other parts of the Arab world, some of the prominent families sent their daughters to be privately tutored by the wives of these schoolteachers. The girls studied subjects such as arithmetic and Arabic grammar and composition. This brief period occurred in the 1950s before the opening of the first state school for girls in 1960. In that year, fifteen primary schools for girls were opened in various cities in the country. While some communities in Najd resisted the opening of schools for girls, ʿUnayzah did not, although some in the community may not have welcomed them. In the first year, 285 girls were enrolled in ʿUnayzah, and in the second year the number of girls studying more than doubled, to a total of 680.

Ten years after the first primary school for girls started, an intermediate school opened, and in 1974 the first secondary school for girls started. There are today twenty-nine primary schools, six intermediate schools, and two secondary schools for girls. The total number of girls studying in 1986 reached 5,893, with 503 teachers. In addition to these, a number of secondary-level teachers' training schools exist. Thus the teachers in girls' schools exceed the number in boys' schools by 78, while the number of boy students exceeds the number of girls by 610.

CHAPTER 6

Occupational Change
and New Institutions

Concomitant with the development of the new state and of modern education, new technology and infrastructure were introduced. Wage labor, salaried employment, and entrepreneurship came to predominate in the organization of work both in ʿUnayzah and other places in the new country. A national currency, the Saʿudi riyal, replaced the Maria Theresa dollar and other currencies which had been used previously. Barter and payment in kind disappeared, and people increasingly relied on obtaining cash in order to secure a livelihood. In the case of ʿUnayzah, all the above variables are associated with the restructuring of agricultural production, occupational change and outmigration, the intensification of the role of the state in the community, and the development of new local institutions to provide welfare and improve physical conditions.

The Restructuring of Agricultural Production

One of the most important early technological changes was the introduction of mechanical pumps on wells for irrigation. In 1925, ʿAbd al-ʿAziz gave three kerosene pumps to members of the amir's family. People in ʿUnayzah comment on this today and consider it to mark an important change. By 1961, there were 523 pumps operating in ʿUnayzah. A year later, ʿUnayzah also had six tractors, eighteen mechanical threshing machines, and seventeen harrows (Sharif 1970: 127–131).

The introduction of pumps had a profound impact on agriculture.

The drawing of water by the *sawani,* which required numerous camels, fodder to feed them, and heavy inputs of human labor, made irrigation an expensive undertaking. Indeed, agriculture had been limited mainly because of the expense and difficulty of irrigation. The introduction of pumps decreased the labor input required by agriculture, made it possible to farm more land, and led to an increase in the size of landholdings. Pumps also led to gender specialization in irrigation, as only males operated the pumps.

As indicated earlier, Sharif (1970:118–121) identified 293 agricultural landholdings as existing in 1961. Of these, at least 20 percent were new. These new farms had a minimum of ten hectares and were thus larger in size than most of the old ones. Most of the new farms grew new crops in addition to the traditional ones. The new crops included oranges, tangerines, grapes, apples, apricots, peaches, pears, grapefruit, tomatoes, lettuce, cucumbers, garlic, and potatoes. The new, larger farms were sometimes farmed by sharecroppers, but many relied on both permanent and seasonal wage laborers. On older, smaller farms, extra labor, which had previously been provided by reciprocal work parties, came to be contracted on a daily basis for wages. Some of this labor was provided by males and females who had formerly worked on the *sawani.*

The following two cases illustrate the change that occurred. When she was fifteen years old in about 1940, Umm Mansur worked on the *sawani* on a farm leased by her husband's brother. Later on, she worked with her husband, sons, unmarried daughters, and sons' wives on various farms that her husband leased. In about 1956, she started working for wages on the farms of others and began to organize work gangs of women. At the time of fieldwork, she was working for wages on a farm belonging to her son, marking an extraordinary change from the domestically organized work of the past.

About thirty years ago and before we gave up the farm we had leased, I started to work on other people's farms and was paid by the day. Usually, when extra hands were needed on a farm, the owner would come by my house and let me know how many women he needed. I would inform women I knew and we would agree on a meeting place, where we would be picked up early in the morning to go out to the farm. I was not paid more than the other women, although I was the one who was in charge of getting them together. Occasionally, if the landlord did not mind, I would go over to a neighboring farm in the afternoon to gain some extra money.

My son Mansur is now the director of a primary school and is also a *mu'adhdhin*. Within the past three years, he leased a farm for 8,000 riyals a year. He is on leave from the school and is studying to get a higher degree. He has two Egyptian and four Pakistani workers on his farm. He also hires women on a daily basis to sort and process the dates and to thresh the alfalfa. I also work for him and he pays me 50 riyals per day for this work.

My daughter's husband also has a sharecropping arrangement with a landlord, and when I work there he pays me. During the harvest season, my son sends some of his workers to help out on my daughter's husband's farm. My daughter's husband also sends some of his workers to help my son when he needs them. When they are working as a large group on these farms, my son's wife joins us on my daughter's husband's farm to help with the cooking, but she is not paid, as this is a kind of festive occasion.

As a girl, Umm ʿAli worked as a member of her family on a small farm owned by her grandfather. In about 1955, she and her husband went to work as day laborers on a big farm. Interestingly, this case also illustrates the hiring of a woman to work on a relative's farm.

When I got married, my husband and I went to work on a big farm nearby. At the beginning, we worked on a daily basis. There were several other women who went to work with us on the same farm. We worked from early morning to noon for 7 riyals a day each. We cut and gathered up alfalfa. We separated and replanted melons. We cut the alfalfa which had produced seeds and gathered it up in our skirts to be sure not to lose any of the seeds. We threshed the alfalfa to get the seeds and put them in sacks.

We worked there for a number of years and then went to work for my maternal uncle, who had gotten a farm of his own. We did the same kind of work and he also paid us.

Then, my husband and I worked throughout the year on a very big farm owned by a man who was not a relative. He paid us monthly. My husband irrigated along with other men who had been hired, and I helped in all the other work. When extra hands were needed, the owner would ask us to arrange to bring in some women. I knew a woman who knew other women who needed to work, and she would bring them to her house, and then my husband and I would pick them up in a truck that belonged to the farm and we would take them with us. At this time, the pay had been increased, and they made 20 riyals a day.

We eventually left this kind of work, and my husband now works as a janitor at a school. Whenever possible, I try to find some work on a farm or even to help process dates in other people's houses. I like to do this kind of work because I can now make 50 riyals a day and, also, I usually work with the same women that I worked with years ago, and we are friends and enjoy being together.

As wage labor became predominant on farms, production increasingly was oriented toward sale for cash in the markets of 'Unayzah and other cities such as Riyadh. A large segment of the local population continued to work in agriculture. However, the agricultural labor force was increasingly composed of illiterate women and older men from the 1950s until about 1975, when expatriate laborers came to predominate as laborers on farms.

Occupational Change and Out-Migration

Technological change spared the labor of many who formerly had worked in agriculture. Motor transportation made the *jammamil* obsolete and contributed to the rapid decline of the *'uqaylat*. Craft production also declined in 'Unayzah as industrially produced goods were increasingly imported and replaced locally produced items. As a result of these changes, occupational change increasingly became common in the 1940s and 1950s. Some found work in other occupations in 'Unayzah while many migrated to other places in the country which were becoming centers of development.

Abu Mish'al, who worked as a *jammal* until the late 1940s, described the impact of motor and rail transportation on the *jammamil*.

When the trucks started to come, they began to take work away from us. They drove across the desert and they could go back and forth to Kuwait or Jubayl. They were faster and could carry a lot. We hated the trucks because they took our livelihood away from us. If we found him dying of thirst, we would not give him a drop to drink—the owner of the truck. But there were the Dahna' sands between al-Ahsa' and

Riyadh, and the trucks could not travel across them. And so we went there and carried dates from al-Ahsa' for the shaykhs in Riyadh. Then the railroad was built to Riyadh and that was the end.

The *jammamil* did not get involved in motor transportation to any significant degree. Some of the older ones settled down and took up farming, mainly as sharecroppers, or opened small shops in the *suq*. However, those who were younger sought jobs in new occupations. The following case is of a man who first worked with his father as a *jammal* and then became an employee in various enterprises before he established himself as an entrepreneur. During this period, numerous young men from *fallalih* and other backgrounds had similar career histories. Abu Yusif is sixty-eight years old and has recently retired in 'Unayzah. In 1932, he started working with his father as a *jammal*.

> I left 'Unayzah as a boy of about twelve years of age. My father was a *jammal* and I worked with him for a few years. Then, I went to Bahrain to [a merchant from 'Unayzah] and worked for a couple of years in his office. I did this work until I was nineteen. Then I worked with a man who had a truck and hauled merchandise in Dammam. I became a mechanic and then became a boss of a garage. Then I went to Kuwait for four years and worked on my own in trade between Kuwait and Riyadh. I made a lot of money in that trade but there was a lot of risk involved and I grew tired of traveling all the time. I settled in Riyadh and opened a shop for selling gold. I stayed there for twenty-two years, and the shop did very well. I had worked for fifty years every day of the week except sometimes on Friday and I decided to retire. I sold the shop and moved back to 'Unayzah.

The use of vehicles not only brought an end to one of the old occupations for which 'Unayzah was famous. It also opened up the city to the wider world on a level that could not have been imagined earlier. Trips that in the past took as much as twenty days could now be made in one or two. At first, the vehicles traveled across the open desert, as there were no roads. This was often quite easy, since large areas of the desert are flat and easily crossed by cars and trucks. However, there are sandy areas, and these cause great difficulty. Vehicles were always getting stuck and sometimes had to be pulled out by camels. Also, sandy areas effectively blocked vehicular communication between different places, as was the case between Buraydah and 'Unayzah and between al-Ahsa' and Riyadh. However, by the 1950s 'Unayzah had been linked by a network of roads to most of the major cities of the country. Most of these roads were paved in the 1960s.

According to Sharif (1970: 172–177), the road that linked 'Unayzah to Riyadh via Shaqrah was paved by 1967. The road that linked it to Buraydah and Ha'il was paved in 1963. By about the same time, a paved road linked 'Unayzah to the Hijaz via Madinah. An unpaved road linked the city to Kuwait, but this was a difficult route, as there were sandy areas along the way. 'Unayzah was also linked by a network of roads to the settlements around it. Most of these were difficult and in bad condition, but in 1965 the Ministry of Transportation initiated the building of a network of modern roads to link the city to its agricultural areas and villages.

Sharif also reports that there was a small "desert" airport in 'Unayzah which received small Dakota planes. In the early 1960s, flights between Jiddah and Riyadh stopped in 'Unayzah four times a week and brought both passengers and the mail. The main Qasim airport, serving both 'Unayzah and Buraydah, was completed by 1964, and numerous daily flights now connect the Qasim to all the many commercial airports in the country and, through its main gateways, to the rest of the world. The city is also now served by a new network of excellent paved highways.

Most of the work involved in the construction of this infrastructure in the 1950s and 1960s was performed by men with backgrounds as *fallalih,* Bedouin, or craftspeople. This work attracted a large number of men from 'Unayzah who worked as wage laborers. Significantly, the construction of infrastructure, which was financed by the state largely with revenue obtained through the sale of oil, also stimulated the development of contracting companies, including several established by men from 'Unayzah with merchant and *'uqaylat* backgrounds. The new roads also facilitated labor migration to the newly developing capital, to the oil fields of the Eastern Province, and to the Hijaz.

Although the city is located far away from the oil fields of the Eastern Province, the discovery and development of oil there had a pervasive, albeit indirect, effect on 'Unayzah, particularly during the late 1940s and 1950s. Exploration for oil began in 1933 in the area of Dammam by a company which later (in 1944) took the name of the Arabian American Oil Company (ARAMCO). Oil in commercial quantities was discovered in 1938, but the large-scale development of this resource was interrupted by World War II.

In the 1940s, men from ʿUnayzah began to go to the Eastern Province in search of work—not only in the oil fields but in numerous related activities. They worked, for example, in the building of the railroad, which began operations between Dammam and Riyadh in 1950, in the building of the Trans-Arabian Pipeline (Tapline), and in the Geological Survey, which searched for oil deposits throughout the Eastern Province and the Empty Quarter.

The following case shows the involvement of men from ʿUnayzah in these activities. Abu ʿAbd al-Muhsin is the owner of a medium-size farm in ʿUnayzah, and he looks forward to retiring there in a few years. He is now a high administrator in PETROMIN, the state marketing agency for oil. He remembers his first work at ARAMCO many years ago.

I started to work for ARAMCO in 1947. People from ʿUnayzah had been going to work in the Eastern Province since the early 1940s, but they began to go in larger numbers around 1951, when ARAMCO really began its work in earnest. We all went there as unskilled workers. Many of us were the sons of *fallalih,* and some had worked a bit as drivers or mechanics. I had first gone to Riyadh and worked there in construction as a laborer. While I was in Riyadh, I stayed with other young men from ʿUnayzah. Some of them had found jobs building the old airport there. This work was under the supervision of ARAMCO, and they heard about opportunities for jobs in the oil fields in the Eastern Province.

A number of us decided to go there, and we left Riyadh as a group. We signed on with ARAMCO and were hired for 3 riyals a day. Altogether, there were about 150 young men from ʿUnayzah in Dhahran at that time. There were also others who worked in the Geological Survey and others who found work in the building of the railroad. The best jobs, however, were with ARAMCO itself, because they gave you special training courses, and it was possible to learn new things and to improve yourself. For example, I was chosen to participate in an intensive training course which started in 1949. I knew how to read and write but that was all, but I attended training courses in both English and Arabic and was able to graduate into a job that required skilled expertise.

Several of the men who went there as workers soon got into businesses that they themselves developed and that supplied a lot of things that ARAMCO needed. One set up a company to provide transportation for ARAMCO. He is now one of the biggest merchants in the kingdom. There was also another who became a labor contractor, and, being from ʿUnayzah, he naturally tried to help the people from his hometown. He recruited a lot of workers, especially for the Geological Survey. There were also quite a number of ʿUnayzah men who went to Bahrain in those days, particularly through the old ʿUnayzah merchant families who had long been established there.

The men from ʿUnayzah stayed together as much as possible. We would meet and eat *mataziz* [a traditional ʿUnayzah dish] together, and at the time of the ʿid we would dance the ʿardah as a group and sing songs that are traditional to ʿUnayzah. We helped newcomers from our city to find jobs. There were, of course, workers from many different towns and tribes, but people would stick together with their own kind.

I think it's fair to say that the men from ʿUnayzah who went to work with ARAMCO were very successful. For example, there are Abu Ahmad and Abu Salih. They both now head very big companies, and Abu Salih is one of the richest men in the world, like ———. But he made his money in a clean way. They were both simple workers at the beginning. Also, people from ʿUnayzah were not afraid to go into the desert. We were very familiar with the desert at home and we knew the tribes and the Bedouin. So, we were not afraid to go and live for more than a month at a time in a camp in the Empty Quarter. The minds of people from ʿUnayzah are open, more so than people from some other communities, and we have always respected learning. Most of us were ready to stay and work regularly and take advantage of what we were taught. And so, quite a number of the bigger jobs in ARAMCO are now held by people from ʿUnayzah, who went as simple workers and eventually moved up. There were, of course, a number who did not stay for long periods, who went only to make a little extra money. They were the ones who came back to ʿUnayzah. Those who were successful did not come back, but maybe they will retire here.

When we went at the beginning, we were all young and most of us had not married. Some people got married there, mainly from families who had migrated from ʿUnayzah and were living there. Others got married from here, and they brought their wives to live with them there as soon as they could afford it. We also, of course, sent money back to our families in ʿUnayzah and they sent things to us, especially food which our mothers made for us and sent with travelers. We also sent them letters.

The above case shows that some were able to take advantage of the training that was offered by ARAMCO and were able to move up in the company and eventually achieve high positions of responsibility. The following case shows how work in this sector did not always directly lead to improvements in type of occupation.

Abu Turki has a construction business with offices in Riyadh and ʿUnayzah. He has become quite rich in recent years, but this was due to business opportunities that have recently come about and had little to do with his earlier work. Abu Turki is now in his forties.

My father used to sell alfalfa in the market. We were very poor then, but I managed to study in the *kuttab* school and to learn to read a little. I went to the ʿAziziyah school [the first state school for boys in ʿUnayzah], but my mother and father were afraid that if I got an education the government might take me away, and so they took me out of the school. I worked in a number of odd jobs here in ʿUnayzah, but I wanted to go to school like my other friends. My parents relented, and I completed the fifth year of primary school. I was about fifteen then and I decided that I wanted to go and find a job.

A friend and I got a ride on a truck going to Riyadh. My mother gave me some *klayjah,* and that was what we ate in Riyadh. We stayed there for two days and slept at the railroad station. We took the train to Dammam and then went to Dhahran. There was a man from ʿUnayzah there who had a company that did business with ARAMCO. He said ARAMCO was looking for youths who had some education. I went, and they hired me. I had a training course and learned some English and I became a car mechanic. I worked there for two years and lived in the camp with others from ʿUnayzah.

My elder brother was working on the building of Tapline and he convinced me to go and work there. I left ARAMCO and got a job on Tapline but I did not like it there. I came back to Dhahran and got a job with the Geological Survey. We worked in the Empty Quarter and all over and we placed dynamite to test for oil. At any one time there would be between ten and forty people from ʿUnayzah in our camp. We all lived together in a tent. There were also Bedouin from the Al Murrah, the Bani Hajir, and the Dawasir tribes and there were people from Haʾil, ar-Rass, and al-Bakariyah. But I don't remember anybody from Buraydah.

Altogether, I worked for eighteen years with ARAMCO and the Geological Survey and at the end I was earning 400 riyals a month. In the Geological Survey we had all been hired by a labor contractor who was from ʿUnayzah. Naturally, he favored people from here. The sons of the *fallalih* and of the merchants seldom did the kind of work we did, but we were from poor families and had to take any job we could find. The contractor paid us our salaries after he had deducted all our expenses. We had to buy all our food from him, as well as the tent and anything else we needed.

I came back to ʿUnayzah in 1968 and worked for a while with a dump truck I had bought cheap. I studied at home at night and took the exams for the primary and intermediate certificates. I became a soldier for a while and earned 205 riyals a month. Then I had a job with the Ministry of ——— here in ʿUnayzah. But I had to quit that in 1974, as I had begun to get involved in private work on my own.

Both of the above cases show the importance of the oil industry in bringing about a transformation of the organization of the work force, as has been argued by Rumaihi (1975) in the case of the Arabian Gulf and by Vasiliev (1986) for Saudi Arabia. ARAMCO initiated qualitative changes in the types of skills required and a new pattern of discipline and routine. It also stimulated further development of changes in the organization of work which had already appeared in Saudi Arabia. These changes included contractual relations and wages and salaries. However, recruitment patterns remained somewhat traditional. ARAMCO attracted workers from among the Bedouin, farmers, and craftspeople; but those who came to work were mainly self-recruited, having heard of job opportunities through kinsmen or friends, or they were recruited by labor contractors who tended to favor men from their own communities.

Throughout the 1950s and 1960s, workers from ʿUnayzah were also attracted to growing urban centers not directly involved in the oil industry. Along with rural and Bedouin migrants, many became semiskilled workers in construction or engaged in commerce or various other service occupations. Although they worked for wages or salaries or to make profits in sales, they did not have the kind of contractual relations or experience the discipline and training that often accompanied work in ARAMCO. Also, their choice of work was often influenced by family considerations.

An example is provided by Abu 'Uthman, who about thirty-five to forty years ago gave up his work in agriculture in 'Unayzah and went to Riyadh in search of employment. He first worked for a prince, taking care of his animals. A few years later, his younger brother joined him in the same work. Sometime later, his brother established a partnership with another man to sell vegetables in the vegetable market in Riyadh. Abu 'Uthman joined in this work and remained there until he decided to start buying and selling real estate during the period of the economic boom after 1975.

Many of those who left 'Unayzah worked as unskilled or semi-skilled wage laborers. In addition, some men were qualified as school-teachers, enabling them to take posts in primary and secondary schools both in 'Unayzah and other cities and villages throughout Najd and the Eastern Province. Similarly, numerous qualified men took up new occupations as employees in the bureaucracy both in 'Unayzah and throughout the country.

Migration out of 'Unayzah has a long history for males. In the past when it was an autonomous community, men migrated mainly to Iraq, Syria, Egypt, Kuwait, Bahrain, India, and to the Hijaz cities of Makkah, Madinah, and Jiddah. While religious scholarship was a motive for some who went to Makkah and Madinah, trade and opportunities for work were the major motives for most. However, as the discussion above shows, the development of the present Saudi Arabian state and of the oil industry changed the main focus of migration away from places outside the Arabian Peninsula to the newly developing cities of the country.

As the national economy and the institutions of the state developed throughout the 1950s, 1960s, and early 1970s, migration out of the community for jobs and for education affected the majority of 'Unayzah families. While some of the males who migrated returned to live in 'Unayzah, many remained in other communities. Many of those who remained outside eventually, if married, brought their wives and children to live with them. If not married at the time of migration, they either returned to 'Unayzah to get married and brought the wife back to the new community or married from among 'Unayzah residents in the new community. Occasionally, they married from among the people of the host community. A few also left wives behind in 'Unayzah and married others in the new community. Thus, migration for males in the past was primarily for job opportunities and, to a lesser degree, for education. The migration of females was almost exclusively due to marriage to a migrant.

Among the large numbers of migrants from ʿUnayzah and/or their offspring who continue to live in other communities within the Arabian Peninsula are many who have maintained a strong identity with ʿUnayzah and have actively contributed to local development activities in the community. Also, as indicated in several of the cases presented above, ʿUnayzah is now attracting a return migration from among its sons and daughters who sought their livelihood "abroad."

Intensification of the Role of the State in ʿUnayzah

Many of those who sought new types of work had to migrate to other communities. Among those who remained in ʿUnayzah, many continued to work in agriculture but mainly as wage laborers or as farm entrepreneurs. The *suq* also attracted people who had formerly worked in agricultural and craft production and from among the Bedouin. Some of the newcomers to the *suq* and many of those who had long been established in it developed larger and more complex business enterprises as the monetization of the economy expanded. However, the major source of new types of jobs and employment in ʿUnayzah was the state, which particularly expanded its activities in the city during the 1950s and 1960s.

The role of the state in opening boys' schools in 1936 and girls' schools in 1960 has already been noted. In the early 1950s, a directorate for agriculture was established first under the auspices of the Ministry of Finance and then under the Ministry of Agriculture and Water when it was established. This was followed in the 1960s by a branch of the Agricultural Bank and an agricultural research center. In 1959, the state opened the first public hospital in ʿUnayzah, although this had been preceded by a state-sponsored clinic. In 1961, the municipality was established by the state. A center of the Ministry of Social Affairs was opened in 1962. During the same period, directorates and other offices of most of the national ministries were opened in ʿUnayzah.

Many of those who worked in the new state offices and in the schools were recruited from other Arab countries. The state offices and schools also employed local men and, in some cases later on, women. Many of the local employees worked as drivers, *farrashin,* "messengers," and guards and doorkeepers. However, as a result of education obtained in 'Unayzah and elsewhere, local people were qualified and worked in staff positions and as teachers. The majority of such positions have now been filled by qualified local people.

The state was, and is, the main source of employment for local people in 'Unayzah. Through its various programs and activities, the state has also played an enormous role in the community since at least the 1960s. An example is provided by the municipality.

Before the municipality was established in 1961, issues of urban development and the maintenance of public institutions such as mosques were the concern of the amir or of private groups or individuals. For example, 'Abd Allah Sulayman as an individual and after he had left government service as minister of finance arranged for and, from his private funds, paid the costs of installing the first public water supply system in 'Unayzah in 1955 (Sharif 1970:242). Also during the 1950s groups of people in different neighborhoods collected contributions and bought electricity generators to provide light in streets and homes.

The first activities of the new municipality were related to promoting cleanliness and to widening and straightening the streets. Its concern with the streets led the municipality to begin the destruction of the old *suq* in 1964 and its replacement with a new one. Since then it has continued to develop modern infrastructure throughout the city. It supervises the new *suq* and controls the quality of food products sold there. It is also responsible for granting licenses and implements rules and regulations designed to control the growth of the city according to central state guidelines and with funds allocated to it by the state. Although the head of the municipality is from the local community, he is an employee of the state.

Another example of state involvement in development in the community is provided by the directorate of the Ministry of Agriculture and Water. Since its establishment, the directorate has administered agricultural production throughout the area of the amirate of 'Unayzah. Although it has greatly expanded since 1975, most of its activities were developed in the 1960s. The directorate is divided into a number of administrative departments with specialized mandates. The department of water provides for the distribution of sweet water for drinking to areas that are without it. It also grants permission to dig wells, is responsible for supervising the drilling of them, and deals with complaints that may arise as a result of drilling. This is a very important function, since it is related to the process of *ihya'*, one of the major ways through which people have obtained private ownership of land.

The department of lands is concerned with studies of soils and is also responsible for giving out public lands to individuals. Only with the approval of this office can one officially acquire the ownership of land as private property through *ihya'*. It thus supervises the patterns of land owning and deals with complaints between landowners over the ownership of land. In the case of conflicts, this department sends a representative to a committee that includes representatives of either the amirate or the municipality, depending on the location of the land in question.

The department of economic affairs is responsible for maintaining an up-to-date census of land ownership and of agricultural production. It also provides a subsidy of 50 riyals for each new palm tree planted, provided that it is planted properly on land that the department considers suitable for palms. This office also administers a subsidy of .25 riyal for each kilogram of dates produced. It supervises the storage of newly harvested wheat by providing the farmer with a date at which he must deliver his wheat to the silo, which is provided by the Grain Silos and Flour Mills Organization, a state agency that pays the producer for the wheat that he brings in.

In addition, there are departments of plant disease control, veterinary medicine, and extension. The first of these inspects diseased plants and provides for the combating of disease, mainly through supervising the spraying of crops with chemicals. The veterinarians obviously treat animals, while those in extension give out information on dates when crops should be planted, types of crops that are most suitable for the soils and climate of the area, irrigation requirements for different crops, and types of chemicals and fertilizers to be used.

The Agricultural Research and Training Center was established in 'Unayzah in 1966 and was originally under the administration of the directorate. It now reports directly to the ministry in Riyadh, through the deputy minister for research, and serves the whole of the Qasim, as well as the regions of Zilfi and Ha'il. The center is currently conducting applied research on such crops as garlic, soybeans, lettuce, corn, asparagus, strawberries, carrots, cucumbers, green peppers, tomatoes, potatoes, yams, dates, olives, grapefruit, lemons, oranges, tangerines, and grapes. All of these are now produced in commercial quantities in ʿUnayzah and the region. The research of the center is concerned with establishing crop varieties, methods of cultivation and irrigation, and timings that will produce the best results in this region. The results of the center's research are communicated to the extension department of the directorate, which has primary responsibility for the dissemination of knowledge to farmers. However, the center increasingly is attempting to have more direct contact with the farming population. It has also started a program for the training of Saudi Arabian youth in modern agricultural techniques.

Agricultural development in ʿUnayzah has also been affected by programs of the Ministry of Agriculture and Water which were implemented at the national level beginning in the 1960s. The ministry commissioned various large-scale studies to investigate underground water resources and soils in order to assess the potential for agricultural development. Significant amounts of geological water, often at very deep levels, were found in various parts of the country. In addition, it was found that improved and expanded irrigation systems, along with mechanization, could increase yields from areas that did not depend on geological water. Also, dams could provide an important source of water for expanded agriculture, particularly in the southwestern part of the country. Given these considerations, a national policy of "food security" was declared shortly after the oil boycott of 1973 and the quadrupling of oil prices in 1974. As will be shown later, ʿUnayzah provides an example of some of the recent agricultural development that has taken place as part of this national policy.

The role of the state in the local community began during the first decade of the twentieth century and has increased in importance since then. Births, deaths, marriages, and divorces must now all be registered with its agencies. Landownership involves registration and must conform to guidelines set by the state, as do commercial establishments. The importation of a laborer requires approval by an agency of the state, and rules and regulations concerning that laborer must be followed once he is employed. The state provides the police force, and there is now a jail. The state provides education, not only in the form of facilities and personnel but the curriculum that is taught. The state is the main provider of health facilities and a contributor to social welfare programs, which it supervises. It has provided roads, the airport, telephones, mail service, and telegraph, which link the community to the wider world. The state also provides a major source of entertainment and the news through its radio and television networks. It has also become the major source for loans and subsidies to build houses or develop agricultural enterprises, as will be shown later. The state has become the single most important employer in the community. Furthermore, it maintains the religious establishment, including the courts.

Community Self-Help and Private Voluntary Organizations

Although extremely important, the state does not dominate everything in 'Unayzah. Throughout all periods, both individuals and groups, whether residents or migrants, have made contributions to address issues of local concern. People in 'Unayzah today acknowledge the major role the state has played in development. They say, "Al-hukumah ma gassart" (The government has not done a little), meaning that it has done a lot but should not be expected to do everything.

The example of 'Abd Allah Sulayman's contribution of the first public water supply system in 'Unayzah has already been cited. This same man, a highly successful migrant from 'Unayzah who played a major role in the creation of the state, also established a *waqf* to support people from 'Unayzah wanting to go on the pilgrimage each year. Since the 1950s this *waqf* has enabled many of those without means to perform the pilgrimage, most of whom today are expatriates resident in 'Unayzah.

Other examples of contributions are provided by migrants who went to India and to Bahrain, where they became very wealthy. These have regularly sent their *zakat* back to 'Unayzah for distribution to the poor members of their families as well as for other poor members of the community and for use in the building of mosques. According to Sharif (1970:196), a member of the Al Bassam family resident in India regularly sent between 250,000 and 300,000 riyals per year in the 1960s. Migrants were, of course, joined by local residents in contributing their *zakat* to meet the needs of the local poor and to build and maintain mosques.

The payment of *zakat* is one of the five pillars of Islam and is thus traditional in 'Unayzah. However, in 1954 a group of local people joined together on their own initiative to establish the Sunduq al-Birr al-Khayri, the Philanthropic Fund. According to one of its founders, the Sunduq was the first organization of this type in the country. It was located in a shop in the *suq* and was open every afternoon to collect contributions from people and to provide aid to the needy if they came asking for help. The Sunduq had its own letterhead, and when it provided someone with aid, it simply informed that person that aid came from the Sunduq. All the contributions at first came from individuals in the community, and each year they collected about 8,000 riyals, which in those days was considered to be a large sum. After several years, ARAMCO heard about it and sent the Sunduq a check for 10,000 riyals.

The Sunduq gave aid to people who needed to travel for medical problems. It also gave out kerosene lanterns to provide light in homes. In the winter, it contacted the mosques in each neighborhood and asked the imams to provide it with the names of the needy in the neighborhood. To these men and women it gave clothing provided by a merchant. It also provided clothes to the imams to distribute to the needy during the month of Ramadan. Other projects that it started and contributed to included the widening of streets and the placing of gaslights in them.

According to the man who directed the Sunduq, the organization kept careful accounts and each year published the amounts of contributions and dispersements. Yet, according to him, things were more informal and traditional in those days. Many would leave contributions under the door of the shop if it were closed. Also, much of the work was done through the imams of mosques who knew everyone in their neighborhoods and who were the traditional channels for providing aid to the needy. The Sunduq continued to operate well into the 1960s and provides an important precedent for a more recent private voluntary organization, the Jam'iyah al-Khayriyah al-Birriyah, the Philanthropic Society, which was established in 1975 and is discussed later.

In 1962 the Lajnah al-Ahliyah, the People's Committee, was formed as a private voluntary organization to supervise and solicit contributions for a Center for Social Services, established under the auspices of the Ministry of Social Affairs, which contributed about half the funds for programs and projects. Both the Lajnah and the center continue to operate today, and their programs have changed over the years as the needs of the community have altered. Until the mid

1970s, much of the work of the center was directed at improving general hygiene, promoting public health, and providing aid and training to the poor to help them improve their livelihoods. The center, for example, ran campaigns to combat and exterminate cockroaches, mice, and other household pests. The center tried to show people how to improve their standards of living and concentrated on housing conditions. It was particularly active in getting families to install more hygienic septic tanks and to improve their water supply systems. The center also helped families obtain refrigerators by paying half the cost. It also provided sewing machines for women to use in their homes as part of a project for productive families that was started in 1972. Women were given training in sewing for a period of six months, during which time they were paid a modest sum each month. The project continued for five years with follow-up studies of the trainees in their homes. Unfortunately, the follow-up studies showed that few were making good use of the machines, which was attributed to the competition of male tailors in shops who produced garments very cheaply. However, prior to the increase in the number of male tailors (who are mainly expatriates), this program was highly popular and had a good potential for providing a source of income for women and a service to the community.

During its first decade, the center provided support for an agricultural cooperative society that had a program of providing loans for the purchase of agricultural machinery and both economic and technical support for farmers in general. The center also established a library and a cultural center for youth which was located on its premises. Moreover, it provided the stimulus for establishing one of the city's two sports clubs, the Nadi an-Najmah, which has been an important contribution to the youth of 'Unayzah.

The case of 'Unayzah demonstrates that, before the economic boom transformed the Arabian Peninsula after 1975, a comprehensive process of developmental change had been well established and was gathering momentum. The state was becoming progressively more complex as an institution. Modern education was consistently expanding. Basic infrastructure had been introduced. Modern health facilities were available. Agricultural production was improving with the introduction of mechanization, new crops, and new techniques. The local population gained new skills and was increasingly employed in wage labor, government service, and teaching or worked as entrepreneurs. At the same time, ʿUnayzah was integrated into the structure of a new and more complex political formation. The city could no longer be described as the "Paris of Najd" or as one of the "great cities of Arabia." It had become simply one among several provincial cities in the country. Up to this juncture, it conforms to a pattern of developmental change common throughout most of the Third World.

PART THREE

Economic Boom and Transformation

CHAPTER 7

The Economic Boom, Expatriates, and Local Development

During a period of about a decade in the latter part of the 1970s and early 1980s, dramatic changes quite unlike those usually experienced in the process of development occurred in 'Unayzah. In its 1969–70 fiscal year, the Saudi Arabian state received 5.7 billion riyals as revenue from oil and other sources (Kingdom of Saudi Arabia 1984). Just over a decade later, in 1981–82, the state's revenue reached a high of 368 billion riyals. This dramatic change was due mainly to large increases in the world market price of oil which began in late 1973 and early 1974.

As revenues increased, the state embarked upon massive development programs and projects. Expenditures accordingly went up dramatically. In 1969–70, state expenditures amounted to 6 billion riyals, but in 1981–82 they had reached 283 billion riyals. Since that time, both revenue and expenditures have declined. In 1983–84, revenue declined by 22.2 percent, while expenditures dropped by 6 percent (Kingdom of Saudi Arabia 1984). The decline in both revenue and expenditures has continued until the present and led to a general slowing down of the economy. Indeed, in 1985–86 the state incurred a budget deficit of 50 billion riyals on expenditures of 181.5 billion riyals (Kingdom of Saudi Arabia 1987).

However, during the years of dramatically increasing revenue and expenditures, a boom of major proportions took place in the country and even the most remote villages and isolated nomads were affected. People refer to this period as the *tufrah,* "boom," and date it from about 1975, when the effect of increasing expenditures began to be felt by the population in general. Major achievements were accomplished during this period. In general, however, these achievements did not contribute to sustainable development, at least in the case of ʿUnayzah.

As Table 1 shows, dramatic changes occurred in many different sectors. Both physical and social infrastructure experienced major expansion and improvements. Agricultural production expanded, largely financed by both short-term and long-term loans extended to farmers by the Saudi Arabian Agricultural Bank which rose from 16.6 million riyals in 1970 to a high of over 4 billion riyals in 1983. Also, a major increase in the construction of housing occurred. Between 1975 and 1984, an estimated 437,000 housing units were constructed, of which 195,000 were at least partially financed by the Real Estate Development Fund. The construction sector showed the highest expansion of all the nonoil sectors in the gross domestic product, expanding at a rate of 18.8 percent yearly between 1970 and 1984 (Kingdom of Saudi Arabia 1984). Furthermore, two gigantic industrial cities at Jubayl and Yanbuʿ were established during this period.

Changes of such vast proportions in such a short time have probably never occurred in any country during times of peace. While the statistics presented above show the magnitude of the changes, they only suggest by inference the social and human dimensions. Saudi Arabia occupies a vast territory, about the size of the United States east of the Mississippi. Its population just before the beginning of the *tufrah* in 1974 was slightly more than seven million, and formal modern education had been in existence for less than forty years. Therefore, the country had to import a vast labor force from abroad to work in the many projects that the state, private sector businesses, and individuals embarked upon. The projects required professionals and skilled, semiskilled, and unskilled workers, who were drawn from Africa, Asia, Europe, and North and South America. As the country developed during the 1940s, 1950s, and 1960s, most of those who came from abroad to work were from other parts of the Arab world, along with a few North Americans and others in the oil industry. But now hundreds of thousands from vastly different cultures and backgrounds flooded the country. Expatriates represented an estimated 14.3 percent of the population and 27 percent of the work force in 1970. Ten years later they had increased to form an estimated 30.9 percent of the population and 53.3 percent of the work force (Sirageldin, Sherbiny, and Serageldin 1984:32).

Table I.
Selected Development Achievements in Saudi Arabia

Item	1970	1984
Paved roads (kilometers)	8,000	24,000
Earth-surfaced roads (kilometers)	3,500	43,504
Registered vehicles (cumulative)	60,000	3,900,000
Schools (number)	3,107	14,146
Teachers (number)	23,000	126,000
Hospital beds (number)	9,039	26,410
Medical/paramedical personnel (number)	6,174	49,639
Eggs produced (tons)	5,000	104,000
White meat produced (tons)	7,000	105,000
Dates produced (tons)	240,000	453,000
Grapes produced (tons)	24,000	60,000
Tomatoes produced (tons)	100,000	286,000
Wheat produced (tons)	130,000	1,350,000
Cement produced (tons)	670,000	8,600,000
Operating factories (number)	207	1,609

Source: Kingdom of Saudi Arabia (1984).

The *tufrah* manifested itself in many ways in ʿUnayzah. While business and the general pace of life have now slowed down, from what people say, things were at that time moving very fast. Men in particular were very busy during the years of the *tufrah*. A whole new town was essentially built after 1975, and most people now live in new housing for which they received loans of up to 300,000 riyals per house constructed. A total of 4,800 loans was extended by the ʿUnayzah office of the Real Estate Development Fund since 1973. The construction of so much new housing fueled speculation in land and also required a large labor force of construction workers, many of whom were Yemenis. Men also opened construction companies, and businesses related to the furnishing of houses received a great stimulus.

The Agricultural Bank extended loans to people who developed land for agriculture, and both farmers and businessmen became involved in the process of establishing new farms and improving old ones. This also fueled speculation in land and led to the importation of a large labor force, particularly Egyptians, to work in agriculture. The expansion of agriculture also stimulated the establishment of drilling companies and other businesses related to the sale and servicing of imported agricultural and irrigation machinery.

Education also continued to expand, and improvements were made in health care and health facilities. Most of the major banks that operate in the kingdom opened branch offices in ʿUnayzah. New roads and major highways were built. The offices of ministries expanded. All of this activity resulted in more employment opportunities for both ʿUnayzah men and women and expatriates.

Bedouin also increasingly settled in parts of the city. The population thus increased rapidly due to the Bedouin, to the increased numbers of expatriates, and to a high birth rate among the indigenous population of the city. This population became quite affluent, stimulating the market and leading to the proliferation of shops and small businesses, many of which also brought in expatriate workers.

Throughout this period, some people who had been quite poor became rich while some of the rich became richer or failed to respond to the *tufrah* and became relatively poorer. A few who became rich lost their money and some are deeply in debt. But almost everybody in ʿUnayzah has benefited and now has a higher physical standard of living. Most families are now living in new housing and most have a car, while many have more than one. Many have also traveled widely throughout the Arab world and to Europe, America, and Asia. While men most often travel abroad ("to recruit workers"), some of the women have also traveled abroad.

Many speak of the *tufrah* as having been an exciting period, but most say they are glad that it is over. One who did not get involved in all of the changes that were going on during the *tufrah* says that people sort of "went away" and that he has been waiting for them to "come back." By this he means that people used to be so busy wheeling and dealing that they had little time for socializing and talking and discussing issues which used to be so much a part of life, at least for males, in urban ʿUnayzah before the *tufrah*. Many now say that it is good that things are coming back to a more normal state, even though the value of property is said to have fallen by 50 to 60 percent in the past year or two and business in the market is slower than before. Instead of the wheeling and dealing, they once again enjoy trips to the *barr* and long evenings of socializing. Yet problems loom on the horizon.

Expatriates in ʿUnayzah

One of the most striking features of ʿUnayzah today is the presence of so many expatriates. When one of the anthropologists (Cole) visited ʿUnayzah in 1968, there was one Englishman and a small cadre of others from Yemen, Palestine, Jordan, Syria, and Iraq. Aside from the Yemenis, who were workers, most of the other Arabs were schoolteachers or in medicine. At that time, one would never have predicted that there would be thousands of expatriates in the city a decade or so later, and much less that there would be large numbers of non-Arabs. Cole's observation about the small number of expatriates is confirmed by Sharif, who reports the following:

> In 1384 [A.D. 1964], the passport office in ʿUnayzah issued 180 residence permits to the following: 51 Jordanians, 43 Yemenis, 35 Palestinians, 24 Syrians, 14 Pakistanis, four Egyptians, four Hadramis, three Sudanese, and two Somalis—and the office still had about 100 passports to process. This would bring the number up to about 280. If we suppose that some of these have children, then the number of foreigners [in ʿUnayzah] is between 300 and 350. These work in government offices like the Ministries of Education, of Health, or of Agriculture, or they are workers in construction or in contracting or in some crafts. (Sharif 1970: 196)

Prior to 1975, expatriates were almost all other Arabs and, with the exception of a few, were employed in education, health, and other government services. Many of these came with their families, and informants say that they were welcomed into the community. Gradually, as the local people acquired modern expertise, they have replaced expatriate professionals in all fields except health and higher education in ʿUnayzah. An example of local professionals replacing expatriates is provided by the Agricultural Research and Training Center, which was established in 1966, before the *tufrah*. According to Abu Nadir, one of the senior staff members at the center,

> when the center first started, it was a small operation run by Egyptian and Syrian employees, who usually stayed for only a couple of years and then left. The director was also an expatriate. They did very little to develop the center. They only planted a few crops and did not develop the irrigation network significantly. Proper research in agricul-

ture takes a long time and thus requires a committed staff that stays on for a long time. In the past, the turnover of the expatriate staff was too rapid to achieve good research results. Now, our staff is all Saudi Arabian and from ʿUnayzah. We have achieved much more than the expatriates did, although our budget is about the same as it was before we came. The only expatriates we employ now are a couple of secretaries and janitors.

No national census has been conducted since 1974, and we have not been able to obtain access to that census. Al-Wasil (1986) presents statistics that he was able to gather from various agencies on the number of people employed in various sectors in ʿUnayzah, mainly for 1984. We obtained similar statistics on people engaged in education. On the basis of these data and on our own observations and interviews in the field, we present in Table 2 "guestimates" of the numbers engaged in various activities in 1986. The reader should realize that these are rough estimates, but they are presented to give an idea of the general magnitude of the various sectors and their composition. These data do not include retirees or local people who work in other nearby cities and villages in the region to which they commute. These probably amount to at least 1,500 Saudi Arabians.

On the basis of these figures, we estimated the population of ʿUnayzah to be about 50,000 people, as mentioned in the introduction. If one includes those who commute to jobs in nearby cities and villages (about 1,000), the total active Saudi Arabian labor force resident in ʿUnayzah would be about 8,200. If one assumes an average nuclear family size of five and that only one person in that nuclear family is actively engaged in the labor force, one could conclude that the total Saudi Arabian population in ʿUnayzah is about 41,000. These assumptions are not entirely valid because it is not uncommon for more than one member of a nuclear family to be active in the labor force. However, we feel that retirees and other nonactive people would make up the difference. Almost all the expatriates do not have family members with them. Therefore, if they are added to the estimated 41,000 local citizens, the total population would be about 50,700.

During the *tufrah*, most expatriates entered the work force in ʿUnayzah as laborers or as nonprofessional employees in private sector establishments. Their entrance as laborers is clearly shown in the case of agriculture. According to al-Wasil (1986:80), no expatriates were employed full time in agriculture in 1974. A decade later, agri-

Table 2.
"Guestimate" of the Size and National Composition
of Main Occupational Sectors in ʿUnayzah in 1986

Sector	Saudi Arabian	Expatriate	Total
Agriculture	1,500	3,300	4,500
Market; commercial establishments	2,500	3,600	6,100
Government establishments	3,000	500	3,500
Construction/"industry"	200	1,000	1,200
Domestic servants		1,000	1,000
Street cleaners/janitors		300	300
Total	7,200	9,700	16,200

Source: Extrapolations from al-Wasil (1986); statistical data from Directorates of Education and Girl's Education; field observations and interviews.

culture employed 2,119 expatriates, of whom 1,699 were Egyptians, 155 were Indians, 121 were Pakistanis, 41 were Sudanis, 40 were Filipinos, 35 were Thais, 17 were North Yemenis, 7 were Bangladeshis, and 4 were Americans. Most of these expatriates replaced ʿUnayzah people on old farms and provided the work force on a greatly expanded number of new ones. Between 1974 and 1984, the local population engaged in agriculture declined from 3,187 to 2,088, although the number of farms increased from 348 to 1,112 during the same period (al-Wasil 1986:79–80). Moreover, most of the local population engaged in agriculture had become owner/managers.

Between 1976 and 1981, the number of commercial establishments increased from 555 to 1,308, with the number engaged in such establishments increasing from 745 to 5,273 (al-Wasil 1986:93). In ʿUnayzah, most commercial establishments are both owned and managed by local residents. However, the majority of workers in them are now expatriates. A similar situation exists in small-scale "industrial" enterprises, which increased from 100 in 1976 to 189 in 1984, according to al-Wasil (1986:97–98).

In addition, observation shows that many (probably about 1,000) Saudi Arabian households in ʿUnayzah employ a female domestic servant. These are all expatriates, and those in ʿUnayzah now come mainly from Indonesia, although formerly they came mainly from Egypt and Sri Lanka. A few come from the Philippines, but these are usually in richer households. There is a strong preference for Muslim maids, but, as can be seen, few of them are Arabs.

Thus expatriates predominate in agricultural labor, as the employees of private sector establishments (whether commercial, industrial, or in construction), in domestic service, and as janitors, garbage collectors, and street sweepers. In addition, they provide almost all the health care services available in ʿUnayzah and all the teachers in the branch of King Saʿud University that is located in the city.

While we cannot specify the exact number of expatriates or how that number has changed in recent years, it is nonetheless true that they are less visible today than they were five years or so ago. At that time, many expatriates were engaged in the construction of houses and buildings and infrastructure. All of these activities made them highly visible in the daily life of the city. Many state that there are fewer expatriate workers now than five years ago. However, according to an informed official in the labor office, this is most likely an illusion. Laborers, he argues, are less visible today because they are mainly engaged in work on farms and in establishments, thereby greatly reducing their visibility. Few laborers today shift from one job to another, as was the case during the construction boom. According to this official, 4,140 new workers had been registered with the labor office in the fifteen months preceding December 1986.

Aside from farm ownership and management and involvement in commerce, Saudi Arabians provide the personnel for the police and security forces and for almost all the staff positions in national and local government offices. In addition, almost all the administrative positions in schools are held by Saudi Arabians, as are teaching positions, particularly in lower levels of the system. Such positions are staffed not only by Saudi Arabians but by people from ʿUnayzah, which is a source of pride for the community. Informants report that about 1,000 local ʿUnayzah residents are also employed in teaching and state administrative positions in Buraydah and other towns and villages of the region. In addition, the Saudi Arabian component of the work force includes men and some women who are engaged in ʾaʿmal hurrah, literally, "free work," "self-employment." Also, a significant number of retirees live among the local population. Furthermore, it is not uncommon for local men to be engaged in more than one type of work at any given time.

Local employers report on difficulties in recruitment of expatriates and complain about their high rate of turnover, which especially poses problems for those who have to be locally trained. However, employers find it profitable to hire expatriates because they do not demand high wages. For example, most of the workers in agriculture come from Egypt and are paid between 400 and 600 riyals a month. Most of these were peasant farmers in Egypt and are knowledgeable about traditional agriculture there, but they have no experience in modern farming. They are mainly attractive to their local employers because they are cheap and speak Arabic. As numerous men in ʿUnayzah commented to the anthropologist, "The present agriculture would be impossible without the Egyptians. They are cheap, and because they speak Arabic, they can communicate with the farm owners here."

Also, a few similarly unskilled workers in agriculture have been imported from Pakistan, India, and Afghanistan. When a more skilled labor force is required, the workers are more likely to be from the Philippines, not because they come with the required skills and expertise but because the owners think that the Philippine laborer has had more involvement with modern work in general and is thus more easily trained to do the work required than would be the case with the peasants recruited from Egypt, Afghanistan, and the subcontinent. Nonetheless, the effort that has to be put into training is seen as a problem by some local employers. Abu Muhammad, the owner/manager of a hothouse farm, said,

> We have to recruit workers from as far away as the Philippines, bring them here, and then train them. When they have been trained and have become good and efficient workers, they leave and return to the Philippines, where the money they have saved from their earnings here is quite a lot, compared to what they could save there. They have benefited a lot from being here. They have accumulated savings and learned new skills. But we are left without a trained labor force, and most of their earnings leave the country.

No matter where they originate, their recruitment is seen as a problem by the owners. It usually involves a trip to the other country, which in itself is seen as quite pleasurable because one can combine recruiting with tourism. In the other countries, both formal recruiting agencies and informal networks provide prospective workers. However, finding the worker is only part of the problem. Before one goes recruiting, one must first satisfy the local labor office of the Ministry of Labor and Social Affairs that one has a need for a worker before obtaining a permit to bring the worker in. Once he is located, the worker has to obtain an entry visa, which takes time because of the great number of visas that have to be processed by the generally overworked consulates abroad.

Once the worker arrives, according to employers, the real test begins. He may turn out to be a poor worker in general, not qualified for the job for which he advertised himself, a troublemaker, or all three. He may become lonely and despondent and wish to leave before his contract is up. Therefore, the employer is very happy when he finds a worker who is suitable. He will normally want to keep him, but most workers stay for only a couple of years and then return to their home country. Although some Arabs have stayed for ten years or more in ʿUnayzah, a high turnover of labor exists not only in agriculture but in other sectors as well.

Expatriate servants have become relatively common in ʿUnayzah. Unlike that which has been reported for the Arabian Gulf states, where expatriate nannies play an important role in the socialization of children and are perceived as constituting a threat to the acquisition of the local culture (Saʿd ad-Din and Abdel-Fadil 1983:153; al-ʿIsa 1983:180), this has not been the case in ʿUnayzah. Here, the maids do household work and do not play an important role in child rearing. In nuclear family households, the maids may care for the children in the absence of the mother; but as soon as she returns, the children are cared for by the mother. Also, women living in nuclear family households usually take their children to a relative when they have to be away from home. In extended families, the care of the children is entrusted to other female members of the family in the absence of the mother.

Interaction between the expatriates and the local population is limited almost exclusively to the work place. While some of the other Arab professionals who have been for long periods in ʿUnayzah occasionally visit socially with people from the community, even this is not common. Occasionally Egyptian workers on the farms share a brief cup of coffee with the owner, but this is not regular. Furthermore, the expatriates mainly interact with people from their own home countries, although this too is rare for those who are on isolated farms.

Almost all the agricultural laborers reside on remote farms, while many of those who work in the city reside in the old mud-brick part of town which has been abandoned by most ʿUnayzah people for new housing in other areas. Professional expatriates are more likely to live in apartments in newer residential areas.

The agricultural laborers invariably live in simple buildings or in barracks-type housing on the farms. Since many of the farms are at some distance from the town, they are physically isolated from the rest of the community. They have one day a week off, Friday, and most of them come into town by any means of transportation they can find. Usually the farm provides the transportation, but it is not uncommon to see workers hitching a ride back late on Friday evening. All the laborers are males, and agricultural laborers are not allowed to bring their families. However, many come from the same villages in their home countries, and it is not uncommon for some to have relatives working in ʿUnayzah, particularly in the case of Egyptians.

From the point of view of the local people, expatriates do not form part of the local society. Although their work is considered integral to the present economy, little cultural exchange actually takes place. This is especially the case for those who do not speak Arabic and are not Muslims. Although socially (and often physically) isolated, the expatriate laborers occupy the position of a working class. However, the temporary nature of their residence prevents the formation of class relations and favors a heightened awareness of their status as expatriates.

Although labor laws exist to protect the rights of workers, some expatriates are subjected to violations of their contracts without de facto recourse to adjudication. From our observations in ʿUnayzah, relations between employer and employee are, of course, regulated by contracts but, in practice, more by community norms than by a specialized institution like the labor office. As in the case of debt relationships referred to earlier, these norms prevent treatment considered excessively harsh.

Nonetheless, a considerable gap separates most expatriates even from the poorest segment of the local population. Most receive very low wages, live in substandard housing of a type that even the poorest Bedouin have now abandoned, and have little sense of security. Isolated on the farms or in the old inner city, their social horizons are confined to their fellow workers from their own countries and class background. Both as groups and as individuals, they are alienated from the society which they serve. For many, their loneliness and social nonexistence are surely bearable only because they are able to save and thus maintain the hope of returning home with the means of starting a better life.

Local Development Through Private Voluntary Organizations

The roles played by the state and by expatriates in the contemporary period are enormous and have been widely recognized by scholars (e.g., Birks and Sinclair 1980; Fergani 1983; Ibrahim 1982; Sirageldin, Sherbiny, and Serageldin 1984). However, the role played by the local people has been largely ignored. Most studies on international migration into Saudi Arabia stress the small size of the local population and its alleged low participation rate in the modern economy. They also claim that the local population is predominantly illiterate and has almost no modern skills. Barsalou, for example, states that "the inadequacy of the Saudi national labor force, which is small and largely unskilled, has resulted in extensive economic dependence on the presence of migrant workers . . . [and] replacement of migrant labor with nationals is not foreseeable in the near future" (Barsalou 1985:5–6).

Although for a single community, our data show a major replacement of expatriates by local people in jobs requiring modern education in all but a few professions. Moreover, many qualified local youth now face unemployment unless they replace expatriates employed in the private sector. This phenomenon has been brought about by the rapid growth of the local population coupled with its acquisition of modern education and the economic slowdown brought about by the end of the *tufrah*. This analysis, which is elaborated later, suggests that scholars concerned with labor migration to Saudi Arabia did not see the transformation of the late 1970s and early 1980s for what it was—a boom that, by definition, had to end. Moreover, they seriously underestimated the potential of the local population to increase in size and to abandon traditional work in agriculture and herding for involvement in the modern economy. The local population's involvement in the modern work force is discussed in detail later. However, the local population has actively mobilized to bring about change at the level of the local community, both through individual contributions and activities and through private voluntary organizations.

Unlike the expatriates, 'Unayzah people have a high degree of identity with and commitment to the local community, a phenomenon which has distinguished them since long before the emergence of the present nation-state and the development of its oil export–based economy. These qualities are manifested in many different ways—through the overriding of tribal identities and loyalties in favor of a common identity with their *watan*, "homeland"; through the preservation of community-based folk songs and dances known as the *sammari*; through a widespread interest and pride in the history of the community; and through individuals and groups taking the initiative to address issues of common concern to the community.

Many migrants from ʿUnayzah have achieved high degrees of success in business at the national and international levels, while others occupy senior positions in the bureaucracy of the state. These have made significant financial contributions to local improvements and development through supporting various private voluntary organizations. They have also used their influence with others in the country to solicit their support as well. Some have also directly contributed by not only providing financial support but by introducing a needed service. To a large degree the Ibn Salih Center, described below, was the gift of a migrant who actively developed the idea for the project and then mounted a fund-raising campaign to finance it, organized the work of building the center, and helped plan its programs.

The local people resident in ʿUnayzah themselves do many things that show their commitment and involvement with the community at large. We could give many examples, but a few should suffice to indicate the kinds of acts that people do as individuals out of concern for the community at large. One man noticed that the prayer callers of mosques sometimes failed to call the prayer at the exact moment at which it was to be called. On his own initiative, he kept track of the time and informed those prayer callers who had made mistakes. Another man has taken it upon himself to lead a movement to preserve from destruction the old mud-brick minaret in front of the new main mosque. He has done this because he says that the minaret is part of the cultural heritage of the community and thus belongs to all; it therefore should not be torn down by a few who believe it is in the way of modernization. Also, when the first group of girls was going to graduate from nursing school, a woman who was not in the program felt the occasion should be marked in some special way. She sent a letter to all the gold merchants in the *suq* asking them to contribute prizes, which they all did.

Another example of local people contributing to the community occurred in 1985, when sixteen female teachers decided to volunteer to teach in a summer program for students who had to sit for their exams a second time. They expressed this desire and received the approval of the ministry. They received about 100 students. The second year they repeated it with 150 students. This time the ministry provided compensation for the teachers. This program has grown and now has two sections, one for academic subjects and the other a cultural program for teaching the Holy Qur'an, holding seminars, and having competitions with prizes. Thus what started as a purely voluntary effort to help students pass their exams is now in the process of growing into a more comprehensive summer program, especially as the teachers plan to coordinate with other institutions in the future.

Perhaps the most impressive way in which community spirit is manifested in 'Unayzah is through private voluntary organizations. In this small city there are six such organizations that collect funds from among both residents and emigrants to promote welfare and carry out a wide range of activities that are designed to provide services to the community at large and that attempt to meet needs that have not been met as a result of other development activities. They all involve the work and time of volunteers, at least part time, and several have volunteers who have devoted themselves full time to this service. Taken together, the private voluntary organizations show the commitment of people to the community and the efforts of many to not wait for needs to be met by the government but to actively provide solutions on their own initiative.

One of the most striking examples of a private voluntary organization in 'Unayzah is the Ibn Salih Center. The center is the result of the effort of a number of people who hold important positions in the country. Some of them live in 'Unayzah, but many of them live in other cities of the country. The center was named in honor of the teacher who opened the first private school in 'Unayzah in 1926. The idea to establish such a center came from among those who had studied in this school, which played an important role in their careers. When Ibn Salih died in 1980, several of his former pupils decided that they wanted to do something in honor of his memory, and they decided to establish a cultural center in his name. They started a fund-raising campaign among people from 'Unayzah and received large contributions not only from 'Unayzah residents but particularly from migrants from the city and from other wealthy Saudi Arabians. Since then they have been able to construct an impressive building on a hill overlooking much of ʿUnayzah where they have facilities for a mosque, a small museum, a library, study and conference rooms, a theater, a restaurant, a swimming pool, sports facilities, and small apartments for guests. The administrative board of the center consists of the mayor of a large city, a director and a former director of education, a retired university professor, the imam of a mosque, and several others. All of these are from ʿUnayzah and are responsible for the overall development of the center.

At the time of fieldwork, the center had not embarked upon its activities, but it has ambitious and impressive plans for programs that are designed to contribute to the cultural life and the development of ʿUnayzah. The general philosophy behind its planned programs is to provide services that are different from those already in existence in the community and at the same time to complement other programs that are already in existence. For example, there are libraries in ʿUnayzah, but the Ibn Salih Center plans to develop a research library that will be fully computerized and have microfilm and microfiche files centering on the Qasim. The sports programs of the center are designed to complement those of the two sports clubs of the city by offering training in sports that are not available at the clubs and for age categories of people that do not have access to the clubs. Anticipating the future needs of their city to be in developing skilled technical occupations, the center is particularly eager to develop training programs for skilled technical workers to take jobs in technical occupations that are now filled mainly by expatriate labor. The center's programs are intended for both males and females, although in segregated settings.

Another example of a private voluntary organization that has recently been founded as a result of contributions and cooperation between both residents and emigrants is the Committee for the Beautification and Cleanliness of the City of ʿUnayzah. At the time of fieldwork, this committee had been established for about a year. The funds for its work come from a voluntary contribution of 1 percent of the salaries of local employees in ʿUnayzah, as well as contributions from private individuals which have varied from 2,000 to 1.5 million riyals. The committee has built walls around all the farms in the city, planted trees along major streets, built fountains and monuments in squares, provided benches and awnings in the market area, and improved streets in the al-Jannah area in cooperation with the municipality and another private voluntary organization. It also has programs for restoring old houses and painting houses. It has plans for reconstructing the gates of the old walls of the city and also plans parks and recreational areas in the western part of the city and in the *barr*. It will also remove the old buildings that are collapsing and reconstruct some of them to preserve the old character of the city, preserving some of its narrow streets and some of the mud-brick houses. It also plans to improve the fronts of buildings in the main commercial streets.

The committee has twelve male members who include the amir of the Qasim as well as various prominent state officials in 'Unayzah. In addition, there is a subcommittee of thirteen female members who are all active and leading figures among educated women in 'Unayzah today. Many of them are headmistresses in schools, and some are wives of engineers and other influential men. They were chosen specifically because they could be of use to the committee. The subcommittee of women uses the schools as a forum to disseminate information about the committee throughout the community and to collect donations from the students and staff. It has conducted feasibility studies and made suggestions for projects that in fact were endorsed and carried out by the committee. Also, the committee has sometimes objected to the plans the subcommittee has forwarded to it and did not carry them out. The subcommittee divided its work among a group in charge of publicity and another in charge of fund raising. The group in charge of fund raising sent letters soliciting funds to the wives of men of 'Unayzah in major cities. However, the women were unable to tell us what the response was since the funds were forwarded to a bank account controlled by men. Now, however, they have established an independent bank account and the subcommittee is getting better organized. The subcommittee was especially active in a special week for cleanliness by intensifying a campaign throughout all the schools in 'Unayzah. It plans to intensify its activities. It has submitted a plan for an artificial lake that is currently under study. Usually male relatives of members of the subcommittee volunteer their expert knowledge, their offices, and other facilities for the projects.

The Ibn Salih Center and the Committee for the Beautification and Cleanliness of the City of 'Unayzah are both private voluntary organizations that developed during the *tufrah*. As shown in chapter 6, the Lajnah al-Ahliyah, the People's Committee, was formed in 1962 before the *tufrah*. This is a committee of male and female volunteers who supervise the work of the Center for Social Services, one of twenty-two centers in the country. These centers involve both state and popular participation to provide programs that address needs in the communities where they are located. Aside from providing its own administrative employees, the government will provide up to a maximum of 50 percent of the cost of a project or program, although it is said that, in fact, the government contribution is often less than half the cost. The remainder of the costs are provided by contributions from members of the community or through fees paid by the beneficiaries of programs. In 'Unayzah, people have donated land for the construction of facilities for kindergartens and other activities. They have also provided buses for use in transportation, and female teachers have volunteered to teach in summer programs. Others have also made significant financial contributions to the work of the center.

The present program of the center is organized into three main fields or specializations. These are social services, health and preventive care, and cultural programs. One of the main activities of the social services field is the running of a preschool program in which there are five kindergartens. At the time of fieldwork, 585 boys and girls were enrolled, and there were 26 Saudi Arabian female teachers and 22 other workers. All these were paid, with the budget for the kindergartens being partially financed by fees and by individual contributions. The contribution to the budget from the state in the 1986–87 school year was said to be 100,000 riyals, while in 1985–86 it had been 250,000 riyals.

There is also a literacy program called Dur al-Fatat, which is designed for females and which is held according to a flexible schedule to meet their needs. Seventy-nine women were enrolled in this program at the time of fieldwork. After two years, participants will have completed the equivalent of the fourth grade of primary school. After three years, they complete the equivalent of fifth grade, and after four years, the equivalent of sixth grade, at which time they take the exam for the primary school certificate. The third and fourth years of this program are run by the Directorate of Girls' Education, while the first two are run by the center.

Other courses that are offered by the Dur al-Fatat program include sewing, Holy Qur'an studies, typing, and English. Also, plans existed to start a program in computer science in March 1987, as many of the women have been asking for such a program. The typing program for women at the time of fieldwork had thirty-four students.

Thirty-one others had completed the program and had passed an exam. The anthropologist met numerous women working in offices who had taken that course in typing. Most of the work in the programs of the Dur al-Fatat is done by expatriate women, as it is said that Saudi Arabian women are not attracted because the pay is poor and because the work involves visiting other people's homes in follow-up work.

In addition, the social services section of the center's progam runs a summer program for girls. This is usually held in the last month of summer and is for girls between six and fifteen years of age. This was started in the summer of 1985 with 100 girls; in 1986, 70 girls participated. They take classes in handwork, art and design, and home economics.

Programs also exist for men, but these are given less importance because, it is said, men have more opportunities and are in less need of special programs. In 1986, there were 41 men studying typing and 137 who were enrolled in Holy Qur'an studies. The center also runs summer camps for boys, and each summer about twenty participate. The center hopes to develop the summer program for boys but recognizes that the sports clubs provide for much of this type of activity.

Within the health and preventive care field, the center maintains a clinic and also has a program that has introduced first-aid kits and fire extinguishers into homes. It has carried out a series of improvements in the sheep market to make the area more hygienic. Furthermore, the center is in the process of collecting files on the health histories of members of every family in ʿUnayzah. It also conducts cleanliness campaigns and hygiene awareness in kindergartens and schools.

The cultural section of the center maintains three libraries, one for women, one for children, and one for men. It has sponsored several competitions between male students in literacy schools and between male and female students of intermediary and secondary schools. So far, seventy-four awards have been given, of which forty-five went to girls—sixteen in secondary school and twenty-nine in intermediate school. It also holds cultural events and programs in the evenings at the schools which house the kindergartens. These are divided between programs for males and others for females.

One of the most popular of the private voluntary organizations in ʿUnayzah is the Jamʿiyah al-Khayriyah al-Birriyah, the Philanthropic Society. This was established in 1975 upon the recommendation of the Center for Social Services. The Jamʿiyah is run entirely by volunteers, with the exception of a paid treasurer. The director is a former schoolteacher who retired after twenty years of teaching and now lives on his retirement pension and devotes himself full time to this activity. (It is said by people in ʿUnayzah that he took his retirement early so as to be free to devote himself to this service.) In the afternoons, the offices of the Jamʿiyah are open to the public, who come to present their requests for aid. The director is joined by several others who work with him, and there is a committee that studies the petitions and takes actions on them. Also, volunteers work as researchers who go to the homes of recipients of aid to be sure that they make use of the aid and that the aid actually reaches the person for whom it was intended.

The original goals of the Jamʿiyah are set forth in a document that also indicates that it is registered with the Ministry of Labor and Social Affairs. The goals include helping the needy and handicapped, contributing to the development of the cultural life of the community, and maintaining and strengthening the society. The money the organization receives comes from three main sources: *zakat,* private contributions, and aid from the state. The state provides 50,000 riyals to start up such an organization and then provides 500,000 riyals per year.

Most of the donations that the organization receives come from *zakat* (70 to 80 percent of the total) and can only be used to directly meet the needs of the poor. It cannot be used for investments or for general-use projects, which depend on contributions from private citizens. Normally the Jamʿiyah expects to receive about 6 million riyals, but these amounts are reported to be going down as a result of the general economic recession and because other private voluntary organizations in ʿUnayzah are competing with it for donations. In 1985, however, the Jamʿiyah received 6,522,390 riyals from the *zakat,* 670,600 from membership fees, 446,250 from the state, 16,110 as contributions in kind, and 290,500 as profit from investment in shares in a company.

Between 200 and 250 needy families regularly receive contributions from the Jamʿiyah to meet their needs. They may be given money to purchase their daily food, to pay the rent of their houses, or to purchase a heater in winter or an air conditioner in summer. In 1985, 191 families received a total of 460,842 riyals in the form of financial assistance to meet their daily needs; 106 families received 733,339 riyals to pay their rent; and a sum of 456,928 riyals was spent to provide refrigerators, washing machines, ovens, electric heaters, air conditioners, beds, and clothing. The people who receive such income are those who are not able to work or who may be able to work but do not make enough to meet their needs. Furthermore, the Jam'iyah does not give the recipients cash money but rather vouchers to take to a merchant who provides them with the item and then collects from the Jam'iyah.

Assistance is also given to men to pay the dower to get married. This may be given to a man for his first marriage or to a widower or to a man whose wife is seriously ill and unable to meet the duties of a wife (in which case he must not abandon her). In 1985, twenty-seven men were given such assistance for a total of 614,000 riyals. The Jam'iyah may also assist a woman to repay her dower in the case of divorce, and in 1985, three women were given 100,600 riyals for this. Assistance for medical treatment for those who cannot be treated in the existing facilities of the government health program is also given. In 1985, four families received such assistance for a total of 107,000 riyals. The Jam'iyah also provides assistance to meet payments for the *diyah,* "bloodwealth," which may result from deaths in automobile accidents. In 1985, 15,300 riyals were given to two families who were involved in such accidents. Assistance is also given for upgrading and repairing a home, for which 155,610 riyals were given in 1985 for sixteen homes. In addition, the Jam'iyah is eager to assist people to start up work in a technical occupation, but few have sought such assistance. In 1985, only two individuals requested it; they were given a total of 5,000 riyals.

In the past, the main focus of the Jam'iyah was on meeting the needs of the poor. However, it is now beginning to focus more on projects that will serve the whole community. One such project is for housing. The Jam'iyah has constructed a number of apartments which it hopes to provide to needy families. It is in the process of establishing a nursing and physical therapy center which will be for both men and women. It is also studying the feasibility of establishing an advanced clinic for eye diseases. Such projects are designed to meet the needs of the community at large and not only those of the poor.

The activities of the private voluntary organizations reflect the economic transformation that has occurred. The generous contributions of people from 'Unayzah were themselves in part the result of income earned during the *tufrah;* now that it is over, the private voluntary organizations report that contributions are falling. Furthermore, the work of the private voluntary organizations has changed its focus. As shown in chapter 6, the first such organization, the Sunduq al-Birr, collected small amounts from individuals in the 1950s and provided basic needs to the poor through neighborhood mosques. Both the Center for Social Services and the Jamᶜiyah were first mainly concerned with meeting basic needs in community hygiene and providing funds for the needy. Now that few are truly needy, they have shifted their focus to providing community services such as kindergartens, summer programs for girls and boys, and a nursing and physical therapy center. These are important projects which contribute to the overall quality of life, and it is perhaps a mark of the progress that has been achieved that meeting more basic needs is no longer required. There is now a private voluntary organization that is concerned with beautifying the city. Yet it is significant that the Ibn Salih Center, named for the man who first opened a modern school in ᶜUnayzah, the first in Najd, has as a priority on its agenda the development of training programs to address what it and we feel is the most basic issue facing ᶜUnayzah: the need to once again fully depend on a skilled and productive labor force that is composed of the sons and daughters of ᶜUnayzah.

CHAPTER 8

The Market Today

The old *suq* reflected the central role that ʿUnayzah played in exchange and distribution in both the local region and the wider area. Today, the *suq* reflects the city's provincial status and the peripheral role it has come to play in the new national economy. Much of the new agricultural production bypasses the local *suq*. Local merchants seldom import directly from abroad for further distribution to other cities or villages as they did in the past. Likewise, they no longer arrange the export of local or regional products, except occasionally dates. Except for agricultural products, almost all the merchandise for sale in the *suq* is manufactured abroad and is mainly imported via large commercial establishments in Riyadh, Jiddah, and the Eastern Province cities. According to Abu Talib, the old merchant who worked as an ʿuqayli and who was introduced in chapter 4, "now the [male] merchants buy their merchandise by telephone or telex. They call up wholesalers whom they know in Riyadh or Jiddah, and sometimes in foreign cities, and order what they want. The merchandise is sent immediately. The wholesalers send them an invoice, and the merchants pay them with a check through the bank."

The old *suq* of ʿUnayzah was not all torn down at once, and large parts of it continued to exist until several years ago. By 1985, however, the municipality had completed the construction of a new, publicly owned *suq* to serve the community. This *suq* includes 234 shops in concrete buildings and 92 places under a tin roof for the sale of vegetables and fruit. They are all run by men. The municipality has also built an area where about 130 women sell, also under a tin roof.

In addition, at least 250 shops are located in buildings that have been constructed by private individuals and rented out to men. The old main mosque of the city was also torn down and replaced with a new one. This mosque, however, is still the major landmark in the central market area of the city.

In front of the mosque is a large open area still known as the Majlis, although the amir no longer sits in court there and none of the old merchandise that used to be sold to the Bedouin and to caravanners is available. Off to one side of this open area are shops where men sell rice and other grains, coffee, tea, cardamom, and sugar in bulk. On one side of the open area men sell vegetables and fruit, which are placed either on the pavement or on handcarts. It is also here that local vegetables and fruit are sold by auction early in the morning. Nearby is the large covered area where vegetable and fruit merchants have stalls. Further on is another covered area where men sell household utensils, toys, clothing, and other products. In this central area of the *suq,* an outdoor market is held on Thursdays and Fridays.

Around the sides of the central market area and in a pedestrian mall that radiates out from the central area to the northeast are many shops that specialize in different products. These sell gold, cloth, clothing for men and women, carpets, household utensils, mattresses, and pillows. These shops are owned and operated by men, but a large proportion of the buyers here are local women, a phenomenon which the men say is recent. According to them, local women have more free time now, thanks to labor-saving devices in household work and the presence of expatriate maids in many households; and due to their salaried employment they also have more money, which they spend on themselves and their children.

To the east of the central area of the *suq* is a street that has numerous relatively large shops. In these, a wide variety of imported consumer durables are sold, including clocks, watches, stereo cassette recorders and radios, video equipment, televisions, kitchen stoves, refrigerators, washing machines, cameras, film, prerecorded cassette tapes, luggage, men's Western-style clothing, women's clothing, personal computers, electrical musical instruments, perfume, stationery and books, and pharmaceuticals. The clientele is to a large degree expatriate, although local people also buy here. The owners of these large shops are local people, but almost all the salesmen are expatriates.

In addition, ʿUnayzah has well-stocked hardware stores, agricultural equipment stores, furniture stores, and places that sell building materials of all sorts. Throughout the town are small grocery stores, bakeries, butcher shops, and a number of small supermarkets. There is also a sheep and goat market (but no camel market) and a used car market where cars are sold by auction. One can buy almost all makes of new Japanese cars and some American models, although Mercedes-Benz and other luxurious cars have to be bought in Riyadh or another larger city.

The only crafts that remain in the *suq* are tailoring, along with those practiced by two old goldsmiths and by a couple of men who still make sandals. Several small modern "factories" make gold jewelry. One of these is located in a house in a residential area and employs about twenty-five workers from Tunisia, Indonesia, Pakistan, and India. Other small manufacturing enterprises make aluminum window frames, metal doors, and wooden products for houses. Like those in the gold jewelry factory, the workers are all expatriates, while the owners are from ʿUnayzah. There is also an "industrial zone" where car and other repairs are made. In 1984, there were 189 industrial establishments in ʿUnayzah. Although the area has recently achieved significant increases in agricultural output, none of the industries are involved in the processing of agricultural products (al-Wasil 1986:97–98).

All the commercial shops described above are owned by men from ʿUnayzah. Most of those who sell in the central area of the *suq* are also from the city, as are those in the gold shops. Some of the cloth shops and most of the other shops employ expatriate men as salesmen. Aside from these, there is also an area of the *suq* where local women sell products to both men and other women. We have chosen to describe and analyze this market in detail below because this segment of the market illustrates some changes that have taken place in the *suq* as a whole. Although this segment remains relatively traditional, it represents one of the links of the past to the present. Of equal importance, the focus on this segment documents the existence of women sellers in a public *suq* in a gender-segregated society.

The Women's Market

In ʿUnayzah, *suq al-harim*, "the women's market," refers to a part of the market where women are sellers. The presence of women selling in the *suq* has been mentioned by various early travelers and the places where they sold in the old *suq* in ʿUnayzah were described in chapter 3. When the old *suq* began to be demolished, women were moved from their old selling areas several times over a period of seven to eight years. At the beginning, they were moved to an open area where it was impossible for them to leave their merchandise overnight. They had to carry it back and forth from their homes to the market, which was inconvenient, to say the least. They were then moved to another open area, but here they were able to store their merchandise overnight in *sanadiq,* "trunks," which in fact were large wooden or tin containers about two meters high. The trunks also protected it from rain and, at the same time, served as a kind of shop.

According to a number of the women sellers, buying and selling were good in this area, but the men who sold nearby became jealous of the success the women were having and of the competition they provided. Therefore, the women were forced to move again—to selling on sidewalks in the same general area. The municipality eventually provided them in 1982 with a covered area which is located to one side of the main *suq* and which is considered to be temporary. This area is covered by a tin roof and is surrounded by a wall about one and a half meters high. The two main gates are closed and locked at night. Inside, each seller has a space of about one and a half by two meters on the concrete floor. These spaces were allocated to them by the municipality, but there are no physical dividers between them. The sellers stack their merchandise in these areas, and some have stands for displaying some items. At night, their goods are covered by canvas. Some of the sellers expand into the spaces allocated to neighbors, and while this is often ignored by the neighbor, conflicts over space sometimes erupt. An extension was added to this area a year later, but women consider that it is less desirable than the original area. As a result, the extension is less crowded. There is also a small mosque for the women to pray in and a public toilet.

Between 130 and 150 women sell here. They sell spices such as cumin, pepper, ginger, cinnamon, coriander, fenugreek, mixed spices, and dried limes; cooking utensils; large containers used in the preparation of dates; flatware; perfume; dye; detergents; biscuits; chocolates; nuts; homemade cookies and cakes; leeks; pumpkins; clothing for men, women, and children; and shoes and sandals. Much of this merchandise is imported from Taiwan and China, although the large containers for cooking and for preparing dates are made in

Kuwait or Buraydah. Some of the spices are locally grown and processed by women in ʿUnayzah. Some of the biscuits and chocolates are produced in Saudi Arabian factories, while the traditional homemade cookies and cakes are made by women in ʿUnayzah who market them through these sellers.

The market opens around seven in the morning. The women are driven there by their sons or husbands. They uncover their merchandise and some go off to bring items from nearby storerooms that they have rented in some of the old houses. They drink coffee and eat dates. Those who sell spices clean and prepare them for sale in small plastic bags. Business is slow in the morning, although it picks up around noon. It then slows down until after the midafternoon prayer, at which time it picks up until sunset, when the market closes. Unlike other shops in the *suq,* this market does not close at the time of the prayers, although the women pray either in their space in the market or in the small mosque. The general pace of the market picks up markedly on Thursdays and Fridays and during Ramadan and the spring and summer school holidays.

The women who sell here are all veiled. Those from the settled community cover their faces with a black gauzelike material, while the Bedouin women wear a face mask under a thin veil. When there are no men in sight, some uncover their faces; but as soon as one appears, they immediately veil. Many of them wear old faded dresses, although the Bedouin women are more colorfully dressed.

Socioeconomic Backgrounds of Women Sellers

Some of the women who sell here used to sell in the old *suq* before it was demolished, while others have more recently taken up this activity. The newer sellers are mainly Bedouin women who have settled in ʿUnayzah. Some of the older sellers say that many of these used to buy from them, but now they have become sellers themselves. Furthermore, many of the Bedouin women have male relatives who work in the more traditional parts of the men's *suq.* However, few of the women from the sedentary community have male relatives who are merchants. All the sellers are illiterate and at least forty years of age. They are all married, divorced, or widowed, as it is considered unacceptable for a young unmarried woman to sit and sell in the market. Many of them are relatively poor, although some are quite wealthy. Almost all live in new housing that has been financed with loans from the Real Estate Development Fund. Women sellers also come from all three descent statuses in ʿUnayzah—*qabili, khadiri,* and *ʿabd.*

Aside from the Bedouin, many of the *hadari,* "sedentary," women who sell in the *suq* today were agricultural workers in the past. Typically, their move into the *suq* was a gradual one. Women who worked in agriculture in the past often made items which they would sell in the Friday market. When her children began to grow up and she no longer had to take care of them, a woman sometimes began to move more permanently into the *suq,* particularly if the family needed extra income or if she became too old to work in agriculture on a regular basis. Illustrations of this process of gradual entry into the market on a full-time basis are shown in the following cases.

Umm Yusif is a grandmother over fifty. Her husband is alive, but he is ill and only occasionally able to work.

When I was first married, I helped my husband in his work in irrigation on a farm. Later on, he traveled to look for a job, and I was left with my son and almost no money. I started making straw mats, which I gave to a friend to sell in the market. It took me about two weeks to make one, which would sell, in those days, for about 12 riyals.

When my husband returned, he worked for hire on a farm. I continued to make straw products and I started to take them myself to the market on Fridays. Four years later, we rented land and took up farming [as sharecroppers]. After eleven years, my husband became weaker and we had to leave farming. However, during this time I continued to go to the market on Fridays. Women sometimes gave me gold to sell for them. I did not always know them, but they saw me in the market, heard about me, and trusted me. If I did not sell the gold on the same day, I took it home. Sometimes, women came to my home to buy these things. In the past, they took the gold and came back a week later to pay. I would then take the money to the woman who had given it to me to sell, and she would pay me my *saʿy* ["commission"]. In those days, we did not know the value of gold and we trusted people too much. I later made them pay for gold immediately.

I went into the market fulltime when we left farming altogether. I already knew a great deal about the market. I rented a shop and started to buy and sell. I observed that women got merchandise from a dealer on credit and I did likewise. This was about twenty years ago.

Umm Yusif is now one of the more successful sellers in the new market. She has a storage room and sells in an excellent location. Clients often seek her out. She predominantly sells spices and kitchenware and is regularly in the market.

Umm Salman provides an example of a woman who used to work as an agricultural laborer for hire on a daily basis. She is about forty-five years of age and is regularly in the market, where she sells a wide variety of items.

> I worked for ten years as a laborer on a big farm. They paid me on a daily basis, although I worked every day for them. I was paid 10 riyals a day. My husband had a shop where he sold sugar and tea, and he also worked as a driver. I spent part of my income on family expenses, but I was able to save some money. While I worked on the farm, I also made straw mats, which I took to sell in the Friday market.
>
> With some of what I had saved, I bought some merchandise, which I carried to the market in a bundle on my head every day for three years. Then I rented a shop which I shared with my sister-in-law. The shop was in a street behind our house. After three years, my sister-in-law got out of the business, and I continued to sell on my own for a year. Then they demolished the building where my shop was. I went to the main *suq* area. They moved us around several times before we came here.

Not all the sellers were originally engaged in agriculture. An example is Umm Hazim, who is about sixty-five years of age. She has been selling in the *suq* for "more than twenty years." Her father was a moneylender, and all five of her sons sell out of two shops in the men's market. She first started selling her merchandise on the sidewalk but eventually rented a shop in the old *suq*. She sold mainly cloth, locally made clothes, and cooking utensils. Now she sells face and hand creams, shampoo, detergents, and imported clothing.

Another case of a woman who was neither a Bedouin nor previously engaged in farming is that of Umm 'Abd Allah. She is about sixty years of age and has one of the best selections of merchandise in the women's market. She is one of the most established sellers and buys much of her merchandise in Riyadh.

> I was married three different times. I lived in Makkah and in al-Ahsa'. My third husband and I came back to live in 'Unayzah about twenty-

five years ago. I took some cloth from the wife of a merchant and sold it on commission. I took it around to people in their homes. Then I began to buy the cloth from her and took the risk of selling it myself. Later on, I used a room in my house as a shop. This room opened onto the street, and I bought merchandise from men who came around in cars. I also went to Buraydah to buy merchandise. On days when the *suq* was busy, like on Thursdays and Fridays, I would display my merchandise on the pavement in the main *suq* area. Then I had one of the *sanadiq* that people had after the old *suq* was demolished. After that, I moved here.

The majority of women in the market sell there on a full-time basis; that is, they are there throughout the day. A minority of about 20 percent only come in the afternoons. Most of these have other jobs that occupy them in the mornings, mainly in the schools, where they are employed as *farrashat,* serving coffee and tea and running errands. Some women also have to tend to their household duties in the mornings.

Acquisition of Merchandise and Credit

Women sellers obtain their merchandise predominantly from wholesale dealers who bring merchandise to them in the *suq*. These are men who usually arrive on Fridays after the noon prayer. They come in big trucks, which they park outside the area of the women's market. They unload samples of the merchandise they have to sell and wait for the women to come and buy. These men are of various backgrounds. Some are from the Qasim, while others are Bedouin who have settled, Yemenis working for Saudi Arabian establishments, or Pakistanis who likewise work for other Saudi Arabians. The Bedouin tend to specialize in clothing that they bring mainly from Kuwait. The Yemenis and Pakistanis bring goods from Jiddah, while those from the Qasim tend to bring items that they obtain within the region.

Some of these men have been dealing with the women in the *suq* for decades and know some of them quite well. As a result, they sometimes give them merchandise on credit. An example is a dealer who comes from another town in the Qasim. He used to be one of the few dealers who brought goods to the women. In the past, he specialized in selling them spices and kitchenware. He has now diversified and brings them items like blankets and clothing. As one of the sellers said,

He is a very good man. He gave me goods on credit. When I bought from him, I asked the price of what I had bought. But he kept the records of my debts. He is a very patient man, and it is usually I who must ask him to tell me how much I owe him. By the end of three years, I was in debt to him for about 50,000 riyals. Some women tend to misuse him. One woman has owed him 5,000 riyals for the past seven years and has still not paid him. He now does not come very often because the women have made him very angry.

In the words of another, "He is so good. If I ask for two dozen of something, he will usually say, 'I know you well. Take four dozen.'"

Although the sellers tend to maintain relationships with dealers over time, it is possible for either party to cultivate new ties with others and to enter into new credit relationships. Dealers who are eager to dispose of their merchandise quickly are likely to give credit to women. Observation has shown that dealers who are willing to negotiate credit sell more of their merchandise than do dealers who are more strict.

Credit is pervasive throughout the women's market, and most women have taken goods on credit from several different suppliers. However, before credit is established, one must gain the trust of the supplier. The women say that the dealer gives them credit because he knows them, yet it is difficult for him to know them since they are veiled and he is often from another town. If he sells to them in the market where they sell, he at least knows their place. But if they go to him in another city, which sometimes occurs, they are just a voice behind a veil. It turns out that the dealer gets to "know" them through their buying from him several times and paying cash for their purchases. In the words of one woman, "I go to a man in Buraydah who sells me things on credit for up to 1,000 riyals. He knows only that I have paid him in the past. I have shown him my honesty. You pay him until he knows you. This is done through buying items from him with cash. This is done several times before one takes merchandise on credit."

Since the women are all illiterate, they do not themselves keep written records. Most of the men, however, are literate and they are entrusted with record keeping. The Yemenis and Pakistanis, who work for companies, give the women bills for the items they have taken. The women show these to others who know how to read to tell them what has been written. The other dealers usually write the amount of the goods taken on a scrap of paper and give it to them. However, some dealers record all the transactions in a *tuftar*, "booklet," that they keep. Whenever a payment is made, they are supposed to subtract it from the total owed. In the absence of record keeping, memory, trust, and public announcements are the only ways that women have to protect themselves. Therefore, whenever a woman pays back a dealer she does not know well, she usually shouts in a loud voice, "Where is your *tuftar?* Scratch out what I owe you. My neighbor here is a witness that I have paid you."

It sometimes happens that there are differences of opinion about what has been paid, as the following case indicates. Umm Salih took clothing from Abu 'Uthman. He used to go to Kuwait and bring back "nice things." She continued to take from him over a period of time, and he kept noting the transactions in his *tuftar*. They both occasionally discussed these. Once, when they were settling the account, it turned out that he said that she owed him 25,000 riyals. When she heard him tell her this, she was stunned. She denied having taken so much and challenged his records. He brought in another man to read the record aloud. In the end, she had to give in and make arrangements to pay over a long period of time. Commenting on this case, other women in the market said, "She is crazy. She takes and does not pay back. It would have been better if she had taken little by little and paid back gradually."

Since these transactions between the two parties are informal, neither party can easily substantiate a legal claim against the other. This is well recognized by both parties and structures the relationship that exists between them. Either party that violates the unwritten rules that govern the relationship will be sanctioned. The dealer wants to market his merchandise, and the woman seller wants to obtain merchandise. The only way that this can be accomplished, in the absence of ready cash, is through credit.

However, the dealer occasionally, at least, has to obtain cash for the merchandise he provides on credit. When he arrives to collect from women in the market, the news spreads rapidly. The women prepare their strategies of how best to deal with the situation. They know that they have to pay him something, but how much they are willing to pay depends on a number of different factors. One is how much cash they have on hand. Another is how many other creditors are likely to come and press for payment. Other factors include whether they need to replenish their merchandise and from which dealer, the history of the debt with the dealer and whether he has asked to be paid previously, and their own personal need for cash. Depending on these various factors, the formula of how they deal with him changes.

A woman owes, for example, 3,900 riyals to four men, and she has 1,500 riyals on hand from sales that she has made. All four descend on her on the same day, which, though unusual, sometimes happens. To one she owes 1,500. She pays him 400, since she has owed this for a long period of time. To another she owes 1,000 and pays him 300, which is proportionately more because she is currying his favor to obtain more merchandise on credit from him immediately. She owes another 500 and pays him 200. To the fourth she owes 900 and pays him 300. This leaves her with 300 in cash. She has no particular reason for paying the last two men the amounts she pays them except that she has to pay them something. This situation becomes even more complex when she has more creditors, and one woman had twelve at the time of fieldwork.

The women say that they do not like to let their debts to creditors become too large. The ideal is to take goods on credit and pay back the creditor in full. But this seldom happens. One of the women who expressed the ideal of having no debts to creditors owed more than 15,000 riyals to twelve creditors. Another owed 8,000 to one creditor. Furthermore, they usually pay back their creditors part of what they owe them and then take more goods on credit at the same time. In one case, a woman owed 10,000 riyals to one dealer. She had 4,000 riyals on hand. She gave him 2,000 to be deducted from what she owed him and then bought and fully paid 2,000 for more merchandise. In another case, a woman owed 6,000 riyals to three different dealers. She paid them a total of 2,000 and at the same time took more merchandise on credit. The difference between the two strategies followed is that, in the first case, the woman was eager to reduce her overall debt, while in the latter case, the woman was responding to the need to pay back something in order to obtain future credit.

One might ask why the creditor continues to give credit. The fact is that he knows that the only way he can continue to sell is through extending credit. He does this, however, only to those whom he trusts—and trust is proven by payment. Furthermore, when he finds a client who is a good risk and has proven that she both can and does pay back, he encourages her to take even more goods on credit. When the creditor comes to the market, he has his intentions, but these have to be accommodated to the ever-changing situations in which the women find themselves. He has to be able to judge the situation and determine his strategy—whether to be firm and insist on payment or whether to postpone his demands for a number of days.

Credit is extended by the women sellers to some of the people who buy from them in the *suq,* and similar principles guide the relationship. Those who normally buy in this market are both local and expatriate and include men and women. The sellers say that, in the past, many of those who bought were from the Bedouin. The expatriates who come to the market are usually men who work on farms, and they come on Fridays when they have their day off, mainly to look but sometimes to buy. No credit is ever extended to them. They pay in cash, and the women say that these men are good buyers because they do not try to negotiate the price. Saudi Arabian men seldom enter this market, but Saudi Arabian women are important buyers. It is to these that credit is sometimes extended. All the women sellers say that they do not like to sell on credit, but they all do. One of the women said that her greatest preoccupation was in keeping track of the items she had sold on credit.

One case that was observed involved a woman from 'Unayzah who came to the market and went directly to one of the sellers. She greeted her and had a little chat with her about family members. She chose several things to buy. She paid for these and gave her 80 more riyals for a debt that she owed. She then went to another seller who had items that the first seller did not have. She chose items from the second seller and then came back to the first one and borrowed 50 riyals from her to pay for these items. She decided to take some other things, and as she walked out of the market the first seller told her that she now owed her 140 riyals.

In the above case, the two women knew each other. However, women report that they also sell on credit to women they do not know. One said that some Bedouin from another town came to buy. They were shopping for a wedding. As Umm Hamad said,

I had never seen them before. I had a lot of nice things and they bought clothes, kitchen utensils, face masks, and lots of other things. The total came to 2,500 riyals, but they could only pay me 1,000. They said that they would return with the rest. They also told me that they needed women to entertain the guests in the wedding party. Since I do this occasionally, I told them I would be willing to come. We parted on a friendly basis. Weeks passed and no one came. I did not have an address for them. One day, one of their daughters came looking for me in the market. She told me that the wedding had been postponed and she wanted to buy more things from me. Hesitantly, I let her buy for 600 riyals. Two weeks later, she came back with her brother and his wife. They were looking for women to entertain in their wedding. A common friend brought them over to me. I reminded them of their debt. The sister admitted that they owed me and promised that, if I would come to the wedding, they would pay me all that they owed and also give me my fee. We agreed, and I went to their village. They paid me everything they owed me, plus 4,000 riyals for my fee for entertaining them.

Not all of the women will take such large risks. When women are not known to them, they are reluctant to sell on credit. Usually the women sellers do not give credit until the buyers have bought from them several times and paid in cash. The women say that most of those who take goods on credit pay them back. In fact, some come and pay back debts that the women sellers have forgotten about. But occasionally people do not pay, as was reported for two different cases. According to one seller,

> a woman had been coming to the *suq* and bought from me a number of times and always paid me. Then, once she came and bought stuff worth 2,000 riyals. She did not have any money to pay with. I knew her by voice only. I remembered that she had paid previously. So I said, "No problem. Come back when you can pay." She told me that she would be back after four months. It has been over a year and I have not seen her.
>
> In another case, a Bedouin woman bought from me for 700 riyals. Her husband bought some things worth 100 riyals. They, too, promised to come back and pay, as they did not have any money with them. They also have not come back. I should have learned from the first case. That woman could be walking around in the *suq* today, and I would not know her unless she spoke.

Selling on credit to people whom one knows and trusts is not unusual and is a well-established pattern in ʿUnayzah. However, selling on credit to people who are from other places and whom one has only encountered within the context of a few previous transactions is much more of a risk, particularly since no written documents are exchanged and the seller has no formal means of redress if they fail to pay. When pressed to explain why they take such risks, sellers say that it is better to sell, even on credit, than to have the merchandise just sitting there—there is always the chance that the buyers will pay, and most, in fact, do pay eventually. Also, selling on credit is a strong temptation nowadays because of the general slump in the market.

The system of taking merchandise from a number of dealers and then juggling to pay off at least part of the credit has its limits. At some point, cash has to be paid. If a seller's debts get out of hand and she can no longer pay an acceptable proportion of them, she has to borrow money from a moneylender. She may also borrow from moneylenders when she is first starting her business and has not yet established credit with the dealers, as the following case illustrates.

Umm ʿAbd al-Rahman now has an established business in the women's market. She sells spices, clothing, cooking utensils, and kitchenware. She has numerous credit relationships with dealers and also sells on credit. She is over fifty and recalled the time when she established her first shop in the al-Qaʿ in the old *suq*.

I borrowed 500 riyals from a man who lent money. I used this to buy merchandise and to start buying and selling. I rented a shop for 30 riyals a year. Later on, I had to borrow more money and once again I borrowed 400 riyals from another man. I was careful and was lucky to be able to pay both of them before the year was up.

Today, many people give me merchandise and wait. I have known one of the dealers for a very long time, and he gives me a lot of merchandise on credit, although he does not do this with the other women. I take up to 15,000 riyals worth of merchandise from him, and no problem. If I asked for three times as much, he would give it to me.

This case shows that women took loans in the past and is an example of someone taking a loan to set up her business. The following case shows a woman borrowing from a woman moneylender to both pay back debts incurred through taking goods on credit and, at the same time, expand her business and establish credit with new dealers. Umm Nayif is about forty-five. She has been selling in the *suq* for a number of years.

> When I moved into the new *suq* here, I borrowed 7,000 riyals from a woman who lends money. I wanted to start selling large pots for cooking, but I did not know the dealer who sells them. I also had several dealers who were anxious to be paid for things that I had taken from them on credit. So, with the money I borrowed, I paid back these dealers all that I owed them and then took more goods on credit from them. I also bought pots for cash from the dealer who sold them and thus was able to establish credit with him. I was lucky and was able to pay back the moneylender before the year was out.

Setting Prices

Some of the merchandise that is sold by women in the *suq* is locally produced by other women in 'Unayzah. This includes various types of traditional cookies and cakes. The women sell these on commission, and the price is thus essentially set by those who prepare them. The woman seller simply adds about 5 percent to the price quoted to her by the woman who has given her the items to sell. The setting of sale prices for the items that the woman has obtained from wholesale dealers is more complicated, and the women claim that they do not know how they set the prices. It should be remembered that they usually take items on credit from a dealer, and they also bargain with him about the prices of the goods he provides them with. They usually know what the cost is of piece goods like utensils or clothing, but items that are sold in bulk, like spices, and that have to be divided into small parcels present them with difficulty in calculating the cost of each small parcel. They know the cost of a large sack of cumin, for example, but they do not know how many small packets they make from the original large sack. They say, "We do not know how many small packets we make, but when we have sold them all, we have a profit." Prices in the market are not uniform; however, they do not vary tremendously from one seller to another.

Umm Sultan sells spices, nuts, kitchenware, and chocolates. She said,

I buy a big sack of pistachios for 750 riyals. I break that down into small quantities which I put into plastic bags. I sell each of these for 10 riyals. I get mixed up if I count all those small bags, especially since I have lots of other small bags for spices. But I do not lose.

A set of cooking pots cost me 80 riyals. I sold them for 110 riyals. Others may sell them for more, but 30 riyals are a good profit for me. I do not care what others do.

Another seller bought a set of fifteen cooking pots from a dealer for 190 riyals. She said that she sold them not as a set but one by one. They were of different sizes. The largest ones she sold for 40 riyals each, while the smallest one she sold for 10 riyals.

Another seller bought twelve pieces of children's clothing for 350 riyals. She started selling each of the pieces for 35 riyals. Another seller, not far away from her, was selling the same merchandise for 50 riyals apiece. These cases suggest that each woman is acting independently of the others. However, they themselves recognize limits to the variations that occur and express this in different ways. As one woman said, commenting on a cheaper price for the same item which she was selling, "If they sell cheaper than I, they will lose and eventually have to stop doing that. Besides, each one of us will get her share of *rizq* ['bounty']." Another woman, commenting on someone who was selling an item for a higher price, said, "She is greedy. In the end, it will be found out that she is too high, and this will make her clients go to others."

The ideal that women project is that of modest profits, of not being greedy, of not cheating the customer on the quality of goods, of not taking advantage of the creditor, and of fearing Allah in their dealings with people in the market. On the other hand, many of them are aggressive sellers and try to keep the creditor at bay for as long as possible. They also say that "business is business" and that each seller is free to do what she likes in setting prices. However, it is clear that they do consult with each other, at least to some degree, and agree on what the prices of certain items should be. One who said that she sets her prices independently of others later on said that she and others who are her neighbors in the *suq* discuss what the asking price should be for a new item that they have all obtained from the same dealer. Another said that she did not consult with her neighbors. She did, however, consult with some relatives in the *suq* who obtain their merchandise from the same source.

Relationships among Sellers

In the process of selling, the women follow a certain etiquette and ad-
here to unwritten rules. They do not advertise and do not try to attract a customer away from another buyer by offering to sell at a
lower price. This is considered highly improper and leads to conflict
if it occurs. Also, a certain solidarity exists among the sellers, expressed by one woman, who said that she does not sell her goods
more cheaply because she does not want to undercut the others.
While she may have been expressing an ideal, solidarity among the
sellers is expressed in other acts.

Within the market, sellers often form small groups that socialize
together, drinking coffee and chatting with each other. Some share
meals together. As one said, "There are seven of us who are neighbors in the *suq*. Every Thursday and Friday, we have lunch together,
and each week one of us is responsible for bringing the meal. On
other days, each brings her own lunch, but we still eat together and
share things with each other." Although some of the sellers go home
for lunch and others eat alone, the sharing of coffee is universal
among them. Sellers mind each other's shops when one is away and,
if a person comes to buy something from the other's merchandise, a
neighbor will sell it for her and make no effort to attract the buyer to
herself, although she has the same merchandise. Also, if a customer
wants something that the seller does not have, she will send him/her
to one who does or she will go and get the item herself. A case that
indicates this type of solidarity occurred when a man came to the
suq to buy cloaks for women. He went to a seller from whom he
had bought several times previously. She did not have the items he
wanted and sent him to a neighbor. He selected five cloaks, each cost-
ing 210 riyals, and asked that they be shortened. The seller agreed and
took them to a tailor, who shortened them for 50 riyals. She paid the
tailor and brought the cloaks back and the man took them. She thus
realized a sale of 1,500 riyals through the good graces of her neighbor.

The women do not like to give loans to other sellers, but occasionally they do. An example is of a woman who gave money to one of
her neighbors who was going to Kuwait. She did not ask her what
she wanted the money for, but felt she had to give it to her because
she was a neighbor and because she herself was in better financial condition than the one who asked for the money. In another instance, one

seller lent another 400 riyals to pay off a creditor who was anxious to collect. This was quite some time ago, and the woman has still not paid her back, which has led the one who gave the money to say that she will not do this kind of thing again. The women also do not like to guarantee another seller to a creditor, and this is seldom, if ever, done because they run the risk of getting themselves in trouble with the creditor if the other does not meet her debts.

Few of the sellers have kin in the market. However, those who do are on amicable terms with them. However, they assert that "the market is the market," meaning that they will heed kinship relations, but not at the expense of their interests in the market. The same is, of course, true for friendship ties that women cultivate in the marketplace.

Relationship to the Wider Economy

The women's market is a well-bounded part of the *suq* in ʿUnayzah and is located in a specific geographical area which separates it from the rest of the *suq*. We have mainly described what takes place inside that localized market, but it is a part of the wider economy of the city and is tied to that wider economy in various ways. One way it is tied is through sellers investing outside the women's *suq* in other sectors and another way is through the institution of moneylenders. Sometimes women in the *suq* are able to save cash. Even if they are able to save significant amounts they do not think of reinvesting in the market and expanding their operations. They lack the know-how which would enable them to deal directly with the bigger suppliers and to set up a shop similar to those in the more modern parts of the *suq* that are run by men. In addition to being illiterate, they do not go to banks and have no experience in dealing with the networks and procedures that are involved in setting up a modern enterprise. Therefore, the few who have been able to amass significant savings have opted to invest them in such things as land and houses. These are traditionally valued areas for investment and it is not surprising that they think of investing in them.

The following cases show how some sellers venture out of the market with their profits. In the first case, a woman who is over fifty has a reputation in the market of being very calculating, stingy, and too businesslike. The sellers say that she would "sell her own daughter biscuits to give to her grandchildren." She is also sharp-tongued and very assertive. She has one son and three daughters and has been divorced by three men. One of her relatives said that she saved the money of her *mahr,* "dower," from her three different husbands. She bought an old house in which she lives with her unmarried children. Over the years in the market, she has saved a considerable amount of money. With that money she purchased a piece of land which she registered in the name of her son to enable him to obtain a loan from the Real Estate Development Fund to build a house. The house has been built, and the son has rented it out. He continues to live with his mother in her old house and gives her the income from the rent of the new house.

Not always are these women able to see this process of investment to its end, as the following case shows. Umm Hazim, mentioned earlier, is one of the richer women sellers and one of the oldest in the market. She has accumulated considerable cash over the years. She bought a piece of land in an auction with some of the money she had saved. She wanted to build a house on this land as an investment, but to do so she needed to obtain a loan from the Real Estate Development Fund. However, because her husband has a house, she does not qualify to obtain a loan. She has asked her widowed daughter to apply for a loan, but the daughter has been reluctant to do so. Therefore, the land is sitting empty.

Another important way in which the women's market is tied into the wider economy is through the institution of moneylenders. Sometimes sellers have to obtain cash. Short of going to a friend or relative, the only way to obtain the cash is to go to a moneylender, since they do not consider going to the bank. They can go to either male or female moneylenders. The cases which we present happen to be with females.

In the words of Umm ʿAbd al-ʿAziz,

> I needed some cash to pay creditors and to buy more merchandise. I heard of a woman who lends money. I also heard of men who lend, but it was said that they take more interest. My sister-in-law had borrowed from this woman before. She confirmed what others had told me about her—that she is patient and kind, although she appears otherwise. I went to her, and she gave me the money. It was understood that I would pay back within a year. I borrowed 7,000 riyals.

This woman's father was a rich man. He had farms, houses, and land that he later sold as real estate. Her mother was rich, too. She [her mother] used to work in the tanning and processing of leather. She also spun wool yarn. The woman who lent me the money inherited a lot of money from her parents. She also had a shop, but what she inherited was her main source of money.

She had a partnership with a male moneylender. She had a lot of money—even men borrowed from her. She could give you even 100,000 riyals. If you wanted money, you would go to her, and she would take you to her partner. He would write a paper and give you a check. Her interest was twelve for ten [i.e., 20 percent].

I got my money cash from her with a paper that said how much I owed her. There is another woman who lends money and she is even better. She is investing her deceased son's money and takes interest, so that it will increase for his children. She does not write a paper, and I have to remind her that I owe her. This woman is good—she is patient.

Another case of a woman moneylender is Luluwah. According to one of the sellers in the women's *suq,*

her mother and grandmother were both rich. Her mother was a money-lender and used to lend people money and expected favors in return. When she visited the people she had lent money to, she expected to be treated well and to be offered a meal. If they did not do this, she would remind them of their debts.

Luluwah inherited her grandmother's house. It was a big house in the Majlis. When the area began to be improved by the municipality, it was one of those to be demolished. The municipality estimated that house to be worth 90,000 riyals. She challenged them and said that it was worth more. The municipality placed the money with the *qadi,* who then summoned Luluwah to collect her money. He advised her to take the money, that there was no way they would increase the sum. He told her that if she wanted more money, she could put it to work in the market. It was about this time that another woman, Munirah, wanted to buy a truck for her son to work with. Luluwah lent her the money with interest. Munirah's son worked with the truck until he had a huge accident and completely destroyed it.

Munirah had not paid anything back on the loan, and her debt had risen to 135,000 riyals. Munirah was in a terrible situation. She could not pay even small amounts of her debt. Luluwah went to the *qadi* to report Munirah's case. Thus she had to either pay or go to prison, and Luluwah got a paper from the *qadi* which said that. Luluwah then went to the amir. She asked him to do something—either to pay her from the funds of a philanthropic society or to force Munirah to pay or to throw her into jail. The amir summoned Munirah, who obviously could not pay. She, therefore, went to make arrangements to go to jail. Luluwah took pity on her and gave her one more week to come up with the money.

Munirah came back to Luluwah after a week—without the money but with a new solution. She offered to give her one of the three houses which she owned. By that time, the debt had increased to 150,000 riyals. After weighing the options, Luluwah decided to accept the offer. They sent a committee to estimate the value of the house and they said that it was worth 125,000. Luluwah took possession of the house and agreed to waive the interest on the remaining sum and to wait until Munirah could pay.

Luluwah has a husband who is blind. He lives alone, and she lives with her two daughters and three sons. Her husband comes regularly to eat but does not interfere with her business. Other women speak of her as a very powerful woman who has neither mercy nor consideration. She is a partner of a male moneylender. They both use each other's money when they need to.

Unlike most of the rest of the *suq,* the women's market continues to be organized primarily by traditional patterns of buying and selling. However, all the women say that in the past they used to sell much more than they do now. They used to have sales of up to 900 or 1,000 riyals a day. "The market was hot," they say. They have brought in new types of merchandise and improved the quality of the things they sell. They have brought in a lot of ready-to-wear clothes for children and trousers for expatriate workers, for example. There are now more dealers who bring them merchandise, and there are more sellers than in the past. But they all say that business is not as good as in the past. As one woman said, "We sold so well that the men were envious."

But since it is traditional, the sellers maintain small operations. The shops run by the men have become larger, and they have better displays of merchandise. These shops are more attractive to the increasingly modernized buyer of today, whether male or female. However, so long as there is a segment of the population that is relatively poor, there will continue to be those who seek to supplement their income with smaller operations. Of course, some men maintain small operations similar to those of the women sellers and sell many of the same kinds of merchandise. But most of the men have modernized their operations to a much greater degree.

CHAPTER 9

The New Agriculture

The popular image of Saudi Arabia in both the Middle East and the West is of a land of deserts and oil. However, the vast majority of the population were farmers, herders, or fisherfolk. Furthermore, no existing evidence indicates significant import in the past of basic food crops into the region. What was imported were such things as coffee, tea, sugar, cardamom, and rice—all of which, including rice, were luxuries which played important roles in the social life of the people but were not essential for basic subsistence.

This is not to argue that, in the past, people had a rich and varied diet of locally produced food. To the contrary, many older informants in 'Unayzah, which was a comparatively rich agricultural oasis, spoke of having experienced hunger when they were young. However, if hunger existed, it was due more to socioeconomic inequalities than to the incapacity of the population to produce enough for its own basic consumption needs. Also, the memory of hunger expressed by older people must be seen in the context of the abundance of imported and locally produced food that is consumed today. While the meals that are regularly served today include vast amounts of food, much of which is not consumed and thus wasted, the meals of the past were simple. They normally included dates, bread or dishes made from wheat, ghee, and milk. On occasion, meals included some vegetables and, more rarely, meat (or fish for those in coastal areas).

As money became more abundant, due to increased prices for oil, and as the state embarked upon large-scale development programs and projects, patterns of food consumption changed. For example, rice became a basic staple; meat became a regular feature of at least one of the daily meals; and fruit, other than dates, became common. Thus, the food requirements of the country increased dramatically in terms of quantity and in terms of quality and type.

With the increasingly large amounts of money that became available, the state invested heavily in the development of water resources and the modernization of agriculture in at least some basic crops to limit the country's heavy dependence on food imports. One of the results of this policy is that Saudi Arabia has become not only self-sufficient in wheat but exports it, at highly subsidized prices or as gifts, to other countries in the region, including Egypt.

Agriculture in ʿUnayzah, as in many other parts of the country, has been transformed. Agricultural production has expanded dramatically as a result of desert land reclamation, the introduction of new crops and new varieties of crops, the use of chemical fertilizers, and mechanization. However, both the technology and labor that have made this expansion possible are largely imported.

The state has played a primary role in determining change in the agricultural sector through a variety of ways that include the institutionalization of rules concerning landownership and the development of agricultural extension programs and administrative structures that were discussed in chapter 6. Since the *tufrah,* it has also played a major role through financial subsidies and loans.

The Role of the State

The role of the state in agriculture began to increase gradually as the institutions of the modern state themselves emerged and developed, especially in the 1950s and 1960s. The directorate of the Ministry of Agriculture and Water, the Agricultural Research and Training Center, and the Saudi Arabian Agricultural Bank established in ʿUnayzah at first had small staffs and modest operations. They provided some technical expertise and a few loans of modest amounts. However, the role of these greatly increased as the revenue of the state from the sale of oil increased dramatically in the mid 1970s. As a result of national policies that were decided upon centrally, the Saudi Arabian Agricultural Bank began to make available more and larger loans for agricultural development and the other institutions expanded both their staffs and programs.

The most profound and direct impact on agriculture in 'Unayzah has been brought about by the bank, which started to extend loans to farmers in 1965. At that time, its activities were quite limited, but these began to expand in 1975–76. The bank provides loans for the purchase of equipment for use in agriculture and irrigation. According to information provided by the bank in 'Unayzah, it extended 1,500 loans between 1982 and 1986 in 'Unayzah for a total of 165 million riyals. These were medium-term loans for the purchase of 1,390 stationary irrigation machines, 1,450 pumps, 930 tractors, and 700 central pivot irrigation machines, as well as short-term loans and loans for the planting of dates. In addition, it extended loans for thirteen special projects, mainly hothouses and chicken and egg farms, for a total of 56,976,000 riyals. As is not difficult to imagine, these loans provided a major incentive for investment in agricultural production. Both farmers and businessmen eagerly jumped into the business of developing new agricultural lands and improving old ones.

According to Abu Ahmad, a young man about thirty who is from 'Unayzah and who is one of the leading administrators in the 'Unayzah branch of the bank,

> to obtain a loan, a citizen must present a request, along with evidence that he/she is the legal owner of the land on which a farm is located or is to be developed. If the request is initially approved, an agricultural expert from the bank visits the farm and prepares a report on it, indicating whether the request is for something that is actually needed. This report is reviewed by three officials in the bank, and if approved, the farmer is instructed to put up his collateral, which may be done through a bank account or through the ownership of real estate or through the auspices of a *kafil* ["guarantor"]. When this is done, a member of the bank staff goes to a private agricultural company, which supplies the equipment and records the identification number on the item. The bank then issues a check to the company and instructs it to provide the farmer with the item he has requested.
>
> For most equipment, the bank deducts 50 percent of the cost as a subsidy paid by the bank. The farmer then owes the bank the remaining half of the loan, which he must pay back in yearly installments over a period of ten years for what are called medium-term loans. The bank subsequently checks to ascertain that the item is actually being used. If it is not in use, the subsidy is revoked, and the farmer is responsible for paying back the whole loan.

None of the state institutions or the services they provide were available to the old agriculture, which was limited by technological constraints, particularly in irrigation, and often encumbered by heavy debts with interest that farmers were forced to take from moneylenders and merchants. While these institutions provide very important contributions to the improvement of agriculture and are highly appreciated by the majority of farm owners, they are themselves relatively new and are still in the process of developing. The employees of the various institutions say that they have become more effective in recent years but also note that there are problems that remain to be solved.

Their increased effectiveness in contributing to the development of agricultural production is attributed by them to the fact that, with the exception of the veterinarians in the directorate, all the professional staff is now composed of trained Saudi Arabian men who are also from the community of ʿUnayzah. The Agricultural Bank has thirty employees, ten of whom are agricultural engineers, while the research and training center employs nineteen agricultural engineers and twenty agricultural technicians. The directorate employs an even larger staff of agricultural engineers and administrative personnel. With the exception of a couple of middle-aged men, all these are young men in their middle to late twenties or early thirties. Some are the sons of *fallalih,* while others are the sons of merchants or craftsmen. Most completed their education through secondary school in ʿUnayzah or obtained secondary school diplomas from the Agricultural Technical Training Center in Buraydah. The agricultural engineers are all graduates of King Saʿud University in Riyadh, and many have attended advanced training programs in the United States. Being of similar ages and having grown up in ʿUnayzah, they all know each other well and form a close-knit group which regularly socializes together.

Commenting on the staff at the Agricultural Bank, Abu Ahmad said,

> The bank has operated here since 1965, but at that time its activities were very limited, and it occupied only a single small office in the directorate. But now we have thirty employees. Since three years ago, they have all been Saudi Arabians, and all of them are from ʿUnayzah except for one driver, who is from Buraydah.
>
> All of us are young, and when we first came to work here after

finishing our studies, most of us were worried about how we would be able to deal with the farmers. Most of them are older, and we were afraid that they would think of us as just kids and not take us seriously. But things have worked out very well. Because we are from here, we know the local people and their needs and aspirations very well. Also, the people in ʿUnayzah are better educated and enlightened than is the case in some other places. They understand that the government has a *nizam* ["system; routine"] and that they have to meet all the requirements to obtain a loan. And we apply the *nizam* equally to all—even to my father.

They also tend to believe strongly in the effectiveness of the programs that they are administering. An agricultural engineer at the bank, Abu Salih, who is about twenty-eight, said,

The bank has played the major role in helping the country to both maintain and expand agriculture. Before the expansion of the bank's role, agriculture was on the decline, and many people were abandoning it. Now, it is not only maintaining itself but it is expanding dramatically. Also, this program has had a major social impact, particularly on the Bedouin. Many of them have obtained land and have been given loans to buy agricultural equipment. They have central pivot irrigation systems and are growing wheat and fodder crops and are responsible for a great deal of the agricultural development that has taken place in villages and remote areas in this region. I would estimate that 70 to 80 percent of the Bedouin in this area—mainly Mutayr followed by ʿUtaybah and Harb—have central pivots for irrigation and grow wheat. This has sped up the process of sedentarization, and now their children go to school and are becoming educated. They are also cleaner now than in the past and are becoming more integrated into modern society.

At the same time, the staff recognizes that problems have occurred and that, while much has been achieved in terms of increasing agricultural output, the costs have been high. Abu ʿAbd al-Karim, one of the older staff members in the directorate, for example, said,

The farmers here are not really in a good situation. They have taken many loans, and even if they are subsidized by the government, they still have large debts to pay off. A few years ago, agriculture was dying off because there was no profit in it. In fact, many were taking land out of agriculture to build houses and buildings on it. There were also studies years ago that showed that the costs of agriculture here are very high and that we cannot compete with the world market. It is cheaper for the country to import onions than to grow them here. Also, there has not been enough planning at the local level, and we now have an overproduction of many crops, including wheat. Furthermore, we do not have a good marketing system or proper facilities for distribution and storage.

They mention other problems, such as overdependence on cheap and unskilled expatriate labor, the rapidity with which the expansion has taken place, and possible overuse of precious water which has taken millions of years to collect. However, in spite of the fact that all the agricultural employees are local men and many of them say that this makes them more effective in their work, some say that one of their major problems is communication with the farmers. This is partly due to the administrative structure of the state institutions and to many of the farmers being older men who were highly knowledgeable about traditional agriculture but who have little understanding of at least some aspects of modern farming. According to Abu Nadir at the research center,

> we have a major problem of communication with the farmers in the area. Most of this is supposed to be done by those who work in agricultural extension in the directorate. The research center gives them the results of its studies and also provides them with seeds to distribute, but the workers there do not know as much as they should. The researchers in the center have developed a lot of knowledge about crops and their requirements in this area, but those who disseminate it are others, and they are under a different administrative unit.
>
> The farmers themselves are also a problem. They want everything very fast. They come in with a question. Sometimes the question can be answered immediately, but more often it requires study and even research, which is something they do not understand. If not answered immediately, the farmer gets impatient and does not want to wait for proper results, and so he goes away mad and does not come back.

New Farms

Various types of new farms have been developed in the ʿUnayzah area within the past decade or even within the past five or six years. These can be distinguished on the basis of size, which also correlates with location and, to a large degree, with the socioeconomic characteristics of those who have developed them. Also, most people who own farms now are referred to as *muzaraʿ*, "farmer," rather than *fallah*, which connotes a peasant. There are essentially four different types of new farms. These are *basatin* (sg. *bustan*), "gardens," developed mainly by merchants; small to medium-size farms developed by *fallalih*; large wheat farms developed by individual entrepreneurs, most of whom had no background in farming; and combined hothouse and chicken and egg production farms developed by entrepreneurs. Within the area of the Qasim, very large new wheat farms also have been developed by members of the ruling Al Saʿud dynasty or by companies. In addition, some small farms have been developed by Bedouin.

With the exception perhaps of farms developed by princes (none of which are in the ʿUnayzah amirate), subsidized loans from the Agricultural Bank have provided much of the financial capital that has made these farms possible. All of them share other common features. With minor exceptions, they are all located on land that was not previously in cultivation such as desert land in the *barr* which was formerly used mainly for grazing purposes by the Bedouin or, in the case of some ʿUnayzah farms, in parts of the wadi that in the past were not farmed because of drainage problems and/or the existence of malaria. Aside from hothouses and chicken and egg production farms, which are a special case, all the farms use modern technology in irrigation and are fully mechanized. The larger farms all employ central pivot irrigation systems called *rashshashat* (sg. *rashshash*), "machine guns, sprinklers," by people in ʿUnayzah. According to information provided by the directorate, the ʿUnayzah amirate has 424 *rashshashat*, the largest of which is capable of irrigating 78 hectares of land. Smaller farms and *basatin* use stationary irrigation machines called *madafiʿ* (sg. *madfaʿ*), "cannons." In addition, drip irrigation is used where appropriate, as is the more traditional basin irrigation. All the farms have their own wells, which in the case of larger farms have usually been drilled to very deep levels and mine geological water. Another common feature of new farms is that they rely almost exclusively on expatriates for labor, as well as sometimes for management. The following cases provide typical examples of new farms.

A Very Large Company-Owned Farm

Although the farm that is described here is not in the amirate of 'Unayzah, it is an example of a very large farm that has been developed by a company, and the farm's project director is from 'Unayzah. It is located to the northwest of Buraydah within the area of the Qasim and is on land that was formerly desert. It is one of several farms owned by a company that was established in 1983 for the purpose of developing agricultural enterprises. The company's owners are said to be Saudi Arabian businessmen who are mainly residents of large modern cities in the country. The project director is twenty-six years old, is not yet married, and is an agricultural engineer with a degree from King Saʿud University in Riyadh.

This farm is located on an area of 16 by 12 kilometers of land, and in 1986 a total of 6,901 hectares were under irrigation from wells sunk to a depth of 800 meters. The main crop is wheat, and in the 1985–86 season it was grown on 88 circles under central pivot irrigation systems. During the season of 1986–87, the farm grew wheat on 67 circles, barley on 20, and alfalfa on 1. In addition, the farm has a breeding and fattening unit for sheep and goats, with about 800 goats and 250 sheep.

This farm employs 86 workers on contract and also uses some additional casual labor. Aside from laborers, the farm employs 4 farm supervisors, an irrigation engineer, a civil engineer, a medical doctor, a veterinary officer, a geologist, a workshop supervisor, and a nursery and research supervisor. All but 2 of the 86 employees are workers on contract from abroad. The only Saudi Arabians on the farm are the project manager and a Bedouin who works as a mechanic.

Three Large Individually Owned Farms

One example of a large individually owned new farm is located about twenty-five kilometers to the west of 'Unayzah and occupies an area of three thousand hectares on land that was formerly desert. Although there was a well of the Mutayr Bedouin on this land, where as many as two hundred Bedouin families used to camp in summer, the owner, Abu Hasan, said, "The Bedouin have no claim to this land because they did not endow it with life [i.e., provide it with water and develop agriculture]. I obtained part of it as an *'iqta'* from the amir thirty years ago, but most of it I have obtained through *ihya'* during the past few years and with the approval of the Ministry of Agriculture and Water."

On that part of the land which was obtained as an *'iqta'*, or grant from the amir, there are some tall eucalyptus trees and several small buildings made of concrete blocks where some equipment is stored and where the farm workers live. Alfalfa is grown here, and there is a large tin-covered area where about one hundred sheep and thirty cows are kept. The major expansion of the farm started in 1980, when the owner said that he obtained a loan from the Agricultural Bank.

At the time of fieldwork, wheat had been grown on the new part of the farm for the past six years. The wheat is irrigated by six *rashshashat*, which use water drawn from nine wells sunk to a depth of 250 meters. When the water comes out of the ground it is hot and, therefore, a basin has been built to allow it to cool, particularly since there are plans to develop a chicken farm on the property next year.

In addition to growing wheat, this farm is also being developed to include an orchard. During 1986, 30,000 fruit trees, which are watered by drip irrigation, had been planted. These include pomegranates from Ta'if in the Hijaz; apricots, figs, oranges, tangerines, and peaches from Egypt; lemons from Spain; and olives from the United States. The farm also produces watermelons, potatoes, green peppers, and white eggplant, in addition to the alfalfa, sheep, and cows already mentioned. In the 1987 season, barley was to be grown on part of the land that has been in wheat production.

The farm is worked by fifteen Egyptian males under the day-to-day supervision of an Egyptian mechanic/driver who has lived in 'Unayzah for ten years. Most of the others stay for one or two years and then return home; however, all the workers are from the same village in Egypt, and they send others from the same village to replace them when they leave. The owner does not labor on the farm, but he plays an active role in its development and management. He is responsible for bringing all the fruit trees from abroad, and he actively reads about agriculture and is keen to introduce new crops.

Another example is a farm that was established in 1980 on land that is located about thirty kilometers to the southeast of 'Unayzah. As in the previous example, this was desert land and was developed with loans from the Agricultural Bank. Ownership was obtained through

the process of *ihya'*. It has sixteen *rashshashat,* and both wheat and alfalfa are grown on the irrigated land. There are nine wells at a depth
of a thousand meters and, unlike that from some other deep wells in
the region, the water is cool and said to be very good.

In addition to the wheat and alfalfa, a fish farm has been developed
with fish that were brought from Egypt and which are raised in seven
lakes, each one of which is three hectares in area. Fish in the middle of
the desert is surely an innovation. The owner said he first learned
about fish farms from one he saw in Syria. According to the owner,
Abu Salim,

> after I saw a fish farm in Syria, I decided to start one here. That was
> two and a half years ago. I went to a research center in Riyadh, and
> they gave me some information and provided me with some stock of
> fish to start with. I also went to Egypt to see what they do there and I
> consulted with some Egyptian experts. But they only have fancy diplo-
> mas and do not have any real expert knowledge that is of any practical
> value. So, I went to Germany and to East Asia to learn about this busi-
> ness. Now, we produce catfish, Nile fish from Egypt, *bulti,* and *garamit*
> [types of fish]. During the fishing season, which is in the warm months,
> we produce one-half to one ton of fish per day, but this will increase to
> about seven tons per day when all of the seven lakes are in full produc-
> tion. The fish we produce are sold live in water tanks which we have
> provided in various supermarkets in the Qasim. Most of the fish is
> bought by expatriates, because the local people are not used to eating
> fish and have not yet developed a taste for it. But that was the case with
> chicken a few years ago: at first, they refused to eat it, but now they eat
> it all the time. I am also developing a project to market this fish through-
> out the kingdom.

The farm also has a small herd of gazellelike animals that were
brought from Germany, bustard, and a few sheep and camels that are
kept in stables. In addition, a large grove of date palms has been
planted near a luxurious house on a hill overlooking the farm where
the owner socializes with his friends and spends weekends.

The labor on this farm is done by twenty-five male workers from
Pakistan, India, and the Philippines. These live on the farm in wooden
trailer houses which are located near several large tin barns where
equipment, seeds, and crops are stored. There is also a Palestinian ag-

ricultural engineer who is the overseer and who has worked on the farm since it started. The other workers tend to stay for only one or two years and then return home.

A third large farm of this general type likewise started in 1980 and was established on desert land that is very near the city. Since much of the farm is on a sand hill, terraces have been built. The farm consists of orchards with fruit trees, date palms, and flowers as well as wheat. In addition, two hothouses have been built where the owner plans to grow vegetables. There are also stables and pens where camels, cows, geese, ducks, and turkeys are kept. In addition, the owner has built a luxurious villa where he lives with his family, a guest house, and a mosque. The labor is done by expatriate males in addition to the owner, who, unlike the owners of other large farms, does engage in some agricultural work such as ploughing with a tractor.

The owners of these farms come from varied backgrounds. Two are of *qabili* status, while the other is *khadiri*. One is about seventy years of age, while the other two are around forty. Only one has a previous background in agriculture. The other two were (and are) businessmen who are owners or partners in drilling and/or construction companies. Two of them agree that they would not have developed these farms if there had not been subsidized loans from the Agricultural Bank and if the government had not agreed to purchase wheat at a guaranteed subsidized price. Like many others in ʿUnayzah, both of these express concern that the government has changed the price it will pay for wheat in 1987 from 3.5 to 2 riyals per kilo. According to one of the owners, Abu Hasan,

> in the past, it was very difficult to develop agriculture here in ʿUnayzah because credit was hard to obtain. The merchants and moneylenders charged a lot for the money they lent out. When I was young, I owned several different farms, but it was difficult to make a profit because of the interest one had to pay. I also worked as an ʿuqayli and bought sheep to sell in Palestine. I used to go as far away as Yemen to buy sheep, and once I walked all the way behind a flock of sheep which I took to sell in Jerusalem during the time of the Second World War. That was in 1942.
>
> I helped develop an agricultural cooperative society here a number of years ago before all the recent development in agriculture. That society was very important and was established to help farmers get ma-

chinery and to introduce new crops and improve agriculture in general. The members all made contributions, and it still has funds. But the need for this is not very great now because all have been able to get loans and subsidies from the Agricultural Bank. Each individual is, thanks to the loans, able to take care of himself. However, government officials still need to be informed about the needs and requirements of the farmers. I often write the minister of agriculture and water to tell him of things that need to be introduced or changed. I have also written the minister of agriculture in Egypt to advise him of things that should be done to improve agriculture in Egypt. For example, it is not right for the government to say that it will pay 3.5 riyals per kilo of wheat and then, all of a sudden, change it to 2 riyals. This makes the farmer nervous. Maybe some day they won't even buy it at all. Anyway, I am going to plant barley this year instead of wheat on some of my land because the Bedouin have become lazy and are buying lots of fodder to feed their animals instead of taking them to graze in the *barr*.

Unlike Abu Hasan, who has always been keenly interested in agriculture and who comes from a merchant-landowning family, Abu Salim said that he had no background or former interest in agriculture.

I have only been involved in agriculture for the past six years, when I started this farm. I am from a merchant family here in ʿUnayzah and none of us have ever been *fallalih*. When I was young, I used to import goods from Kuwait. Later on, I became the general manager of a company that was formed by myself and others from my family. We have offices in Riyadh and ʿUnayzah. Our original main work was in drilling artesian wells, which continues but on a smaller scale than before. It is also a trading and contracting company. The company drilled all the wells here and also built the roads and other heavy work that had to be done here. But I took loans from the Agricultural Bank which are very good because you only have to pay half of it back, and they do not charge interest. Financially, it was a good deal, but we are all worried about the government lowering the price it will pay for wheat. One of the main problems I confront is finding workers and supervisors with skilled expertise and experience in modern farming. But developing this farm has been an interesting experience, and I am learning as we go along. I travel a lot, and whenever I see something new abroad, I always say, "Why can't we do that at home?" And then I try it out here.

While Abu Hasan developed his new farm partly as a result of a long-term interest in agricultural development and because of the availability of subsidized loans, and while Abu Salim developed his because it seemed like a good business opportunity, the owner of the third farm, Abu Ziyad, gave a more personal explanation for why he decided to develop a farm.

I was born in ʿUnayzah, but when I was a very small baby I was taken with my family to the Hijaz, which is where I grew up. I had a large company in the Hijaz, and we had a lot of very big projects in construction. I traveled a lot and lived for seven years in Europe. I used to work very hard and was always busy. I did not sleep regularly and did not eat regularly because of the pressure of work. My relations with my family and with my religion were affected by this kind of life-style. I became ill with overwork and felt that life was becoming meaningless. I was tense all the time and had severe headaches and a problem with my back, and there was something wrong with my kidneys.

When I saw the development taking place here in ʿUnayzah, I decided to return to my *watan* ["homeland"] and to develop a farm. I turned my company in the Hijaz over to a relative and returned here. Now I am much better and do not have any of the physical symptoms I used to have. I was in London a year ago and decided to have a checkup. The doctors could not believe that I was the same man they used to see a few years ago.

I myself work on the farm and drive a tractor and participate in all the physical work. The Qurʾan teaches us that agriculture is very good. Also, ʿUnayzah is a good town because it is small and the people are good. The society is good, and religion is respected. There is none of the pollution that exists in the big cities. One is able to live a quiet and peaceful existence here and make the land grow.

I don't think of this farm as an investment or as a business operation. Anyway, the first ten years of a farm are likely to be ones in which there is little profit. It takes a long time to build it up before it will produce a profit and pay off the heavy investments that have to be made in the beginning. However, I want to make this farm a success. Allah willing, it will bring a profit in the long run.

Small and Medium-Size Farms

In addition to large wheat farms with numerous central pivots for irrigation, many small to medium-size farms have been developed in

the past decade with loans from the Agricultural Bank. Most are between about ten and fifty hectares in size and are mainly located in the
wadi or other areas near the city. A few have one or two central pivots
but most rely on stationary irrigation machines that, as mentioned
earlier, are called *madafi* by people in ʿUnayzah. Most of these farms
also utilize more traditional forms of basin irrigation. Each has its
own well, and in the wadi most of these are at depths of about sixty
meters. As people in ʿUnayzah say, "The wadi has good soils, good
water, and those who farm it know agriculture."

Farms with central pivots grow wheat on the circles irrigated
by them, but most of the farms are devoted to dates, other fruits,
vegetables, and alfalfa. Many of them also grow a local variety of
wheat. Unlike the "government" wheat of the big farms, this variety
is marketed locally and sells for about 6 riyals per kilogram. It is processed locally and is used in making a number of traditional local
dishes. Indeed, these are the farms that supply ʿUnayzah with most of
the food it consumes, although some is also sold in other places in the
country.

The people who have developed these farms are mainly from *fallalih* backgrounds and were either sharecroppers or owners of small
old farms. Many are also currently employed in other occupations or
have retired from employment and receive pensions. These include
men who have lived always in ʿUnayzah and others who were migrants to other cities in the country and who have returned to retire in
the city. The income from the farms is seen as an important supplement to their salaries or pensions. However, they have also developed
them because of a commitment to a way of life that always involved
agriculture, although they may have been engaged in other types of
employment. When loans were made available, these men took advantage of them to develop farms not only because they promised
economic benefits but also because they were in line with what they
considered themselves to be—*fallalih*.

An example is a farm of about ten hectares in size which was developed on desert land by Abu Hamad, who is a low-ranking employee
in a state office. About thirty-five, his father was always a sharecropper, and he grew up on a farm. He himself does most of the work
with the part-time assistance of one Egyptian, who also works on a
farm belonging to a relative. This farm, he says, "is an important
supplement to my salary. It is also important to me because I own the
land and the farm is mine. In the past, we always worked on the land

of others. This has all been possible because of the loans from the Agricultural Bank."

There are many others like this. For example, there is a date palm farm that has been established by a man about seventy who was a sharecropper and, more recently, the manager of a big farm owned by wealthy merchants who, though originally from ʿUnayzah, are settled in Kuwait. Another such farm has been developed by a man who retired after more than thirty years of government service but whose family had always been in agriculture as sharecroppers. For these, the loans provided by the bank have allowed them to achieve something that their fathers before them were seldom able to do— own a farm of their own.

Invariably these farms established by *fallalih* are neat, the crops are carefully planted, and the date palms are of the finest varieties and are well looked after. Each farm usually also has a few simple farm buildings, a stable with a few cows and sheep and goats, a place for sitting, usually out of doors, for drinking coffee and tea and socializing. Unlike the old farms, families do not live on the farms and family members do not work on them. The work of the farm is done by one to seldom more than three workers from other countries—usually Egyptians, but occasionally Pakistanis or Indians. However, the owner is there every afternoon and often in the morning to actively supervise every detail of work on the farm, often doing some of it himself.

The Basatin

Aside from the new small to medium-size farms developed by the *fallalih* and the big commercial wheat farms, there is another development in agriculture that has more to do with social factors than with farming. These are the *basatin,* which have been established by men who are either merchants or highly paid employees. These, too, were developed with loans from the Agricultural Bank.

One example of a *bustan* is that of Abu Muhammad, a man about fifty who used to be the headmaster of a school in another city. He returned to ʿUnayzah to take a new highly paid position in a government job. He has developed one of the more elaborate *basatin* on land that used to be covered with ʾathal. He has a house on the land and there is a swimming pool. There are about fifty recently planted date palms along with vines, roses, and some vegetables. There are stables with about ten milk cows and a number of goats. He says that the cows provide milk for his household, while a young male calf might be slaughtered, as are the goats. According to Abu Muhammad,

> this *bustan* is not for economic gain. It has been very expensive to establish and involved a lot of hard work. The land here is sandy and so we had to bring in mud from the wadi and to mix it with the sand. Also, it has taken a lot of time and effort to find all the right palms and to plant the vines and flowers.
>
> I have done this not because I expect to make money from it but because I enjoy it. I love having the date palms and the animals. I have never worked in agriculture myself and there are three Egyptians who do all the work here.

The *basatin* are mainly located to the west of ʿUnayzah in sandy areas that used to be covered with ʾathal trees. People who owned trees in these areas eventually obtained ownership of the land. As ʿUnayzah began to expand during the boom, several individuals bought up this land from others and subdivided it into parcels of between five and twenty hectares. The area was provided with electricity and telephones. Furthermore, it was easily accessible because the highway to Madinah passed through it. Numerous tracts of this land were bought mainly by merchants and wealthier members of the community, who developed the land mainly for recreational and social purposes.

Each *bustan* has a building which is used for socializing. Many of these buildings have only one or two rooms, but others are much larger and have several bedrooms, reception rooms, and sometimes a swimming pool. Whether large or small, these are frequented by men in the late afternoons and evenings for drinking tea and coffee, talking and telling stories, playing cards, etc. They are also the sites for meals where men invite guests on the weekends. Since they are mainly used for social purposes, the fact that they are no more than ten to fifteen minutes from the *suq* in ʿUnayzah is one of the main reasons for their having been developed in this area.

The area was also attractive because it was not rocky and because water was both close to the surface and of good quality. Mud from the wadi, however, had to be brought in to mix with the sand in order to develop agriculture. The main crops that are grown here are vegetables and alfalfa. Most have a few *sukkari* date palm trees and also keep a few animals. While some of the crops grown here are sold in the market, most are consumed by the family of the owner or the worker who does the farming. Each of these farms has one or two workers, most of whom are Egyptians and who live on the *bustan*.

Hothouse Agriculture and Chicken and Egg Farms

The new agriculture also includes hothouses and chicken and egg farms. There are at least three such enterprises in ʿUnayzah. All three have been developed by men in their late thirties. One of these was established by a man who had been mainly involved in contracting. He constructed a hatchery and a number of hothouses for growing vegetables, but only the hatchery was operating at the time of field-work. It was operating at only half capacity because, according to the owner, the market was not large enough to absorb all the possible production. He said he had not yet been able to put the hothouses into production because of lack of both expertise and a trained labor force. However, he hopes to recruit a farm manager from abroad who will be able to develop this aspect of his new farm.

The other two enterprises are working at full capacity. One hatchery, according to its owner, supplies both ʿUnayzah and Buraydah with all the eggs consumed there. Both enterprises have hothouses which are controlled by computers. In these are grown tomatoes, green peppers, cucumbers, squash, and other vegetables. One of these operations has seven glass hothouses, each one of which covers an area of 5,200 square meters. This farm employs a specialist from Holland, along with forty workers from the Philippines who have had to be trained to do this kind of work.

The other hothouse farm also employs workers from abroad, a mixture of Pakistanis, Afghanis, and Filipinos under the supervision of an Egyptian foreman. The only Saudi Arabians actively involved in either of these two farms are their owners. In both cases, they come from families with backgrounds in the old agriculture of ʿUnayzah, but they both are educated and have never worked in the old agriculture. According to one of them, Abu Muhammad,

> my family has owned a farm here for generations, but my father has mainly worked in trade in Riyadh. I grew up in both ʿUnayzah and Riyadh and I have always been interested in agriculture. I saw hothouses in Holland and in America and I studied up on them. I formed a

partnership with my father's company and obtained a loan from the
Agricultural Bank for 13 million riyals. The actual cost of establishing
the farm was 15 million riyals. This was extremely expensive. But we
decided to install the very best greenhouses that money could buy.
And, of course, the prices for everything went up a lot during the
tufrah. If we were to start it today, it would cost less.

All the produce of this farm is sent to Riyadh and to the Eastern
Province cities of Dammam, al-Khubar, and Dhahran. The owner
has arrangements with supermarkets there and supplies them directly
in trucks that belong to the farm. The main competition, he says, is
with produce from other Arab countries like Egypt, Jordan, Syria,
and Lebanon. In his opinion, Saudi Arabia should limit its imports
from these countries, which have lower production costs that make it
difficult for the local growers to compete.

New Crops

The new agriculture has involved the introduction of new crops or
new varieties of them. The wheat that is grown on the big new farms
is a variety known as Yecora Rojo and is imported. Seeds are provided
through the agricultural supply companies, and in the 1986 planting
season there was considerable concern among many farmers because
the seeds were late in arriving. This wheat is grown with heavy appli-
cations of fertilizers and chemicals, considered by most consumers in
ʿUnayzah to be unhealthy. Furthermore, this variety of wheat, according to local residents, is not appropriate for use in the preparation
of traditional local foods. Instead, they buy a local, traditional variety
of wheat at about twice the price of the new wheat. As mentioned
earlier, the new wheat has been purchased by the government at 3.5
riyals per kilogram, but it was said that in 1987 the government would
only pay 2 riyals per kilogram. Even so, this would have been much
higher than the world market price for such wheat.

Because of the fall in the government guaranteed price of wheat, at
the time of fieldwork farmers were beginning to introduce barley,
which would also be purchased by the government for later sale at
subsidized prices for use as fodder. This, of course, will benefit the
Bedouin, who have become sedentarized to a high degree and who
now prefer to feed their animals fodder instead of engaging in the

more difficult task of taking them to distant pastures to graze the natural bushes and grasses that depend on rainfall.

New vegetable crops were mainly introduced prior to the recent agricultural development, but their cultivation has greatly expanded in the past decade. The same is true for citrus fruits like oranges and tangerines. Dates also have experienced a renaissance, and the cultivation of two high-quality varieties—the *barhi* and the *sukkari*—has accelerated dramatically in ʿUnayzah.

The *barhi* was brought from Iraq a long time ago and was considered to be the best-quality date produced in ʿUnayzah. However, when freezing became possible, it was discovered that the *sukkari* responded extremely well to freezing. As a result, the *sukkari* is becoming more popular. Many new groves of both *barhi* and *sukkari* have been planted. A sapling costs between 1,000 and 3,000 riyals and begins to produce dates after about three years. A full-grown *barhi* tree annually produces dates worth 1,000 to 2,000 riyals, while a *sukkari* produces dates worth up to 3,000 riyals. By contrast, the dates produced by the more ordinary varieties of palms are said to be worth an average of about 300 riyals per tree.

As indicated in chapter 2, the planting, fertilizing, pruning, insemination, and harvesting of dates all required expert knowledge, which in the past was provided by the farmer or by an expert who was brought in. None of the foreign and other Arab workers who make up the major part of the labor force in agriculture today have this knowledge. Therefore, this work is still performed by ʿUnayzah men who specialize in it and who are paid about 200 riyals per tree.

An example of a relatively new farm in the wadi that is devoted mainly to dates is that of Abu ʿAbd al-Muhsin, who is about seventy years of age and who used to deal in the buying and selling of sheep and goats. He acquired the land for this farm seventeen years ago and has planted about six hundred palm trees, half *barhi* and half *sukkari*. The farm also grows various types of fodder crops under the trees. The farm employs three Egyptian workers who have been specially taught to care for the palms, which, because they are young, are not too tall and can be climbed easily. Taller, older trees are more difficult to climb and thus always require special workers. According to Abu ʿAbd al-Muhsin, the dates here are sold by auction, and for the past two years people from as far away as Najran have come to buy. They bring in about 700,000 riyals a year. The wages paid to the workers do not exceed 24,000 riyals a year. Aside from the original start-up costs of the farm, there are no other regular expenses other than the cost of running the pump for the seventy-meter well which provides water for irrigation.

Marketing

Labor in agricultural production by the local population has all but disappeared, but the output of the agricultural sector has increased. This increase is due not only to cheap imported labor but to mechanization and the expansion that was stimulated by the availability of state programs of subsidies and loans. Not only is the now larger city of ʿUnayzah still self-sufficient in all but a few agricultural products (like rice, tea, coffee, cardamom, and some fruits), it produces a surplus, and at certain seasons of the year the market is flooded with locally produced items to such an extent that prices become very cheap. All the farmers complain about the marketing system and speak of the need for a marketing cooperative and for the provision of more storage and processing plants. While these issues have been the subject of both formal and informal discussions in ʿUnayzah, nothing in this regard had been resolved at the time of fieldwork.

Aside from dates, which are sold by auction at the farm site, and government wheat and other grains, the marketing of the vegetables and fruits produced on all the farms of ʿUnayzah is done through the central market. The following description by Abu Ibrahim, an auctioneer who plays a key role in this marketing process, shows what happens when the farm produce reaches the marketplace.

The farmers or their workers bring their vegetable and fruit produce into the market packed in crates which they leave in the market, with a slip of paper with their name on it. Another auctioneer and I come at about 6:00 A.M. in the winter or 5:00 A.M. in the summer and start to auction off the crates of the farmers that sell through us. I have two assistants who work with me, one a Saudi Arabian and the other an Egyptian. I also have another employee who works in my office and keeps the accounts.

I only auction the crates which have slips of paper on them and only those of the farmers who work with me. The other auctioneer has his clients. I may also auction produce brought in by people from outside

'Unayzah if they are present. Once the produce is under auction, it is sold and the owner has to accept the result. He cannot withdraw his produce if he does not like the price.

The produce is all sold to sellers in the market. These then sell it to consumers, who come to the market throughout the course of the day, preferably early, as that is when the produce is fresh. These sellers sell at whatever price they can get from the consumer. Prices are not controlled by the municipality, and the seller is free to ask any price. He does not advertise what he paid for it in the auction. As the day goes on and supplies become depleted, the prices usually go up, although the sellers can also be left with a lot of unsold produce at the end of the day.

Farmers generally complain that these sellers make too much profit, and they want them to be controlled or for the growers to get more money to better cover the costs of production. But many of the sellers sometimes do not get enough to cover their own costs, and at the end of the day they cannot pay for what they bought in the morning. This is especially the case of sellers who buy a lot—those who buy little sell it all and make a profit.

In the late afternoon, those sellers who bought from me in the morning come to my office and pay me the amount of their purchases. I have a register for each seller, and we record the payment or lack of it if they do not yet have enough to pay. Likewise, each grower has a register, and the details of the sales of their produce are recorded. The grower may take his money in the afternoon of the same day, but this is seldom done unless he is from out of town and is leaving. The growers from here usually take their proceeds every month or so or at the end of the season. They usually prefer to take it all at once as a lump sum because that way they will get a lot of money that they can use for investments. If they take it in small amounts, they will spend it on odds and ends and will "lose" it that way.

I also arrange to buy seeds for the farmers. I used to also buy them chemical fertilizers, but I no longer do this because there are a lot of problems with the chemicals.

I have been doing this work here for about fifteen years. The main change is that in the past five or six years there is much more to sell. Before, the auction used to last about half an hour. Now it lasts about two hours.

At the very beginning of the season, for any produce, the price is very good. This is also the case at the end of the season. But in the middle, the prices go down to almost nothing, and even so there is a lot of produce that is turned over to the municipality as waste because it is not sold. Watermelons are particularly worthless at the height of the season. Also, during the season, some growers take their produce to Riyadh, but Riyadh also sends produce here. The problem is that they produce too much of the same thing and it all comes in at the same time. There have been discussions about setting up a marketing cooperative, but how will this work? Who will organize it and control it? And what will happen to people like me?

A massive amount of change has occurred in the agricultural sector of ʿUnayzah. If the goal has been to increase agricultural production, this has obviously been achieved with great success. However, some people in ʿUnayzah have reservations about different aspects of what all recognize as a phenomenal growth in agricultural output in a short period of time. These reservations are shown in the following comments.

Abu Khalid, the twenty-six-year-old director of a large agricultural project and an agricultural engineer, said,

> All this agricultural production has occurred very rapidly and has incurred vast amounts of expenses. The government has paid out much more money than it should have cost to achieve this expansion. Money has been wasted. And the people here do not realize that this money that has been spent is their own money. The government gets money from the sale of oil and then gives it out to individuals and companies to develop agriculture. The people think that they are getting money for free, but since the money belongs to the society, they may be losing it in the long run. There is also the problem of the technical aspects of modern farming. Most of those who are involved in it do not know much about the new techniques and requirements.

Abu Nadir, also an agricultural engineer and an employee in one of the agricultural offices, said,

> Most of the new agriculture has been developed by investors and by old farmers very quickly. The old farmers know a lot about dates and the old traditional crops, but they have little if any knowledge about the new crops and their requirements. They do not know when to plant some of them, and they do not know when and how much to

irrigate them. This is even more true for the investor who has no background in agriculture.

All of these, both investors and old farmers, have gotten loans and subsidies. This means that society as a whole has helped them. Because of this, they should be responsible to the society and develop agriculture on a sound basis. But I fear that many of them think only of their own immediate gain. They hire expatriate workers because they are cheap, but these have little if any knowledge of modern agriculture. Furthermore, they take their earnings out of the society here, and—even more important—they stand as a block against the employment of Saudi Arabian workers in agricultural enterprises. Unfortunately, the expansion in new agriculture, while producing a large output, has not significantly led to developing the Saudi Arabian population or its capacities.

Though not an agricultural specialist, Abu Salih, who as a boy worked as a *jammal* and later tried his hand at many other jobs that range from being a mechanic to being the owner of a gold shop in Riyadh, raised a more basic and fundamental problem, that of water. He said,

> I know they say that there is a lot of water deep down under the ground here. There was a man from the University of Petroleum who said the other night on television that there is the equivalent of the flow of water of the Nile for five hundred years here in Saudi Arabia. Maybe so, but how can we really know? What we do know is that it does not rain very much here. The water has to be limited. What they are using now for all this agricultural expansion took millions of years to collect. And every year the wells have to be dug deeper and deeper.

CHAPTER 10

Salaried Employment and Its Social Impact

One evening a small group of men from ʿUnayzah were sitting around the coffee hearth of a *majlis* in one of the *basatin*. An Egyptian agricultural laborer was sitting with them, and the talk turned to the issue of work. Someone asked the Egyptian for his opinion about Saudi Arabians working. He said, "The old ones know all about work, and they used to do everything. But the young ones don't know how to work at all. They can't do anything that involves work." An old man from ʿUnayzah spoke up and said, "I witness that it is true. By Allah, we used to work hard and do everything. I remember walking all the way from Jiddah to Jerusalem in 1942 behind a flock of sheep I was taking to sell in Palestine." In another setting, an old man said, "When the city of ʿUnayzah was under siege early in this century, it was possible to hold out for several weeks. We had everything we needed right here. I wonder how long we could survive now if under siege or if things from the outside were cut off."

These remarks point to two different but related aspects of the transformation that has occurred in ʿUnayzah. Very few local people engage in work that involves regular physical labor. They do work, of course. However, most of them now work in air conditioned offices and shops, mainly as employees of the state or as owner/ managers of private agricultural, commercial, or "industrial" enterprises. The working class, so to speak, is now composed of expatriates. The majority of the actively engaged local population now works in middle-class occupations.

The foundations for this change were established in the period before the *tufrah* and include modern education and the development of state institutions and modern private-sector enterprises. However, the *tufrah* included a major expansion in private-sector enterprises, the ownership of which is legally restricted to Saudi Arabians. Our observations also indicate a probable overemployment of local people in state institutions in the city. The employment of more personnel than is needed to meet the requirements of the work load in many state institutions is related to the huge amounts of revenue the state obtained during the *tufrah*. Such employment represents an attempt of the state to redistribute some of its revenue among the local population rather than simply the filling of needed positions with qualified local people.

Nonetheless, many qualified local people have replaced expatriates in all but a few positions in state institutions in ʿUnayzah. However, most of those now occupying such positions are young and, barring some unforeseen change, can be expected to remain in them until they retire fifteen to twenty years from now. The increasingly large and educated younger generation in ʿUnayzah is currently confronted by almost no employment opportunities in the types of jobs their parents and older brothers and sisters have obtained. This younger generation must, therefore, either accept unemployment in ʿUnayzah or migrate. Alternatively, and what is more likely, they will have to take lower paid and less secure employment in private-sector enterprises. By doing so, they will replace expatriates. It is unlikely that they will fall back into working-class jobs involving physical labor, at least in the foreseeable future.

Dependency on imported labor and on economic factors over which the local community has little control will remain. The city certainly could not withstand a siege today. It is unlikely to ever have such self-sufficiency again. However, a diminution in its dependency may be possible through a restructuring of the local work force to include employment in skilled technical work. Such restructuring will require changes in attitudes toward work that developed as part of the *tufrah*. It will also require the creation of enterprises different from those which came to predominate during the *tufrah*.

In this chapter, we discuss the patterns of modern salaried employment for both local men and women that came to predominate during the *tufrah* and indicate the new types of enterprises that were established. We also show how the prevalence of cash income has affected social relations, particularly in the case of women.

Modern Employment of Women

Work patterns for both men and women are, in fact, structured by gender segregation. However, such segregation did not in the past, and does not now, limit women's work to the confines of the home.

Both men and women have always participated actively in economic transactions in the *suq,* although their worlds have remained spatially and ritually apart. In the old *suq,* women tended to cluster in certain areas; however, their place of work was less segregated from the general activities of the *suq* than is the case at present in their temporary covered area. Women did not, and do not, sell only to other women. Women sellers deal exclusively with male wholesale dealers, and they deal equally with both male and female moneylenders. As buyers, women purchase from shops run by either men or women.

Although the two sexes come into contact with each other in the marketplace, their worlds remain separate. This is marked by the use of veils, which women strictly observe as sellers and as buyers. Other mechanisms for observing social distance are, however, more flexible. Women sellers will engage men in haggling over prices, argue with them over credit, and negotiate credit extensions with them. Frequent interaction between the two partners in the exchange reduces further the social distance between them. For example, women sellers even joke with some of the older creditors with whom they have worked for long periods. However, women strictly observe the use of the veil in the marketplace. It is relaxed only in the absence of men from the market area and during lulls in buying and selling when the presence of men is not expected.

Although older female informants asserted that they always covered their faces while working on the farm, further probing revealed the reality to be different. When a woman's work on the farm involved cooperation with men whom she was barred from marrying, she clearly did not have to observe the veil. Sometimes, however, the extended family may include men to whom a woman must veil, as, for example, a husband's brother or father. In such situations, the veil was used but in a more relaxed fashion. The women would, for example, only cover the lower part of the face and leave the eyes bare so as to be able to see better to work, or they would move the veil to one side, separating themselves from the view of the man but allowing them to see. Women say that, in these situations, one was among one's own family, but, when strangers appeared, "we veiled completely." When women worked as hired labor, even when in the presence of strangers, the activities they performed required that they relax the veil to see more easily. However, in these situations women worked separately from men though on the same farm. Thus, the ideal of male-female segregation and the actual practice of it did not hinder the ability of men and women to both work at the same site in the past.

Segregation of men and women has also not kept women from being employed in the modern economy. In contemporary Saudi Arabia, women are employed in various fields and work outside the home. However, for such work to be legally sanctioned, it must be done in a setting that does not result in contact with men. Modern employment for local women in 'Unayzah is mainly in the field of education as teachers. They are also employed in administrative positions and as nurses, typists, cashiers, bank tellers, journalists, and *farrashat*.

As shown in chapter 5, modern formal education for girls did not begin until 1960. This field has expanded rapidly. In 'Unayzah there are now 503 teachers and 101 administrative and other personnel employed in 37 schools with a total student body of 5,893 girls. All teachers and administrative and other personnel (376 women) in the primary schools are Saudi Arabians and come from 'Unayzah. In the intermediate schools, 110 out of 117 teachers are Saudi Arabians from 'Unayzah, while in the secondary schools 28 out of 64 are likewise from the city. Although statistics were not available on the nationalities of administrative and other personnel in the intermediate and secondary schools, observation showed that they are all Saudi Arabians. These schools also employ about 70 Saudi Arabian women as *farrashat* and about 150 Saudi Arabian men.

Several teachers' training schools were opened in 'Unayzah after 1960. These have now been replaced by a teachers' training college for women that requires two years and a general secondary school certificate. This college was opened in 1980, and by 1984 a total of 408 women had graduated and were qualified to teach in primary and intermediate schools. Since 1984, a total of 221 have graduated and qualified for primary schools. Intermediate and secondary school teaching now require a university degree. At present, the teachers' training college employs 29 teachers, of whom 5 are Saudi Arabians. There are also 7 administrators, all of whom are Saudi Arabian women.

The Inspectorate of Girls' Education was established in 1964 and was first staffed by expatriates. Since 1980, Saudi Arabian women have been employed there, and they now number 16 out of a total of 30 women who supervise all aspects of girls' education in the primary, intermediate, and secondary schools, as well as literacy programs for women.

Thus, public education for girls in 'Unayzah employs a total of at least 1,090 people. Of these, 876 are Saudi Arabian women, 150 are Saudi Arabian men, and 64 are other Arab women. In addition, numerous male employees work in the Directorate of Girls' Education and a large group of expatriate males clean the premises of the educational institutions.

In addition to the primary, intermediate, and secondary level public schools, 'Unayzah has 1 private school at the primary level with 35 girl students, 4 teachers (one of whom is Saudi Arabian), 3 administrators, and 1 worker. Furthermore, there are 5 kindergarten/nurseries, of which 3 are governmental and 2 are private. The governmental ones have a total of 118 children with 5 teachers, 3 administrators, and 4 workers, all of whom are Saudi Arabian women except for 1 male worker. The 2 private kindergarten/nurseries have 150 children, 8 Saudi Arabian women teachers, and 8 administrators and workers, all of whom are Saudi Arabian and include 2 men. In addition to employment in girls' education in 'Unayzah, approximately 375 women from the city teach in other schools in the region. These include about 300 who go to Buraydah.

As the above figures show, many women in 'Unayzah are employed in the field of education. They are well paid by local standards, and informants report that teachers with long experience may earn up to 13,000 riyals per month, which is a significant amount of money. It is also remarkable that given their late start (in 1960) so many local women are employed in the system, which now only requires the employment of a few other Arab women in the higher levels.

Aside from education, nursing is a field which has attracted women in 'Unayzah. In 1981, a nursing institute was established in the city, and in 1985 the institute graduated its first group of 48 nurses. About 43 of these were employed in hospitals, clinics, and health units attached to schools in 'Unayzah and other nearby towns and at the Social Affairs Center. In 1986, a second group of 16 students were graduated, and in the 1986–87 academic year there were 67 girls enrolled in the institute.

While employment in girls' education presents no difficulties to women because they are in a segregated situation, nursing presents a more difficult field for women's employment. This is in part due to the ideology of gender segregation, but it is also due to a more general view that sees nursing as equivalent to the semiskilled work of maids and, in addition, may cause the nurses to be exposed to ritual pollution in the process of patient care. Attempts have been made to make nursing an attractive field both for students and for later practice. Each student receives a scholarship which pays 1,800 riyals per month, considerably more than the 800 riyals given to students studying arts and the 1,000 riyals given to those in sciences. Graduates are appointed at grade five in the state employment scale and are paid a starting salary of 4,500 riyals per month plus fringe benefits. Special arrangements are provided for Saudi Arabian nurses. For example, they are exempted from night duty. Also, at their request, they have been placed in situations where their contact with men will be minimized and, if possible, limited to male professionals.

Many of the nurses are from low-income backgrounds in ʿUnayzah. For these, the salary has been a major attraction. However, there are others whose fathers or husbands are merchants who are educated and quite well off. Prominent old families do not generally consider nursing to be a preferred occupation for their women, but there are a few from such families who have become nurses or are in training.

Although we have noted that some women take up employment because of financial need, women who are employed in education come from all social and economic backgrounds. Some take up jobs that are difficult and do them not only for financial gain but also out of a sense of dedication and commitment, as the following case shows.

Fatmah was a very successful student throughout her school days. She entered one of the teachers' training institutes but had some problems during the last year and withdrew. A friend of hers in the same class convinced her to apply for a job as a teacher in primary school. A few months later, in 1974, they were appointed to teach in a village outside ʿUnayzah. Fatmah insisted on accepting the job and convinced her father to agree. She was the eldest of her siblings and wanted to help her father with her salary. In her words,

> the school was in a village not too far from ʿUnayzah, but the road was not paved. In those days, it took two hours to get to school. When it rained, it would take up to four hours, and sometimes the car would break down. We usually started out at four o'clock in the morning be-

cause the driver who took us there had to bus children to schools later on. It was really a tiring journey every day to the school. But I liked my work and so did the other Saudi Arabians who were with me. I often visited the villagers and convinced several of them to send their daughters to school. With the help of Allah, we were very successful. From that small village we managed to get twenty-nine girls enrolled. Some of them went on to intermediate school and to secondary school, and a few are now enrolled in the university.

We were not paid very much, at least not in comparison to what we make now. Our salary was 1,000 riyals plus 60 percent as compensation for working outside of ʿUnayzah. I remember when I collected my first pay. They gave us our salary for three months. That was a lot of money at that time. I gave it to my father, who had no idea of what to do with so much money. He said, "What shall we do with it? Buy a car?"

Recently the road was paved, and it takes no more than twenty minutes or half an hour to get to school. Our salaries have also greatly increased.

Many women still teach outside ʿUnayzah. Although transportation is now much easier since paved roads have connected ʿUnayzah with the villages and towns in the region, it is still a problem, as they have to rely on communal transport. Often they have to leave home by five o'clock in the morning regularly. Such commitment and hard work are reminiscent of the pioneering attempts of the first girls in ʿUnayzah to obtain higher and higher certificates and degrees. Many of them combined teaching with studying, and some of those who wanted a college education had to go to Riyadh for that. It was not possible for them to enroll regularly in the university and a system was devised whereby girls could take final examinations and receive university degrees. The girls who did that had to put in an extra effort, as they had to find a relative to take them and a relative to stay with in Riyadh. A number of women managed, however, to arrange trips to Riyadh and temporary residence with relatives there over a period of four years for the sole purpose of obtaining a university degree. Since the opening of the Imam Muhammad Ibn Saʿud University in Buraydah, they no longer have to go to Riyadh, but the same system of working and studying continues.

Many of the women employed come from well-to-do families where the salary is clearly not the main motivation for employment. In fact, some of the women who have been employed the longest in education come from such families. It is perhaps not surprising that young women who have completed their education in recent years should expect to follow it with a career. However, it is remarkable that the parental generation encourages such employment even when there is not an obvious need for the income the women receive. In one case, for example, the daughter of a very wealthy man who had earned his wealth through trade in Bahrain, Dammam, and Riyadh and who greatly increased his wealth through speculation in real estate in ʿUnayzah during the *tufrah* completed secondary school and became engaged quickly thereafter. Her fiancé, who was also a wealthy young man, lived in another city in Najd and planned to bring her there to live with him in his father's household. When the young man came to ask for her in marriage, her father agreed, but with one condition—that he allow her to work if she should so desire in the future.

Commenting on this case, another employed woman who comes from a rich family expressed her surprise that "big" families would engage in such negotiations prior to the marriage. However, another young woman, also employed and also of a wealthy background, recalled that upon drawing up her marriage contract the *maʾdhun* (a religious official who performs marriages and assists in writing the marriage contract) entered her occupation as schoolteacher and then asked her father and her husband-to-be whether any conditions should be specified in the marriage contract concerning her employment. Both men declined to specify any conditions, and the young woman continued her career as a schoolteacher. Other girls in wealthy families who are still students expressed plans for their careers and made choices in accordance with these plans and with employment in mind.

When asked why wealthy fathers support their daughters' employment, most women responded that it was out of a desire on the part of the father to please his daughters. The ideal of father–daughter love, they insist, is behind the encouragement given by the father. Also, they recognize that the additional income is not unwelcome, even if not a necessity. These two reasons rather than that of their fathers valuing work as such are the reasons they support as being most applicable. While recognizing the importance of parent–child love in general as an ideal in the culture, there are some things that children sometimes want which their parents refuse. If parents themselves did not accept employment, they would neither encourage their daughters to be employed nor would they prepare them for such employment through special education. The fact that women work is a combination of a desire on the part of the woman, an agreement by her parents, and a general acceptance of such behavior by the society at large.

The employment of women beyond the requirements of economic need must also be understood in the context of the relative increase in women's physical mobility in the society and the limited opportunities they have for extrahousehold activities. Many of these women have more leisure time because their families employ domestic help. At the same time, the values governing women's movements outside the house have been relaxed somewhat to allow even single women frequent visits to other members of the family, friends, and the *suq*. These, however, are the limits of a woman's social horizon. Work under these conditions must also be understood as an attempt to extend these horizons. In fact, when young women were asked why they worked, they often said "to widen my chest," meaning to widen their social contacts. In her place of work, a woman meets others, cultivates friends, picks up information about community events, and engages her time, which has been spared from household duties. In this process, she also gets paid. Work for these women is not so much a means to a livelihood as it is a way to build up wider social networks and to relate to the world outside the home.

Work as social expression is also an ideal that the less well-to-do groups express, but for them the income is a more critical reason for working. Women from such backgrounds recognize that the income itself is important and also point out that it sometimes exceeds that of the men in their family. That employed women make more money than men may be due to several factors. Sometimes a father is illiterate and has a low-paying job. However, as a result of education, the daughter has a job as a schoolteacher which pays very well. Also, a husband may have an educational level similar to that of his wife and have a similar job in state employment. If the wife is a schoolteacher, her salary will be higher than his (if they are at the same level), because teachers are given an extra percentage over and above the basic salary which is not given to other state employees.

Modern Employment of Men

The involvement of ʿUnayzah men in modern employment in the city is similar to that of women, although men would probably put it the other way around. Men's formal employment has a somewhat longer history, and they are employed in a larger number of institutions. But both men and women are primarily employed in state institutions that are now staffed primarily by members of the community, although they earlier depended on significant numbers of employees from other Arab countries. The same kinds of qualifications are required for both men and women in state employment, and both men and women receive equal pay for jobs at the same level in the civil service, assuming equal formal qualifications and years of service. Men resident in 'Unayzah, like the women, work in state employment not only in 'Unayzah but in Buraydah and other towns and villages of the region. Not only do men work in other places in the Qasim, but many have been and are employees in state service in cities throughout the country and quite a few have reached the highest levels, including those of minister and ambassador.

Within 'Unayzah itself, the largest sector which employs men from the community is education. The first government school for boys was established in 'Unayzah in 1936 with some 150 pupils. There are now 31 primary, intermediate, and secondary schools for boys, with a total of 5,700 pupils and 604 teachers. At the primary school level, all but 3 out of a total of 298 teachers are Saudi Arabian by nationality. At the intermediate level, there are 86 Saudi Arabian teachers and 21 other Arabs, while in the secondary school for boys there are 19 Saudi Arabians and 11 other Arabs. Aside from the teaching staff, there are a total of 230 administrators and other personnel, almost all of whom are from the community.

'Unayzah also has a secondary technical institute for boys which is one of eight such centers in the country and which serves all of the Qasim. This institute was started in 1974 with 70 students in the first class and now has a total of about 250 students in three grades. More than half the students are from 'Unayzah and enter this institute after completing intermediate school. Upon graduation, they receive a diploma and are then able to go on to a technical college or higher institute for training. They study theoretical issues related to technical knowledge and then have practice in workshops where they specialize in automotive mechanics, machine tools, and electrical systems. The institute has 37 Saudi Arabian teachers (most of whom are technical assistants), 23 Saudi Arabians in administration, and about 30 Egyptians and 7 Germans who are involved in teaching. While, according to one of the administrators, this type of technical training has been less popular in 'Unayzah than in some other parts of the country, it is now becoming more popular, and a major effort is being made to attract students to study here.

'Unayzah also has a college of the Qasim branch of King Sa'ud University where students study economics and business administration. At the time of fieldwork, this college had been operating for four years and had about four hundred male students and fifty female students, the girls all in the first year. While the college is open to students from all over the country, many are from 'Unayzah. Students who would formerly have had to go to other cities or abroad for university education are now able to stay at home and complete their university education in 'Unayzah or in Buraydah, where King Sa'ud University has established a college of agriculture and a teachers' training college and where there is also a branch of the Imam Muhammad Ibn Sa'ud University. All the professorial staff in the college in 'Unayzah is of other Arab origin, while the administration includes both Saudi Arabians and others. According to a leading administrator in the college, it is difficult to recruit university teachers because most of the qualified Saudi Arabians prefer to teach in a university in one of the larger cities. The college has to rely primarily on expatriate Arabs, mainly from Egypt.

Aside from education, 'Unayzah men are employed in all the offices maintained by national ministries in the city. Examples are the three offices related to the agricultural sector described earlier. With the exception of the police and security forces, all the state institutions formerly relied on significant numbers of employees from other Arab countries. At present, however, all state institutions in 'Unayzah, with the major exception of those related to health care, are staffed by Saudi Arabian employees, almost all of whom are from 'Unayzah.

New Enterprises

Between 1976 and 1981, the number of commercial enterprises increased by 753 to a total of 1,308. "Industrial" establishments increased by 89 to a total of 189. In addition, most farms became organized as agricultural enterprises. Almost all the new enterprises developed during the *tufrah* employ expatriates, while the owners work as managers.

Most of the new enterprises have been developed by men; however, a few have been developed by women. Aside from a few new shops in the *suq,* an occupation that is attractive to some women is tailoring and embroidery. This is a traditional line of work that women formerly did at home. In 1982, an institute was opened to train women in design and tailoring. This institute has several Egyptian trainers and six Saudi Arabian assistant trainers, all of whom are women. At the time of fieldwork, thirteen women were enrolled and a total of sixty-four had graduated. While in training, which is for a period of two years, each trainee receives a stipend of 400 riyals per month. Many of the fathers of the trainees are small-scale illiterate merchants; some of them are teachers or other state employees; and occasionally one is a mechanic or large-scale merchant.

Upon graduation from the institute, many of the women do not go on to work in this activity or even apply their knowledge to sewing at home for their families. However, the state encourages graduates of the institute to establish independent enterprises by extending loans of up to 200,000 riyals from the Saʿudi Credit Bank. These loans require collateral, and women see this as the main barrier to their participation in this program. Furthermore, women say that all these projects require full cooperation with male relatives, which may not be forthcoming. Although few have attempted to set up a tailoring enterprise, the following case is an example of one attempt. When the attempt proved unsuccessful, the enterprise was changed and became a hairdressing salon.

Umm Saʿd is a married woman over thirty years of age. She has several children, has a primary school certificate, and is a graduate of the tailoring institute. She said,

> The idea to set up a workshop came from my uncle, who is a schoolteacher. He suggested that we become partners in the enterprise. He actually put in most of the work. He borrowed 60,000 riyals from a friend. With that we bought equipment—ten machines plus some other things. We rented a flat to house the project for 12,000 riyals per year. My uncle went to India to get dressmakers. He returned with four of them, each receiving a salary of 700 riyals per month. We gave them one room in the flat to sleep in, and the rest of the flat was for the workshop. Something went wrong in the recruitment, because when they arrived, we discovered that they did not know how to cut patterns. I was too busy to check in regularly. So we hired a Saudi Arabian woman to supervise them and gave her 1,000 riyals per month.
>
> We were having lots of difficulties with the Indians. Another uncle of mine has a tailoring shop in which he employs several [male] Indian

tailors. He helped us out by sending one of them in the evenings to do some work for us. But our problems did not go away. The shop was not getting an income. My uncle suggested that we give the employees a percentage of the price of the pieces that were sold. The Saudi Arabian did not agree and left us. We sent back three of the Indians and hired a new Saudi Arabian supervisor, a young unmarried woman who had more time to work and who agreed to our terms of payment. She had very good ideas for a hairdressing shop, which became an extension of the workshop. She became interested in establishing a partnership with my uncle in that enterprise and the Indian who remained helped them with that. In fact, that second enterprise brought in enough income to cover its capital investment.

We have decided to improve that whole business. We rented a new flat for 8,000 riyals and have divided it between dressmaking and hairdressing. My uncle will go to the Philippines to bring some workers. We can't really hire Saudi Arabians because they will ask for much more, and they may not even come in regularly. The problem for us now is to get a loan from the Credit Bank. When we went to the bank, we found that all our papers are in order, but they want collateral. How can we get collateral? If we had collateral, we would not need a loan. We got into this venture hoping to get the loan. We have borrowed with that in mind. Now we have spent too much on the project, and it is unlikely that we will get the loan.

Relatively more successful have been the self-employed women who have set up tailoring enterprises in their own homes. One main problem for them, however, is to find a market for their production. There is a lot of competition from male tailors who are employed by Saudi Arabian enterprises owned by men. Many of these exist, and they are relatively cheap. Graduates of the institute even take things to the men's shops for them to sew instead of doing the work themselves.

Aside from those who are in state employment, most local men in ʿUnayzah are best described as self-employed as the owner/managers of enterprises. Many of these may also be state employees as well or men who have taken early retirement from state service and receive a pension. While there are a few branch offices of large companies whose headquarters are elsewhere, most establishments are small. Some of these establishments are "industrial" and include such things as workshops for making jewelry, metal doors, wood products, and aluminum window frames. 'Unayzah has a print shop, a number of car repair shops, and numerous butcheries, grocery stores, and bakeries. There are about half a dozen pharmacies and a number of shops for developing film. Several restaurants and two hotels do business.

All of these are owned and most are managed by men from the community, but the customer will almost always be served in them by an expatriate male. In 'Unayzah, the man who changes the oil of one's car is most likely a Yemeni, while the one who fills it with gasoline will be from Hadramawt. If one goes to buy some milk (produced in Saudi Arabia) from a grocery store, one will be waited on by a Pakistani or some other Asian. Needing to have clothes made, one will have to deal with a Pakistani or Yemeni tailor.

Almost none of the small private establishments hire other Saudi Arabians. One of the main reasons is that expatriates can be hired very cheaply compared to what Saudi Arabians demand. Also, according to numerous owners, the better qualified Saudi Arabians have all obtained state employment or own their own enterprises. Any Saudi Arabian who would work as an employee in a small enterprise would, they say, probably be third rate and not work regularly.

The presence of such large numbers of expatriates in the work force is thus related to a large degree to economic considerations. If more people from 'Unayzah do not work in agriculture, in skilled technical jobs, or in service occupations in the private sector, it is because they have been able to obtain high-paying jobs in state employment. The older members of the community say they do not now engage themselves in agricultural work, for example, because they have become too old to work the long hard hours that agriculture requires. The young say that they have gone to school and do not want to do work on farms because there are easier and better-paying jobs in state offices. In these offices, air conditioning and a comfortable environment make work more enjoyable. The employees usually have little work to do and the work hours are not long. They are thus able to drink tea and cultivate friendship networks that might be activated in other occupations—like business.

While agriculture does not carry any traditional social stigma against it and now only has the stigma of hard work, other occupations can be associated with traditional stigmas. For example, occupations like butchery, metal working, and leather processing were not favored in the past and were done by people of *khadiri* status. This situation has been modified now but mainly for people who own and manage their own shops. For example, a family of traditional metal workers now has only two old men who continue this work, while all their children have become educated and obtained employment in government offices.

A man of tribal status who is a merchant, on the other hand, has established a workshop to do metal working, which in the past was considered highly improper for such a person. Another has opened a butcher shop. However, neither of these two men do any of the work but employ expatriate men. These cases are indicative of a trend for people to want to be their own bosses, at least in the small-scale private sector. A man may be a mechanic, but if so he will be the owner or a partner in the shop. He will not recruit Saudi Arabians because foreign labor is cheaper and because, as indicated earlier, people in ʿUnayzah prefer to be the owner rather than the worker and, in fact, have been able to do this because they can generate income from other employment and from subsidized loans. That this is so is due to the rapid influx of cash and the rapid growth of the state sector (as shown in education), which have transformed the local labor force and its work ethics.

Social Effect of Cash Income

The prevalence of cash income is very different from the past when labor was, to a large degree, organized by the domestic unit and members—male and female, young and old—worked without cash remuneration. There was, of course, wage labor for both males and females in the earlier period, but this was not a predominant mode. A high degree of market exchange also existed and money was an important medium of exchange. But there was also barter, and while the value of commodities was usually quoted in terms of money, they were often exchanged without the actual use of money. For example, the cost of a door built by a carpenter would be quoted in terms of money. The agricultural produce of a farmer who wished to buy the door was also quoted in terms of money. However, instead of giving the carpenter money for the door, the farmer would give him an amount of, say, dates equivalent to the money value of the door. Members of the carpenter's domestic unit, some or all of whom would have helped in the production of the door, all participated in the consumption of the dates. In this system, there was no need for placing a monetary value on the labor of individuals. They all worked together to produce a product and, as members of a social unit, they shared in the results of that production, which, for most, ultimately meant food. In the transition to the contemporary period, men increasingly received money for their labor, and, at present, almost all work is remunerated with money. It is the disposal of money earned as a result of work outside the domestic unit that has mainly caused tensions and conflicts within the domestic unit rather than an ethic that says that women should not work outside the home, although some do hold to such an ethic.

What women do with the money they receive from their employment constitutes an area of great variety within the community. There are no set patterns or agreed-upon acceptable uses for such income. Because such income is relatively recent, women and men are experimenting with various alternatives in the use of the money. The description that follows reflects this variety and attempts to place each alternative within a wider societal context.

Commenting on the rising income of employed women, a woman from a rich family who has been a schoolteacher for many years said, "I suspect that in the future women will be richer than men in ʿUnayzah. We do not want this, but that is what will happen because women save their income and men spend their's [on household expenses and maintaining the family]." This woman is divorced and lives with her widowed mother and is not expected to contribute to the financial upkeep of her household, as the mother is heir to a large fortune. On the other hand, another woman from a less well-to-do family implicitly acknowledged the contribution that employed women make to the household when she said, "In that family, four women are employed in schools. Their combined income contributes a lot to the standard of living enjoyed by the whole family."

Throughout the society in ʿUnayzah, the ideal is that men are the providers for the family. In their role as head of household, men are expected to provide food, shelter, clothing, schooling, health care, and some entertainment for all the family members. Their ability to do this depends on the means available to them. In the old society, however, it was usual that women made significant contributions through work in agriculture, crafts, and the market, aside from their housework. Ideally and also in Islam, a woman is entitled to her own property and income, and, at the same time, she is entitled to maintenance and support from her father or, if married, from her husband.

Increasingly, women have obtained a significant amount of income which they themselves directly control without having to depend on a male intermediary. All women recognize the rights of parents to a claim on their income. This is reflected in the symbolic gesture employed women make of turning their first income over to the father or buying gifts for the family. Among the well-to-do, the father is expected to save the income of his unmarried daughters for their later use. Some of the daughters of such families, however, deduct part of their income for their immediate use and then turn the remainder over to their fathers for safekeeping. Among the less well-to-do, women usually give all their income to the father to spend on the family as a whole. There are cases where unmarried daughters have contributed to the down payments for new houses and to the furnishing of new homes. There is also a case in which a woman paid off all the debts that her father had incurred in days past when income was limited for almost all. Women have no reservations about such use of their money due to the strong family ties that bind them to their parents and that are stronger than marriage ties. The same strength of ties binds the son to his family and he, too, is expected to contribute to his parents.

When an employed woman is married, the disposal of her income shows more variation than is the case between women and their parents. Conjugal relationships are undergoing changes, and while there is relative consensus concerning the disposal of a daughter's salary in her father's household, the disposal of a wife's salary shows more variety. Observations show that among younger couples there is now less role segregation than in the past and there are more joint activities involving husband and wife. Furthermore, the expectations of each marriage partner have been somewhat modified. No longer does a wife who is employed expect that her husband be the sole provider of the household. How much she will contribute, however, varies. This is an area of much ambiguity. Different expectations by husband and wife sometimes lead to confrontations and possibly even divorce. Both men and women discuss these issues, and they are written about in newspapers. This has reached such proportions that in drawing up a marriage contract for a woman who is employed, the *ma'dhun* often asks the parties to the contract to specify in the marriage contract the conditions related to such work.

These considerations must be understood also in the context of marital ties, which are perceived by women to be brittle. Divorce is not infrequent, and marriage to more than one wife occurs. Both of these lead some women to acknowledge the insecurity of their status as wives. Consequently, they tend to view their salary as a potential security against adverse changes in the future. In spite of this, a man can abuse this situation and demand that the wife turn over all her salary to him. The variations in the disposal of women's salaries are also influenced by the relative economic status of the family.

In some families, the wife spends a part of her salary on her own clothes, possibly on jewelry, and perhaps on her children and saves the remainder. In other families, a woman may spend on herself and her children and contribute to general household expenses and, at the same time, save something. In poorer families, she may seldom be able to save anything, as her income is required by the household. Although women work, to do so is conditional upon the agreement of their husbands, and some men may use this as a way to control the disposal of their salaries. The variations in the way in which their salaries are disposed of are shown in the following cases.

Hamdah is a schoolteacher who was employed before her marriage. Her father was keen for her to work because she helped him with her salary. This practice continued even after her marriage, but her husband decided that he did not want her to work. A period of fights and disagreements followed. Other schoolteachers reported that when they passed by in the morning to pick her up, her husband would make a scene and insist that no employed woman lived in his house. Usually Hamdah showed up at the school sometime later. She would normally wait for her husband to leave and then have her father pick her up and take her to work. Her furious husband often threatened to take a second wife, but he could not do so since his marriage contract stipulated that a divorce would automatically follow his marriage to a second wife. He loved his wife and did not want to divorce her. Thus a compromise had to be found. Women reported that sometime later things seemed to have settled down between Hamdah and her husband. She now comes regularly to the school without problems.

Commenting on this case, all women, old and young, agreed that it was wrong of the father to take the position of insisting on her working against her husband's wishes. A woman's employment, they agreed, is a matter that must be worked out by agreement between husband and wife. They all agreed that a woman has a right to work and that, if a husband did not agree to this, he should indicate it prior to marriage. Women who know Hamdah say that she probably gives less money to her father now and uses it for expenses in her husband's household. This case is unusual, and while it indicates that theoretically a woman's employment is conditional upon consent of husband or father, this is usually not an issue and thus does not lead to conflict.

Some men make no effort to control their employed wife's income. This is especially the case among the more well-to-do, as is shown in the case of 'Asma'h, who comes from a prominent and wealthy family. She is married to an established and wealthy merchant. She has a university degree and is a high-ranking administrator in a school. She lives with her husband in his father's household, and her sister-in-law is also employed as a schoolteacher. She has three children. 'Asma'h makes a handsome salary because she has been working for a long time and has a university degree. She said, "My husband is a generous man. We have everything we need. He would give me more if I asked. But since I have so much money from my salary, I am embarrassed to ask for money to spend on myself, for my clothes. I usually take from my salary for that. Sometimes, I may buy things for the children, but I have saved all the rest."

While this is an individual case, it is not unusual for women of similar backgrounds and economic status. The following case is more typical for people in middle-income ranges. Bathah is a teacher in primary school. She was working before she was married. She married a man who had been previously married and who has children by his first wife. She lives with him and their four children. Her husband works as an employee in a government office. As a schoolteacher, she makes more money than he does. Describing the family budget, she said,

When I first married my husband, I used to give him all my salary every month. Later on, I changed. Now I keep my salary, but I spend a great deal on the family. For example, whenever I go shopping and buy things for myself and for the children, the expenses come out of my salary. I have a maid, and I pay her salary. Some things we share together. For example, we split the telephone bill, the electricity bill, and the monthly payments on the house. I also pay half the monthly payments for some of our furniture. My husband, however, does the household shopping weekly, for vegetables, meat, etc., and he pays for that. When we buy provisions to last a long time, the bill could run up

to several thousand riyals. We usually split that between us. Whatever
is left of my salary is mine, and I do with it as I please.

The principle here can be generalized to many in the community, although people have different formulas for how they split the payment
of expenses.

While the above cases suggest that there is some attempt at equity
in contributions to the family budget, this is not always true, as the
following case shows. Umm Muhammad is about fifty-four years old
and has been employed as a *farrasha* in schools for fifteen to twenty
years. She now makes a monthly salary of 3,193 riyals. Her husband
has a farm and a few animals and works as a doorkeeper in a school.
He makes a salary of 3,210 riyals. For as far back as she can remember,
he has always neglected his household duties. A stingy man, he never
wanted to support his family, "although he is from a *qabili* family."
She tolerated this situation for many years because she had children,
two sons and a daughter. She worked to support them. The girl
has recently married and moved out. One of the boys lives outside
ʿUnayzah. Her second son works in the Ministry of Telecommuni-
cations and makes a monthly salary of 5,000 riyals. He married a
schoolteacher who was employed for some time and who makes a salary of 6,500 riyals. They all live in a new house built with a loan from
the bank. Umm Muhammad's husband provided the land, and the
house is registered in his name. She has an Egyptian maid working
for her who receives 500 riyals a month. She specifically employed
her to relieve her daughter, who was living at home, from household
duties. After the daughter married and left, the maid continued. Describing the expenses in that household, Umm Muhammad said,

> My husband pays the monthly payments on the house. That is all he
> does for us. In fact, he lives in an independent apartment in the house
> and expects to be served alone. My son sometimes buys food for the
> family and on occasion he pays the electricity bill. He buys his chil-
> dren's clothes but pays very little else. His wife buys her own clothes
> and she buys lots of them. She also buys clothes for her children. The
> rest of the money she gives to her father to save for her. She has a sister
> who is also a schoolteacher and the father has used the savings of the
> two girls to buy a house for them as an investment which they now
> want to remodel. My daughter-in-law has about 300,000 riyals in safe-

keeping with her father. I buy the regular staples—even the sugar and the meat and the vegetables. If I invite my daughter and her husband to eat with us, then I pay for all the extras. Just today I gave my husband my whole salary for last month to go and buy food for the house. But he took the money and paid the electricity bill for two months.

As can be seen from the above discussion, some women are able to save part of their salaries, which can add up to significant amounts. Some of this money is invested in gold jewelry, a traditional form of savings among women. The gold shops in the *suq* are very busy with local women actively buying gold. Some have also invested in land, in stocks, or in joint ventures with husbands or male kin, while others sometimes lend money to their husbands for business ventures.

An example of a woman investing in land and giving loans to her husband is shown in the case of 'Asma'h referred to above. She loaned her husband 100,000 riyals and took a receipt from him. Explaining her behavior, she said,

> I took a receipt from my husband because he has a partner in the business. His partner is his brother, and I trust them both. But it was easy for me to obtain a receipt because he has a partner. Perhaps if he did not have one, it would have been more difficult for him, but then I probably would not have wanted a receipt anyway.
>
> When there was an auction on land nearby, I asked my father-in-law to bid on a piece of land for me. That is registered in my name.

Buying land is not limited to the modern employed woman, as was shown in the case of a woman seller in the *suq* who bought land. Many women transform their savings into shares in various Saudi Arabian companies. An illustration is the case of Sabhah, who has been employed as a teacher for many years and who makes a substantial salary. She lived in an extended family, but for the past two years has been living neolocally. She also has a Filipino maid. She said that her husband pays for all the household expenses and that she just buys things for herself. Consequently, she has a lot of savings. She said, "Now I have shares. One day my friends and I in the school read about a company in the newspaper. We all decided that it was a good idea to buy shares in that company. So, when I went home, I asked my husband for his opinion. He advised against it. However, I decided to go ahead and asked him to buy some shares for me. I still don't know which of us was right. It's much too early to tell."

While this case indicates that a woman may sometimes act contrary to her husband's advice, it is not unusual for women to discuss their plans for investment with their kinsmen. Some delegate this authority entirely to their kinsmen, while others take a more active interest and usually act in accordance with the advice of kinsmen. However, a woman's friends provide her with more information on investment possibilities through their contact with other parts of the community.

Sometimes women enter into joint ventures with their husbands or kinsmen. However, very few keep legal records of these transactions. Luluwah is the headmistress of a school and has been working in the field of education for many years in another city and in ʿUnayzah. She is married to a wealthy official and has four children. They live in a very large new house which was not built with a loan from the Real Estate Development Fund. She says that all her salary goes to the house. She had an investment with her brother and her husband. Each of them contributed 10,000 riyals to start a shop, but no papers were drawn up and nothing official was recorded. She was supposed to look after the enterprise and to supervise it, but she was much too busy with her duties at home and at school. The shop lost substantially, and they decided to liquidate it. Her brother and her husband said that she should see to the liquidation of it and take all the money that remained.

Despite a woman's modern education, business ventures with kinsmen are based more on confidence than a legal basis. Even in the past, her relationships with her brothers in settling their common estate was always based on verbal agreements and "confidence." Men also rely on verbal agreements in business deals with kinsmen, but they, like some women, are beginning to formalize such deals. A case is that of Tarfah, who was a schoolteacher for many years before her marriage. When she married, she moved to ʿUnayzah. She had a lot of savings from her maiden days. Her husband was married to another wife who has children, but he only visits the first wife and lives with Tarfah. From her savings, she took 200,000 riyals as partial down payment in buying the house in which they now live. She was concerned, however, that her husband has another wife and children and, therefore, Tarfah was eager to establish her own rights. She discussed the matter with her husband, and he refused to register the house in both their names. He, however, had another solution. He brought in a number of witnesses, and, in their presence, drew up a paper saying that she is entitled to half the house.

Tarfah elaborated that as far as she could tell no man in ʿUnayzah would agree to register a house jointly in his name and that of his wife. She was not even sure that the paper she had has a legal basis. But, she said, "It's better than nothing, and it will be proof to people with honor who fear Allah."

CHAPTER 11

Changing Patterns of Social Life

Since the beginning of the *tufrah,* change in ʿUnayzah has included a new and expanded agriculture, a major increase in salaried employment among the local people, and the influx of expatriate laborers. Change has also included the building of a new town, mainly on land that was in the desert or covered with ʾathal trees outside the boundaries of the old city.

Most of the new town is composed of housing that was built with loans from the Real Estate Development Fund, a national program that provides loans of up to 300,000 riyals to individuals who own the land on which the house will be built, can show that they have the intention of building a house (e.g., an architectural plan), and can provide collateral. The loan is to be paid back in yearly installments over a period of several years. According to data obtained from the offices of the fund, a total of 5,400 loans was granted in ʿUnayzah between 1973 and 1986. Almost all loans have been granted to men as heads of household, although 311 have been given to women, who, in order to qualify, must be either divorced or widowed.

The building of the new town contributed greatly to the *tufrah* in ʿUnayzah. Some individuals who obtained ownership of large tracts of land divided it for real estate development and made fortunes as the price of land skyrocketed. This development fueled land speculation, and it was not uncommon for a piece of land to pass from owner to owner as people bought and sold land in the hopes of making large profits. The city was flooded by a large group of construction workers, and numerous small establishments related to the construction and furnishing of houses sprang up. People say that the costs of materials and of contractors' fees went up dramatically during the period of the building of the new areas. There were also large projects for the building of new roads and streets and the installation of sewerage, water, electrical, and telephone networks.

By the time of fieldwork, the building period was over, and only a few people were still in the process of building new houses. People were well established in comfortable new homes with all the modern conveniences and were developing new patterns of social interaction that are associated with both the new physical setting in which they live and the new employment patterns they have adopted.

In this chapter, we describe and analyze changes manifested in some major aspects of social life within the family, in neighborhoods, and in visiting patterns. As will be shown, social life neither was nor is limited to primary ties to family and kin. Neighborhood ties have been extremely important, and ties based on occupation, employment, and peer groups also manifest themselves.

Neighborhoods and Changing Residence Patterns

The neighborhood in the old town was comprised of both rich and poor families. People say that a great deal of solidarity existed among neighbors, who did not necessarily correspond with their kindred. Within each neighborhood, there were common areas where people interacted with each other. Small alleyways were the scenes of socializing, and children played in the narrow streets. The mosque was a major center for men in the neighborhood, and the imam of the mosque knew all of its people well. Wealthy people donated generous contributions to the upkeep and maintenance of the mosque or mosques in the neighborhood. Also, sometimes collective actions were taken to improve conditions in the neighborhood. For example, before the establishment of the electrical company, people in various neighborhoods pooled their resources to buy a generator and provided electricity for a few hours each night to the houses of all, whether or not they had made contributions.

Within these neighborhoods, the traditional residence pattern was patrilocal; that is, in the household of the husband's father. Because of demographic features, particularly male labor migration, the composition of many households in the past often included an old man, his wife, and their sons' wives and children. The extended family household continues to be an ideal that many cherish and some continue to follow. Increasingly, however, neolocal residence and the nuclear family are becoming a reality in ʿUnayzah. This new phenomenon has occurred within the past ten to fifteen years, and no clear patterns have yet emerged. Furthermore, no consensus exists within the community on the preferred alternatives.

As in other areas of change, postmarital residence reflects the lack of consensus. On the ideological level, the community appears to be divided between those who support the son's right to an autonomous and independent household and those who interpret this practice as a betrayal of family loyalty and not fulfilling parental obligations. This issue engages the attention of men and women alike, who in social gatherings discuss the pros and cons of neolocal residence. It is discussed in the mass media and emotionally debated by people.

For example, an educated and leading figure in the community who is about fifty years old commented that he had recently been involved in a conflict between a son and a father in his family because the son wanted to live in a new residence with his new wife. He also spoke of a conflict between himself and his wife about where their son should live when he gets married.

> Last night there was a conflict between a man and his son who are both members of my family. The son will get married in the spring and wants to live in a new house with his bride. His father does not want to allow him to do this. I told the father that it is the right of the son to live where he wishes and that the father must let him go.
>
> Also, my wife, who is not very educated, wants our son to live with her when he gets married. But this is not right. We both love our son, but neither the father nor the mother has the right to force him to live with them. If he wishes to establish his own independent household, he should do so. And it is better for him in the long run.

In other people's minds, the issue is not so clearly resolved, as the following debate indicates. A woman about sixty years of age has one son who was married and lived with her and his father in an extended family. His father had borrowed to provide the dower and the expenses for his marriage. Recently, the son and his wife moved out. His mother was very upset and complained to one of her friends, saying, "He is an ungrateful son. After all that we have done for him, he deserts us in this manner." A younger friend replied, saying, "No, you told him that you did not mind if he lived elsewhere. He left you on good terms. That is why he still comes to visit you. You probably interfered too much in their lives when they were living with you."

The statement of the friend reflects a growing recognition of the right of a young couple to be autonomous. However, such a right is not recognized by everybody. Therefore, some young couples resort to discrete strategies that will lead to the establishment of independent households. For example, in less well-to-do families, it is expected that sons and daughters-in-law contribute, if needed, to the household budget. Young couples sometimes manipulate their contributions or even withhold them in order to polarize the situation within the family, thus leading to a confrontation and the consequent breakup of the extended family. This is a slow process, however, and is not an immediate declaration.

Among the more affluent families, conflicts between children are sometimes used as a rationalization for establishing a nuclear family household. However, conflict has not been great, partly because it has happened during the period in which people, including the parental generation, were constructing new houses and because the move to a nuclear family has often been preceded by a few years of residence in an extended family.

In the new nuclear family, women have realized a measure of autonomy from their mothers-in-law and men have achieved some independence from their fathers. This status has been achieved at the cost of a great deal of nostalgia for the old extended family. More concretely, it has also meant the loss of the daily assistance and support that were provided by the extended family. The most blatant example of this is in the socialization and care of preschool children whose parents are both employed. Although the young working mother often takes her children to her mother's house, this practice is seen as a burdensome shuttling back and forth that is tiresome to the mother and to the children and is, at best, a temporary solution.

Furthermore, the older generation of grandparents has been to a large degree isolated from friends, neighbors, and age-groups, due both to the new houses which are located far away from old friends and old neighbors and by the increasing incidence of the nuclear family. The old people are often lonely, as expressed by an old woman who said, "When I close my door in the morning when the children leave [to go to school], it is not opened until they come back." Some of the old men complain bitterly about their isolation and say they want a club where they can all meet. They suggest that buses should come and pick them up every morning, "just like they do for children going to kindergarten."

Some people feel that, because of the new living situation, it is essential that children be put into kindergartens as soon as possible. They say that in the past children grew up surrounded by many other children, both within their extended family and in the neighborhood as they played in the streets. In the nuclear families in new houses, the children are isolated from other children. For some, the kindergarten is therefore seen as a kind of replacement for the older scene in which both family and neighborhood were the main socializing elements. But some also see the kindergarten as a symptom of more basic changes in society. As one man, the headmaster of a school who is about forty-five years of age, reflected,

> a problem has developed in the way in which basic values are passed on to the younger generation. What happens now is that, in the morning, the child gets up and goes to the kindergarten. The father goes to his work and the mother to hers, while the foreign maid stays at home. Child, father, and mother come back for lunch, which is followed by naps. Then the father leaves to go to another job or to go visiting and does not come back until late at night. The mother, it is true, takes care of her children in the afternoon, but the father has little contact with them. What is happening is that outside institutions are doing the socializing of children rather than the family. As a result, the younger generation does not know its origins, does not know its own family, and does not respect family members. These have been basic values of this society for centuries. For the first time in the history of Arab society, we have a major generation gap between those who were brought up in the family and the neighborhood and those who have been socialized in kindergartens, schools, sports clubs, and special religious groups.

His is an extreme opinion in the view of the community. Nevertheless, he implies that the old society no longer reproduces itself. This view is corroborated by the role that the new school system plays in disseminating ideological and cultural knowledge, as well as in teaching scientific knowledge of the world. The grandparental generation now plays a much smaller role in the socialization of its grandchildren than in the past. Dissemination of cultural knowledge by means of storytelling and the recounting of past events and family episodes and by providing models of behavior for the children are now done much less by the old. Their interaction with the younger generation, although not eliminated, is greatly reduced in the nuclear family situation. The new messages and the new life-styles, modified values, and changing norms acquired from the school, parents, peer group, and media all serve to make grandparents respected but irrelevant or, at best, marginal to grandchildren's present lives.

For families in ʿUnayzah, the emergent pattern of neolocal residence is, as noted earlier, associated with a measure of autonomy for men and women alike. A man can raise his children and run his household independent of the direct supervision of his father and mother. The physical separation permits the modification of norms and of values without direct confrontation between the two generations. As the head of a household, a man gains in status in the community at large. He has his own *majlis,* where he receives his guests without having to relinquish it to his father and his father's guests, as is the case in an extended household. At the same time, respect for the parental generation continues to be a value inculcated in the young and actually extended to the old. Yet he becomes the source of authority for his own immediate family, although he may defer to his father in "major" decisions like marriage of his children, change of domicile, or whether to send a son abroad for education.

For the young wife, neolocal residence has translated into independence from the supervision of her mother-in-law, who, in the past, closely monitored her actions and controlled her life. Even in the presence of her husband, a woman usually obtained permission from his mother to go out or to engage in certain activities. It was the husband's mother who controlled the budgets, dispensed the provisions for the day, and allocated household tasks among the women in the family. Remembering those old days, a woman said, "In the past, a wife of a son was like a servant. She was very oppressed. Everyone in the family oppressed her." In dramatizing this, women often relate stories of when their husbands migrated to work in other places and left them behind in the household of the husband's father for several months if not years. During such a period, they worked in the husband's father's household under the supervision of his mother. All of this is a thing of the past.

Expectations of marriage have now changed among young people. A man does not expect that his mother will interfere between him and his wife. A woman, on the other hand, does not expect that her mother-in-law will interfere in the running of her own household or in the socialization of her children. Her own physical mobility is now negotiated with her husband and not his mother.

A young, educated woman today expects more out of married life. She expects to be engaged in common activities with her husband and children, and she often participates in decisions regarding the schooling of the children, the furnishing of their house, and travel plans of her nuclear family. These conditions are enhanced when she is employed and contributes to the family budget in some form or another.

Many young women today no longer blindly accept their husbands' decisions but question, discuss, and negotiate with them. It is perhaps in the field of physical mobility where most of this negotiation is now taking place. Also, a woman no longer tolerates a husband leaving on his own for long periods of residence away from the community, although she does not question his right to travel on his own. As a result of these changes, the family that can afford it now is likely to travel together in the summer, a favorite place being Abha in the mountainous area of southwestern Saudi Arabia. This is not due to individuals' decisions alone but also to economic conditions that now make it possible for families to travel together on vacations and feasible for a man to take his family with him to a new town if he moves there to work.

Women's Socializing

In the old ʿUnayzah, women from *fallalih* families moved back and forth from their houses to the farms. Likewise, the women who sold in the *suq* and others who carried water from sweet wells to houses were obviously not secluded in their households. As shown in chapter 1, there was also the *hasu,* an area around a well in a house where poorer women from the neighborhood gathered for socializing and other activities. The women of wealthier merchant families, however, were more restricted to their homes. The daughters of such families almost never left the house from the time of puberty until after they had been married and had children. When they went out, they left home before the *suq* opened in the early morning and did not return until after it closed at night in order to avoid contact with men. They were always accompanied by another woman. So restricted was the movement of an unmarried girl in the past that women of today are fond of reminding us that a girl did not even have an ʿ*abayah,* the cloak required for movement outside the house, because she had no need of it. If she did have to go out, she wore that of her mother. After having children, the women of such families became much more mobile and went to the *suq* wearing dark clothes under the *ʿabayah* so as not to attract the attention of men. They sometimes visited relatives and almost daily saw their neighbors.

The daily routine of women from merchant families in the old ʿUnayzah of about forty years ago was recalled by Umm Turki, who is over sixty.

I used to wake up very early in the morning, prepare coffee and tea, and drink it with my husband and his mother. Afterward, my husband would go out to his shop and I would clean the house. We had two meals only in those days. The first one needed no preparation because it consisted of dates and milk. We were usually free by mid-morning to go visit our neighbors. Because I did not want to leave my mother-in-law alone, my neighbors usually came to visit me in the morning. These were usually very brief visits.

We drank coffee together and talked about our children. One of my friends was especially clever in curing, and whenever one of my children was sick she would tell me what to do and it worked. We would sit around preparing various things for the main meal and chat about the events of the previous day and what happened to people we knew. Sometimes Umm Khalid would come with a bundle on her head. She is the one who brought cloth and other things to the houses of women who did not go to the *suq*. If we wanted something, we would buy it from her. She would also tell us about the women she had visited, and some of what she told us was new to us because we did not go to all the places she went to, and so it was nice to chat with her. We usually bought from her because, after all, when she entered your house you would be embarrassed not to buy. But things did not cost too much in those days. Whenever I had extra wheat or dates, I also gave her some.

I was back home before my husband returned home at noon for the first meal. He would then return to his shop, and I would begin to prepare for the main meal. We did not have to grind our own wheat, as this was done by others for us. I prepared everything else for the meal. We usually had our main meal just before sunset, and after that we had time to visit friends again. Those of us who had work to do brought the work with us, and we helped each other. We worked and chatted and usually returned not too long after the last prayer. If the men were away, we would stay longer, and some of the older ones who did not have husbands or whose husbands were away might even spend the night there. We usually used this time for preparing the next day's meal and did some sewing. In the summer, we had much more work to do. The days were long, and we had to process the dates, and many were busy with the wheat. We helped each other a lot in those days. If my husband had guests [for the main meal], my neighbors would come and help me prepare the food, and I would also give them some. Those of us in the neighborhood who visited each other were not too many, but we were really like sisters.

In the old ʿUnayzah, neighborhoods were close-knit units, and the homes of friends and relatives were usually within walking distance. As a result, it was easy for women to visit each other. The new ʿUnayzah is spread out over a large area, and most visiting requires transportation. Unmarried daughters today must get permission from either their father or mother to leave the house. When they go out, it is usually to visit friends or relatives or to go to the *suq,* just about all the options open to them in ʿUnayzah. When they go to the *suq,* they have to be chaperoned. The ideal is that unmarried girls do not go out often, not more than about twice a week.

For a married woman, outings can be more frequent. Although theoretically she is supposed to get her husband's permission, in practice she usually just informs him. It is usually he who gives her a lift. The main barrier to women's mobility now is not the direct authority of a kinsman or husband but the lack of transportation. Women are at the complete mercy of male drivers. This not only constrains them in their ability to visit but also prevents their full mobilization in the labor force and restricts their pursuit of their own independent business activities. Hiring male drivers is not a viable alternative for many families, as it is generally believed in ʿUnayzah that for a man and woman to be alone in a car is *khilwah,* "to be alone in a private place," which is forbidden for all except a husband and those one may not marry. For this reason, schools and other institutions that employ women hire a driver along with his wife to provide transportation for the female employees. While many husbands or brothers make an effort to take their female relatives to places, they generally see this as a burden, and the women have to accommodate themselves to the men's schedules. While there are public buses that serve the city, most women do not find them convenient and almost never take them. Furthermore, some husbands forbid them to do so.

With the building of the new town, old neighborhood groups were dispersed into many different areas that are often distant from one another. This dispersion has made it difficult for women to maintain old ties of friendship and has seriously affected their social networks. There are now more than fifteen new residential areas which vary according to economic criteria. Some closer to the old town are more expensive than others on the peripheries. While there are socioeconomic differences among the inhabitants of each area, there is less mixture of rich and poor households in a single area than was the case in old neighborhoods. Also, while each area has a number of mosques, men often have to drive to them. There are no common areas where children play or residents gather to visit as in the old neighborhoods. It is also possible that neighbors know little about each other.

The new residential areas do not form neighborhoods as was the case in the old town. However, people still value neighborhood relations, and many have made attempts to create those ties in spite of the changes that have occurred in the physical environment. Although some relatives and some old neighbors may live in the same residential area today, there are many others who are neither relatives nor old neighbors. Women, however, have particularly made a conscious effort to create and maintain ties among new neighbors.

When a new family moves in, women make an attempt to initiate its women into the ongoing friendship networks that they have recently established. Usually, a number of women go to visit the women of the new family to welcome them to the neighborhood. Then each of the women in the network invites them to a meal. When this circle is completed, it becomes the task of the women of the new family to formalize their options. If the women in that family wish to continue the exchange, they will formalize this by giving a meal themselves. Henceforth, they will be members of the network in the neighborhood. If, on the other hand, as sometimes happens, the women do not wish to do so, they will not give a meal but will still maintain amicable relationships with others.

When a neighborhood-based network has been established, it rotates from home to home on a weekly or biweekly schedule and always on the same day of the week, usually in the mornings. These groups are primarily composed of women who live within walking distance of each other. While consanguineal or affinal ties often exist between some of the women in a network, the raison d'être of the social gathering is their membership in the neighborhood. Occasionally, however, consanguineal or affinal ties may cut across neighborhood networks. For example, in the home of the hostess, a relative from another neighborhood may be present. Also, at any given gathering friends of the regular participants in the network from their old neighborhoods may be present. For example, there may be in the gathering two women married to two brothers who occupy different homes or two co-wives or a woman and her husband's mother or two patrilateral cousins married to two different men in the neighborhood. There would, of course, be other women who are unrelated. Some of these women may have known each other as girls in the old neighborhoods in the old town and some may be new acquaintances they have met as members of the neighborhood network. Almost all are married, divorced, or widowed, since unmarried women seldom come to these morning meetings. They may bring their children along.

These gatherings are not very formal occasions. Women trickle in, informally dressed, around 10:30 in the morning and gather in the main reception area or in the men's *majlis,* if there is one. The hostess, assisted by a relative or a close friend, serves coffee, dates, tea, and some snacks. The hostess is usually busy with the serving. The other women begin their conversations by asking about each other's health and that of their families. Topics of discussion vary, with a number of them talking all at once and in loud voices. A favorite topic is their children and what is happening to them and what they are doing. They often ask a woman how many children she has, and that initiates commentaries on the ideal number of children for a woman to have. Opinions vary. Some say that large numbers of children, say twelve, are desirable and bring rewards from Allah. These are usually older women. Others say that at least five is the minimum that one should have. A woman, for example, who had six children could not be persuaded by the other women to have more even though all her children were adults and were living in other places. A woman who had only five was the subject of joking in which the others said that they should encourage her husband to take another wife.

Other topics include servants and housework in general. The women complain about the language problem with the servants, all of whom are expatriates. As in the case with other workers, the servants have to be trained and when this has happened they tend to leave. They discuss the salaries of the servants and new agencies that can recruit them, and generally they agree on how best to monitor their goings and comings and whether the servant should be allowed to go out on her own without a chaperone. They discuss events that have happened in the community, especially those that involve people whom they know. Women who know each other well may raise family issues related to potential conflict. Especially problematic, as indicated earlier, is the attempt by younger couples to establish neolocal residences.

The older women in these gatherings will sadly comment on how times have changed and how things were much better in the past. One will say that her son and his wife are trying to make or may, in fact, have made plans to live by themselves. This is a problem that usually touches every woman in the group and consequently an animated discussion follows. An older woman may complain that things have changed to such a degree that the younger women now run the show at home. She does not feel confident to go down and buy anything for the household—not furniture or even a dress—because her taste is often criticized by the younger women. In the midst of discussions of change, individuals who have explored new alternatives in almost any field of behavior are discussed and evaluated by the various generations present. Some may be praised, as, for example, an employed woman who paid off her father's debts. Others may be criticized for not showing enough deference to parents. Others may be censored for behavior that is judged as shameful. These evaluations of new behaviors spread beyond the small gathering, as each woman is likely to be involved with other groups.

Another topic of discussion is that of literacy and the relevance of it to the lives of adults with children. Some women are enterprising and have profited from the literacy schools in their neighborhood. Such women often use the gathering as a place for recruiting women to study in the literacy classes. However, not all of them join, and the experiences of those who have joined are constantly being assessed. When an attempt is made to recruit even more women, they acknowledge that they would love to learn how to read and to learn some arithmetic and certainly religion, but they are not interested in some of the other subjects. Some see that the prime value of the literacy classes is to teach the Holy Qur'an. To this, others will add to be able to learn new recipes and new ways of cooking and, more importantly, to learn to use the telephone and perhaps to be able to receive a letter that needs a receipt. As for the question of literacy being related to better child rearing, women often joke about that. Having grown children of their own, they obviously fail to see how literacy programs can help them in that direction.

These gatherings usually break up after an hour and a half or two hours, by 12:00 or 12:30, after confirming the place for the next visit. Occasionally, such meetings are held in the afternoon. Under these conditions, some employed women may participate in them. Usually these women are recruited into these networks by a husband's mother who is already a member or by another relative in the neighborhood. If unmarried girls participate, it is more likely that they attend in the afternoons rather than in the mornings. However, daughters of the hostess are always present and assist their mother. Even in the presence of maids, women of the house usually serve their guests. Whereas the morning groups are likely to be composed of illiterate women, the afternoon meetings will include literate and sometimes educated women. These groups all include women of all three generations— grandmothers, daughters, and grandchildren.

In some social gatherings that are of the relatively well-to-do, the afternoon gatherings have been elaborated to include an evening meal. Although the residential areas tend to include people of similar economic status, they are not absolutely so; and in the neighborhood groups there may be both rich women and women of limited incomes. Within the group, the pattern of interaction, however, is strictly egalitarian, and people interact as a group and not as individuals. These gatherings are usually small circles and topics are discussed by everyone, often at the same time. Although they may intermittently engage the person sitting next to them in a private dialogue, most conversation is shared by all those present. When a woman fails to attend, others inquire about her, and if it is found that she is ill, members of the neighborhood group will go to visit her collectively. Solidarity in the group is also shown when a member is seriously ill and social gatherings are canceled until she improves.

In addition to the neighborhood gatherings, women participate also in gatherings held regularly for the clan; that is, people who share the same surname. These meet regularly but over a larger span of time—about once a month. These gatherings may include both male and female members, who are, however, spatially separated in different quarters of the house. These also usually include an evening meal and are held at a different house each time. Sometimes, however, they are held at the home of the eldest male member, assuming that he can afford it. These gatherings bring together relatives who are otherwise not in contact with each other and sometimes include relatives from other cities such as Riyadh.

Family gatherings of this kind are usually held on weekends and are usually quite formal. Both men and women are more formally dressed on these occasions, and the meal is quite elaborate and usually includes a sheep or goat that is slaughtered for the occasion. Typically, these gatherings include people of various generations and provide all, especially the children, with an opportunity to renew ties with one another. They include both rich and poor members of the clan.

Economic differentiation within a clan is not uncommon. Even among the old wealthy merchant families there are many who are considerably less well-to-do. It is also possible that in the case of two brothers one is very wealthy while the other has a limited income. From among the old *fallalih* group there may be some who are poor and others who have achieved high positions in state service with very high pay. However, if the person is in a very high position, he is likely to live in another city and will seldom attend clan gatherings.

A more usual differentiation is between two members of a clan, even within a single extended family unit, in which one is the director of a state institution and the other is a driver or *farrash* employed in the same place. What determines the interaction between them is the kinship link and the age of the person rather than financial status or job position. Differences in status are highly visible in ʿUnayzah because change has been recent and has involved major qualitative changes, as, for example, when a person from an illiterate farming background becomes not only educated but employed. That person may receive a very high salary that allows a dramatic change in both the style and standard of living. In this it has been individuals rather than kin groups that have been the actors and beneficiaries. At the same time, kin ties have remained strong and highly valued, although there are cases in which wealthy and prominent people have not acted to help improve the status of kin who are in poor circumstances.

Much more frequent are the visits of a married woman to her natal family. One day a week, usually on the weekend, a woman will take her children to spend the whole day with her parents. Her husband may or may not come for his meal there, especially if his own parents are in the city. Couples who live in a neolocal residence will spend one day at her relatives and the other day at his. Visits to their natal home are much cherished by women, who look forward to them with eagerness. So important are these visits for the young women that, in an extended family setup, the various women have to synchronize their visits so that someone will be with the mother-in-law, although she too may be receiving her own daughters. These are usually family affairs, but close friends may drop in if they are not themselves caught up in such visits.

Occasionally, a neighborhood gathering may over the years include younger women who happen to now have the same occupation. Of course, a woman can be active and involved in more than one network, as the following case indicates. Munirah is from an ʿUnayzah family which had migrated to the Hijaz. About twenty-five years ago, she married and came to live in ʿUnayzah. She participates in a social gathering which has been meeting together regularly for the past ten years and is composed of the following: her patrilateral cousin, who is a schoolteacher; her neighbor in the old town and her daughter, who later became a teacher; and women from two other families. This group meets once every fortnight and sometimes once every week. Munirah also participates once a fortnight in a gathering which is held for her husband's family. This usually meets in the evening and sometimes includes the male members of the family. In addition, Munirah is a member of a neighborhood group which also includes old friends who are not her neighbors. Over the years they have come to include the daughters who have become schoolteachers like Munirah and her cousin. This is a much bigger group that includes twenty to thirty women who meet in the evenings, often over a meal, and rotates from one place to another. This group consists of women of the older generation, most of whom are illiterate, along with others who are schoolteachers. In addition, Munirah also visits her "close friends," who may not be in any of these groups.

The participation of women in activities outside the home is somewhat limited. In the past, the physical mobility of unmarried girls was minimal and was contained within the neighborhood. For the married woman of the past, the social horizons were wider. For the working woman, much of her time was absorbed by the requirements of her work. The contemporary women, as we have shown, participate in various kinds of activities outside the house. But their world is predominantly restricted to other women and is severely constrained by the lack of transportation.

The woman's ties with her natal family are very important as a source of emotional support and other forms of assistance. She remains identified with her natal family and returns to them in case of divorce. When marriage ties are tenuous and easily dissolved in divorce, a woman's natal family becomes her prime source of security. The frequent visits of a married woman to her natal family thus strengthen these crucial ties on which a woman depends throughout her life. Her participation in the gatherings of the wider family conforms with the ideals of family relations in the community and provides her with a wider network from which she can also draw help and assistance. It is, however, the neighborhood that sees the social world extended beyond the limit of kinship. These groups and the women she meets in her place of work are the prime sources of extra-kinship relations. All these combine to reduce her isolation.

In these gatherings of various sorts, women pick up information on events in the community and discuss their various concerns. Frequently, women discuss their children, their schooling and care. They also discuss family events and changes that are now taking place. Occasionally, women will air family conflicts, but only among close friends. Often the aim of such an effort is to clear the air and mend bridges through obtaining the advice and counsel of others. Such communication becomes particularly valuable when norms are changing. Occasionally, women discuss the behavior of other women who are not present. Deviation from expected behavior is usually discussed, sometimes criticized, and occasionally censored. These meetings may present opportunities for some women to sell items that they have bought or made. Occasionally, women will also pick up information on marriage prospects for their sons and daughters in the community.

These ties, thus cultivated in various ways, link women to several others with whom support and assistance can be exchanged. Women become friends and even confidantes, lend money to each other, assist in times of sickness, and provide companionship to one another. Major events like death or severe illness draw support visits from neighborhood members who may not be participants in social visits. The same is true of marriage and birth.

Men's Socializing

The social visiting that men engage in is similar in a number of important ways to that described above for women. Through visiting, men reaffirm ties with kinsmen and develop networks that are based on friendship, peer groups, and occupational ties. In their meetings, men exchange information about the community, discuss issues that are related to changing values and patterns of behavior, and sometimes conduct business. Unlike some of the women's groups, however, the men seldom discuss issues related to family conflicts or issues of a personal nature, particularly if they involve women, for the discussion of mothers, sisters, wives, or other women in the community is considered *ʿayb,* "shameful," and unmanly. One may speak of foreign women one has known, but reference is seldom made to local women as individuals or by name by men in a group setting.

Men's visiting is different from that of women in that it is a much more common everyday event that they normally do without any special effort or thought. Unlike women, men have no restraints on their mobility in the community. Every man who can drive (which includes almost everyone except some old men) has a car of his own, and he is often in it going from home to work, to the *suq,* and to visit, looking for anyone who is "sitting" (i.e., receiving guests) if he has nothing else to do.

As is the case with women's socializing, that of the men has changed with the development of the new ʿUnayzah. In the old days, as mentioned earlier, the *suq* was the major scene for socializing among men. Both men and women recall that men used to go to the *suq* every afternoon whether or not they had any business to transact. They would put on their *bisht,* "cloak," and go there immediately following the mid-afternoon prayer. There they would meet friends, observe what was going on, drink coffee and tea in the various shops, and perhaps, but not necessarily, buy something or settle an account with a merchant. The *suq* was a focus for all the males from different neighborhoods and from different occupational sectors, and if a man was looking for someone in particular he would go to the *suq* to find him rather than to his house. The *suq,* therefore, was not only an economic institution but it was also a social field which brought together men from the whole community.

This practice began to break down with the development of the contemporary town. Demolition of the old *suq,* as mentioned earlier, began in 1964, as the newly established municipality began its program of widening and straightening the streets and introducing new infrastructure. At the same time, teachers and other employees began to increase and form a new occupation category in the social fabric of the community. Cars became more numerous, and many of the young employees and other young men began to go on outings to the nearby desert sands in the late afternoon, where they would make a fire, brew coffee and tea, and talk. Electricity was introduced, and in the latter part of the 1960s there was television. The hours of the *suq* began to change, and it stayed open after sunset and until the last prayer. The younger generation of men that was becoming more educated began to abandon the *suq* as a social center, and by around 1970 it had lost its former social character. Many mark this as the end of an era in ʿUnayzah that was symbolized by the discarding of the *bisht* as an element of clothing by young men except on very formal occasions. Men about forty-five years of age say that they never went to the *suq* to socialize.

Since then no other institution has taken the place of the *suq* as a secular place that serves as a focus for the men of the whole community. Since that time, relationships have increasingly become less face to face. Expatriates began to appear on the scene in larger and larger numbers, and people from outside the community began to move in and settle in new neighborhoods that began to spring up. Today, the only institution that brings men from the whole community together is the main mosque, where most men gather for the noon prayer on Friday. While this is a religious setting, it also has a communal aspect about it, and men who do not regularly see each other briefly meet there, exchange greetings, and ask about common acquaintances who may not be in sight.

As the town has expanded and changed, it has not developed public places for socializing or entertainment. The few coffeehouses and numerous small restaurants are seldom frequented by men from the community. While such places are no longer considered shameful by the majority of men as they were in the past, they are nonetheless mainly frequented by expatriate laborers. There is no public entertainment, with the exception of sports events and an occasional parade. Also, at the time of the ʿid, some men may congregate to dance the ʿardah, a traditional dance. Two sports clubs attract youths, and there is the Ibn Salih Center, which has recently been established as a cultural center for the community but which has not yet embarked upon its programs. Therefore, the socializing that men engage in all takes place in private settings.

The men's *majlis* in old houses was described in chapter 1. As people have moved into new housing which conforms more to a Western-style house than to the traditional houses of old ʿUnayzah, many men have built a *majlis* that is separate from the rest of the house, often in a separate building. While the large new houses have large reception rooms, many of the men actually spend most of their time in a small room about five by ten meters where they sit on the carpeted floors with pillows against the wall for backrests. At one end of the room, opposite from the entrance door, is a hearth where in the past coffee and tea were prepared on charcoal fires. On the wall to one side of the hearth there is often a row of shelves known as the *kamar*, built and carved with traditional designs by one of the few old craftsmen who still work in the city.

The men almost never prepare their own coffee and tea anymore as they always did in the past. Now it is sent to them from the women's kitchen, where it is prepared either by the women of the household or by a maid. Both coffee and tea are now invariably served from plastic thermoses which are made specially for the Arabian market in other Asian countries and which have almost completely replaced the copper coffeepots which used to be made locally by master craftsmen. While the men no longer use the coffee hearth for the preparation of tea and coffee, they nonetheless often build a fire there in the cold winter months and enjoy leisurely evenings of warming themselves around it. The smoke of the fire escapes through an opening in the roof, but with time the walls of these rooms are slowly becoming blackened by the smoke, as were those of the old houses.

In these *majalis,* whether at homes in town or at their *basatin* outside of town, men meet and socialize in a number of different kinds of social settings. One type of gathering is the *daʾirah,* "circle." This is composed of a group of between five and fifteen men who meet each night, usually after the last prayer, on a rotating basis at the place of a different man each night. The men who participate in these are always the same each night, although an occasional outsider might be present. The men may or may not be related, may or may not live in the same area, may or may not have similar occupations. The group may have members who range in age from twenty-five to seventy. It is said that most of these groups were established long ago and have been in existence for as long as anybody can remember, although they used to meet in the daytime rather than at night, as is the case now. Although some of the participants may be related to each other or have a common occupation, they are thought of as groups of men who are friends and enjoy being together. In many of these gatherings, the most common activity is playing *balawt,* a card game that the men seriously concentrate on. Often little is said in these gatherings as men devote themselves to cards; but whenever there is any news of a political nature, some business activity that someone has heard about, or some event of mutual interest, it is discussed and opinions are expressed.

People say that the daily *da'irah* is gradually becoming less common and is being replaced with *dwa'ir* that meet on a weekly or twice weekly basis. This is due to the increase in opportunities for socializing and the establishment of a new pattern of gatherings that attract men on the basis of different criteria, especially ones of occupational specialization. For example, a group of older *fallalih* meet once a week in a *majlis* on the farm of one of the men. Each week a different man provides the meal of a goat that has been slaughtered and is served on big platters filled with rice. Around the platters are served leeks, whole heads of lettuce, and fruits in season. Most of the men who participate in this gathering are sixty years old or more, although there are a few who are younger. Some are from *qabili* status, while others are not, and there is a Bedouin who regularly attends and participates.

Before and after dinner, the men, who have known each other for years, enter into animated and lively discussions, speaking in loud voices and often all at once about issues that usually have to do with agriculture—often stories about the past and descriptions of planting palm trees or tales of what so and so did when he was presented with a difficult problem in farming. They also discuss issues of current concern, like whether the locusts will come this year or whether one should take seriously the amount of medicine the veterinarian prescribed for curing one's camels. On this latter issue, one old man proudly reported that he had taken the medicine from the veterinarian but tripled the dosage and thereby cured his animals. Other topics that are discussed include information of when one should plant some of the new vegetables that have been introduced and how much one should water them. They also sometimes complain about how the sellers in the market are taking all the profits on their produce, and once, in the presence of the anthropologist, they drafted a letter to the municipality complaining about the vegetable and fruit sellers. They may also have heated discussions about whether someone is really of *qabili* status or not.

Another example of an occupational group meeting together is that of young men who are employees in the state agricultural offices. About twenty-five of these, which does not include all the employees in this sector, meet once a week and have a dinner similar to that described above at the farm of one of them. Some of them play *balawt*, and others sit around and talk and drink tea and coffee before and after dinner. Many of these men were in school together, both in ʿUnayzah and later on in the university. They have thus known each other for a long time. Topics of discussion range widely and include topics related to the work place and to agriculture, as well as topics of a wider social interest. Like the old farmers described above, they obviously enjoy themselves, laugh a lot, and speak animatedly in a situation of male camaraderie. There are similar groups that are based on other occupations such as teaching and the employees of the municipality.

Aside from groups based on employment and occupation, some groups are based on an extended family but include nonfamily members as well. There are also the dinner meetings of members of a clan described above for women. In addition, some groups have formed to study and discuss religious issues. Others meet to discuss poetry and other topics of secular knowledge, while one group meets weekly to perform the *sammari,* traditional ʿUnayzah folk songs and dances, an activity that is often preceded by a meal and that involves social interaction before and after the performance.

In addition, a few men keep a kind of open house where any man can drop by at any time in the morning or evening. Others visit on an irregular basis, and it is not uncommon for groups of male friends to spend a Friday or a holiday at the farm of one of them. The host himself slaughters and cooks a goat, and they spend the whole day drinking tea, talking, and playing *balawt*.

Many young and some middle-aged men regularly go on outings to the *barr* to enjoy themselves in the outdoors away from town in the

desert sands. They especially go on weekends and spend long evenings in talk and storytelling and, for some, in boisterous activities
such as racing their vehicles up the side of a sand dune. During the
springtime when the weather is cool and the desert blooms with
flowers and a lot of greenery, patterns of recreation in the *barr* include
the family, which camps out for several days or even weeks at a time.

All these socializing activities are mainly seen by men as entertainment, but they accomplish a number of different things. They provide major sources of information and knowledge both about the
community and new ideas and new technologies, and they provide
the settings where traditional values are expressed and reaffirmed or
discussed and challenged. They also tie men together in larger and
larger networks that go beyond the family and kin to include peer
groups, occupational groups, and even the community at large.

Although many participate in a number of different groups, some
men actively go from one group to another and carry news of events
of general interest. In addition, men in these gatherings share information about financial matters and business opportunities. A company that has recently placed shares on the market will be discussed
and evaluated. Various investment alternatives at the national, Arab,
and international levels are compared and evaluated, and sometimes
decisions are taken on the spot to invest in one activity or another.
These types of social settings were also the scenes of a great deal of
business activities during the days of the *tufrah,* when men were buying and selling land, setting up new companies, and exchanging expatriate laborers from one place to another. Business partners met
here and sometimes even borrowed money from men in the social
gathering.

Not all men participate in such socializing to the same degree, but
almost all have some contact with some group. Some men spend only
an hour or two in the early evening with their men friends, but others
are busy in them almost every night of the week and seldom go home
until around 11:00 P.M. or later. Such men spend little time at home
with their families. While they sleep at home, they leave early in the
morning to go to their jobs at the office. They come home for lunch
in mid-afternoon, take a nap, and then embark on what for many is
an important activity of the day—attending social gatherings which,
however, are more than social because they are where one hears the
news and also may do some business.

The participation of men in prolonged social activities that extend late into the night has increased in recent years. In the past, business and socializing took place during the day and probably ended by the time of the last prayer. However, with the advent of electricity and the automobile, both the business and social hours of the community have been extended, particularly for men. The frequency of social outings has intensified, and since access to the *barr* has become much easier, young men in particular make more frequent trips there.

Whether in ʿUnayzah or in the *barr,* the young or middle-aged man is today away from his home for more hours than his young wife may find acceptable. This is especially the case if the couple is living neo-locally rather than in an extended family. The regular absence of the husband in the evening leaves the wife for long periods of time by herself. If her family is also in ʿUnayzah, one solution has been for her husband to take her to her family and pick her up on his return. As they have more children, her movements become more cumbersome. A woman is especially alone if her family is not in ʿUnayzah, as is the case with many whose parents have migrated to other cities in the country. Also, as shown earlier, the young woman today has different expectations of marital life.

In the past, it was not expected that husband and wife would engage in joint social activities; also, they lived in extended families where there were always others present, and the husband was seldom gone for long periods unless he had migrated for work. Women today grant that it is a husband's right to go out or to travel, but they expect more joint activities with their husbands and expect to spend more time with him. The younger men share these expectations with their wives and some return home early to be with their families. Many also have allocated Friday as a day to spend with the family. Others, however, have to be coaxed into such accommodations. Women who object to their husbands' long absences discuss the subject and may even quarrel with their husbands about it. Although the men do not give up the right to go out, they sometimes compromise and come home earlier. Those compromises known to us have usually been among couples in which the woman is educated and employed and contributes to the family budget in some way or another.

The social scene in ʿUnayzah is in a state of flux. As people moved from old neighborhoods into new ones, they gained new buildings but lost the common grounds of the old neighborhoods that were the centers of collective actions. With these they lost the social ties that wove every neighborhood into a web of people who knew each other on a face-to-face basis and who were often kinsmen, affines, or friends and who sometimes acted as a single group. People still value neighborhood ties and are trying to create them in the new areas, although these neighborhoods have isolated women, old people, and children. Women have consciously reduced their isolation by relating to other women in the neighborhood through regularly held social gatherings. Very young children are now taken to kindergartens where they spend their time rather than in the neighborhood. The old women remain at home with the door closed while the old men sit on the steps of the house alone. Men react to the loss of the old neighborhood and of the *suq* by increasing their social visits and sometimes combining business and socializing in private settings. Schools and sports clubs have become major institutions for the socialization of youth, and peer groups that cut across neighborhoods are formed.

In terms of family residence, the old extended family pattern is now changing. Increasingly, young couples are opting for neolocal residence. Still, the extended family remains as an ideal in people's minds as evidenced in the gatherings held by them. One cannot predict the total breakdown of the extended family because economic conditions are uncertain and because the ideology favoring the extended family remains strong. The nuclear family continues to emerge among the young, and the partners involved in it continue to explore alternative solutions to new problems which they now face. Predominant among these are the education and employment of wives. In consequence of both, along with other factors such as travel and the media, husbands and wives are redefining their expectations of and obligations to each other in their roles as spouses. Within this context, it is significant that two of the most absorbing concerns in the community revolve around neolocal residence and the disposal of a wife's salary.

CHAPTER 12

Analysis and Conclusion

Various conclusions drawn from this case study bear reiteration and further analysis. The first set of conclusions relates to the complex structure of Arabia prior to the initiation of developmental change. The second set addresses change associated with development, while the third set leads to an analysis of the transformation brought about by the oil boom.

Arabia Prior to Development

The commonly held view that much of the Arabian Peninsula, and especially Najd, was an area of tribal organization is not only wrong but has led numerous scholars to misinterpret contemporary structures and behavior as holdovers of a tribal past. A blatant example is the following statement by Palmer, Alghofaily, and Alnimir: "In societies of tribal origin, manual labor tends to be disdained. In Saudi Arabia, for example, construction trades such as carpentry and plumbing are generally regarded as ʿaib or shameful by traditional norms" (1984:20). They wrongly attribute the disdain for manual labor allegedly expressed at present by some Saudi Arabians to a past that did not exist. The origins of the present society are not tribal. Moreover, manual work as such was not considered shameful even by those elements of the old society who called themselves tribal.

For hundreds of years before the initiation of developmental change in this century, the Arabian Peninsula had complex formations that integrated society at much higher levels than those of individual tribes or local communities. At the highest level was Islam, which provided not only an integrating structure of religious beliefs and practices but also a body of rules that, along with customary norms, regulated social relations, commercial transactions, and law and order. Islam further provided an ethos which informed and guided behavior. Practically speaking, Islam also tied the Arabian Peninsula to a much wider area, large parts of which became Arabized following the spread of the religion.

Cities and states have existed in the Arabian Peninsula since long before Islam. Although pre-Islamic states no longer continue to exist, the origins of the present state of Oman go back to A.D. 751, while those of the Yemeni state go back to A.D. 900 (Harik 1987:25–26). It is true that central state authority was often weak and sometimes nonexistent in large parts of the peninsula such as Najd; however, the indigenous process of state formation in Najd predates the present Saudi Arabian state by several centuries.

The absence of continuous and effective central state authority did not translate into a condition of acephalous tribal organization based on segmentary lineage structures alone. Such structures existed. However, even the tribally based nomadic and sedentary communities had higher forms of political organization that transcended the segmentary lineage system. For example, so-called tribal amirs were supported by slaves and sometimes by mercenaries. They also extracted *khuwah*, "tribute," from villagers and occasionally other groups as well. In return, the amirs provided a number of functions such as defense, mediation, and adjudication that are usually associated with states. In this regard, the amirs acted not as tribal elders or shaykhs but as the heads of de facto political formations.

In the absence of central state authority, the market acted as a major centralizing structure that linked the various systems of specialized production followed by Bedouin, farmers, and craftspeople. The market provided a level of integration that transcended the boundaries of autonomous political systems. Rules and organizational structures involving the payment of fees allowed for the uninterrupted movement of trade and transport throughout the Arabian Peninsula. Examples of these rules and structures are *wajh* and *rafiq,* both of which guaranteed safe passage across the desert without reliance on armed caravans or the protection of states.

The complexity of the Arabian Peninsula was also manifest in the division of labor, the stratification system, and the existence of production for exchange value. This complexity involved specialized knowledge and skills, risk taking, a high level of work organization, as well as manual labor. It also included a significant degree of migration of laborers and traders.

Developmental Change

The processes of developmental change began before the discovery of oil and long before the recent boom. The first major step in the process of developmental change was the establishment of the contemporary state of Saudi Arabia. In addition to the well-known roles played by ʿAbd al-ʿAziz and the Al Saʿud, this study calls attention to the roles of merchants and urban groups from Najd in the process of state formation. In developing the institutions of the new state, educated men from old communities like ʿUnayzah along with similar men from the Hijaz were principal actors, although members of the Al Saʿud tended to hold ministerial positions, barring most notably those of finance and of petroleum and mineral wealth.

The foundations of the modern school system were also established decades before oil began to be exploited in commercial quantities after the end of World War II. Education and the new state, which unified four-fifths of the Arabian Peninsula under a single political structure, prepared the way and provided the framework within which oil revenues came to play a crucial role in development. Although the foundations of modern education predated the exploitation of oil, revenues from oil were used to finance its expansion along with the building of modern infrastructure. The oil industry also contributed to local development. Most significantly, this contribution had to do with the development of new skills and the training of a cadre of workers.

As Vasiliev (1986) shows, the establishment of the oil industry by ARAMCO initiated qualitative changes in both the organization of work and the types of skills required. Although recruitment remained somewhat traditional, ARAMCO introduced contractual relations, a new pattern of discipline and routine, and wages and salaries on a large scale. The oil industry also stimulated the development of industries and businesses around it which attracted local workers and entrepreneurs.

As the state developed and the oil industry was established, the economy increasingly became monetized. This monetization, in addition to technological change, led to the disappearance of local crafts, the traditional transportation system, and the principal long-distance traders of the old social order. Domestically organized work was also largely replaced by wage labor.

With a modern educational system and modern infrastructure largely in place and with an expanding modern economic structure, the country was well prepared to reap prodigious benefits from the dramatic increase in oil prices which Saudi Arabia and other members of OPEC engineered in the mid 1970s.

The Boom—Development Truncated?

The case of ʿUnayzah indicates that many benefits did accrue to most people—in the short run. The data, however, raise serious questions about the sustainability of the improved standards of living. The long and, in our analysis, largely successful process of developmental change that began in the first decade of this century was, at best, seriously compromised by sudden affluence, by the rush to build new housing and set up new agricultural and commercial enterprises, and by the associated replacement of local labor with imported labor. At worst, the development process was truncated, as evidenced in ʿUnayzah.

The reasons for this compromise—or truncation—are directly related to the characteristics of the boom, which was brought about by vastly increased sums of cash. As an energy source, Saudi Arabia's oil has mainly been used by developed capitalist countries, some of which are heavily dependent on it. Although domestic consumption of refined oil products has increased significantly, Saudi Arabia's oil has mainly been important to the country itself as a source of revenue. When this revenue was relatively moderate, it tended to stimulate the development process. However, the magnitude of increase in revenue between 1974 and 1982 introduced a qualitative change of transformational proportions.

The affluence provided the means for the state to dramatically expand its already existing development programs and to embark upon new ones. Through the extension of interest-free loans, the state became a major creditor to the local population. It also provided large-scale subsidies and, as Sirageldin, Sherbiny, and Serageldin (1984) show, became a principal employer. The state's programs stimulated the private sector and led to marked increases in the amount of money available to wide segments of the population.

The rush to develop brought about by the rapidly acquired affluence often led to compromises in the quality of work that was done. The rush also meant that little time existed for comprehensive planning, and the implementation of some development programs was not coordinated in such a way as to derive maximum benefits. Affluence allowed for the selection of programs and projects on other than purely economic grounds. The rapid changes also had many unintended social consequences. Moreover, the rapidly achieved affluence has rapidly evaporated.

New Housing

The most dramatic symbol of transformation brought about by the boom in ʿUnayzah is new housing. This phenomenon is an example of the redistribution of national wealth among a broad segment of the local population. New housing also illustrates many of the negative consequences of the boom. Interest-free loans encouraged people to build new houses. Since they usually built them on new land, spectacular inflation in land prices occurred, leading to a great deal of land speculation. The building of new housing also led to the importation of a large expatriate labor force and the mushrooming of construction companies and numerous other supporting enterprises. The rush to build new housing was often at the expense of applying strict standards of construction and supplying the expertise to carry it out properly, with the consequence that many of the new houses in ʿUnayzah now stand in need of repair.

Old architectural lines which gave ʿUnayzah its distinctive urban character and architectural specificity were ignored in favor of a completely new style. Neighborhood ties were disrupted. Especially affected by this disruption were old people and preschool children as well as women. The building of new housing also contributed to the weakening of the extended family, as many—with the help of loans—were able to establish neolocal residence.

Now that most of the new housing and the associated infrastructure have been built, the construction sector is faced with depression. Moreover, the operating and maintenance costs of the new housing are substantial.

New Agriculture

As in the case of housing, the state provided interest-free loans to individuals to improve and expand agriculture. In addition, the state heavily subsidized agricultural expansion in a politically motivated effort to achieve food security (cf. Nowshirvani 1987). The expansion also aimed at diversification of the national economy. Although a wide range of people, including *fallalih* and Bedouin, have benefited from the loans and subsidies, those who especially benefited in ʿUnayzah include a number of local businessmen. Moreover, the agricultural expansion benefited import companies, which supplied the machinery and equipment used on new farms, as well as drilling companies. It also led to inflation in land prices and fueled land speculation.

As a result of the state investments in agriculture, a spectacular increase in a wide range of agricultural products has occurred in ʿUnayzah. This increased production came at very high financial cost, and the continuation of subsidies is dependent on the state's ability to maintain or increase the national budget, which has already been adversely affected by the fall in the price of oil.

Aside from its high cost, agricultural development has involved the introduction of very sophisticated technology without the concomitant training of the local population to operate and maintain it. Although the state employs a cadre of skilled and knowledgeable agricultural engineers and technicians, their impact in the transfer of technical skills and knowledge to farmers has been limited. Production in ʿUnayzah has contributed to Saudi Arabia's ability to export wheat; but the machines, their spare parts, and much of the expertise and labor required to operate and maintain them are imported. This importation has led to greater dependency on external sources for both labor and technology.

Moreover, increased agricultural production was not accompanied by the development of an appropriate marketing system, particularly in the case of smaller agricultural enterprises. Thus, an increase in agricultural production has occurred, but a better marketing system would have brought greater benefits to small- and medium-scale farmers.

One can only speculate about the future of this sector, particularly if the state is no longer able to subsidize it. It is, however, clear that development of new agriculture at the scale observed in the central and northern parts of the country would not have occurred if large sums of money had not been made available by the state. Evidence for this is that those who developed exceptionally large-scale enterprises were mainly businessmen (including princes) who had no previous background in agriculture but who sought secure and high profits.

Women's Employment

Affluence permitted a degree of selectivity in the course of change and for choices based on ideological, social, or political priorities rather than economic ones. For example, the strict segregation of men from women in the contemporary work place has been possible due to the financial ability of the state to duplicate many of its institutions. With affluence, the state has been able to maintain separate schools, separate libraries, separate university campuses, and separate administrative structures in the educational institutions for males and females.

Women's full integration into the modern labor force was also restricted by affluence. The low employment rate of women is because their economic contribution to the household budget was not required. However, where a woman's contribution to the household budget has been needed, women have sought and obtained salaried employment. Numerous women have worked for mainly social reasons; but if economic conditions continue to change and women's contributions to household budgets from work outside the family become necessary, it is expected that gender segregation in the work place will be reduced.

The Rentier Model and the New Work Ethic

Some economists (e.g., Mabro 1969; Mahdavy 1970; First 1975; Beblawi 1987; Abdel-Fadil 1987; Chatelus 1987) have applied the concept of a rentier economy to the major oil-producing countries of the Middle East and North Africa. They correctly stress the overwhelming importance of income derived from the sale of oil abroad for the domestic economies of these countries. They are likewise correct in pointing out that the production of crude oil requires little local manpower, that the state allocates revenue derived from the sale of oil, and that large numbers of people benefit from this revenue without having worked to produce it.

However, it is misleading to call income from the sale of oil rent. Moreover, these economists fail to show the causal relationships between the various components of what they call rentierism. Beblawi (1987), for example, posits a relationship between a rentier economy, a rentier state, and a rentier mentality, suggesting that this cluster of features is mechanically interrelated and arises automatically from the extraction and sale of oil when it is a main resource of the country. This analysis obscures the process of decision making and selectivity that has taken place at the local and national levels. More seriously, the rentier analysis ignores the crucial role played by foreign states and multinational and transnational companies in influencing development in countries dependent on the sale of oil. The role of such external forces has been demonstrated by Amin (1973, 1982), among many others, to be instrumental in determining the course of development in Third World countries in general.

Largely because it does not take the world system into focus, the rentier analysis goes widely astray by positing that a rentier mentality or work ethic exists that is derived from indigenous tradition rather than present economic circumstances. Palmer, Alghofaily, and Alnimir (1984) claim that rentierism is not only an economic phenomenon but has cultural and social dimensions as well. In discussing the case of Saudi Arabia specifically, they single out what they call "behavioral correlates" of rentierism which they say "make it difficult for the rentier state to increase its productive capacity and to maximize the economic and political advantages at its disposal" (1984:20). In particular, they identify three sets of what they call "traditional work values," which they claim serve to maintain and perpetuate rentier economies. These sets of values are the disdainment of manual work (which they associate with tribal societies), the attachment of traditional individuals to their extended families (which they claim hinders both geographic and occupational mobility), and the tendency of individuals reared in traditional societies to rank low in terms of risk-taking or achievement-oriented behavior. Based on three social surveys conducted in Saudi Arabia on random samples of high school youths, university students, and middle-range civil servants, they conclude that "prevailing behavior patterns in Saudi Arabia pose a serious obstacle to the government's efforts to break the rentier pattern" (1984:33).

We do not question the results of the surveys; but the analysis and interpretation of them are clearly at odds with the findings of our study. Furthermore, the assumptions on which they base their study are open to question. The implicit assumption that guides their research and the questions they pose suggest that, to achieve development, societies must approximate what are, in fact, idealized social, economic, and political structures of modern industrialized states.

Evidence from Saudi Arabia itself, in fact, suggests alternative routes to development. For example, the extended family need not be incompatible with the occupational mobility of individuals.

If by "traditional" (which they do not define) they refer to the society before the establishment of the present Saudi Arabian state and the development of its oil-based economy, the values which they say are present today were clearly not there in the past. Examples from ʿUnayzah show that manual work as such (e.g., in agriculture and house building) was fully acceptable for both men and women, including those of tribal descent. It is, however, accurate that some manual work (e.g., leather working and smithery) was disdained by people of tribal descent. Nonetheless, such disdain did not inhibit the existence of flourishing craft production, which contributed to the development of significant regional trade.

Almost all people in ʿUnayzah were strongly attached to their extended families. However, such attachment clearly did not stop men from migrating as *ʿuqaylat, jammamil,* and workers in the developing oil industry for long periods of time. Furthermore, and while no sophisticated tests were administered to them, it is clear from their career histories that they were risk taking and achievement-oriented to a high degree. Recognizing that, we do not assume that high scores with regard to risk-taking and achievement-oriented behavior is a sufficient condition for the achievement of basic and sustainable development, as the case of the Swasa in Morocco clearly demonstrates (Waterbury 1972:185–187, 193–199).

Nonetheless, the transformation brought about by the boom does include the emergence of a new work ethic. In ʿUnayzah, this ethic is manifested mainly in job preference. Local people opted to abandon manual work in favor of state employment or managerial/ownership positions in private sector enterprises, whether agricultural or commercial. The new work ethic both reflects and reinforces these changes. It places value on acquiring wealth fast from "clean" work that involves little financial risk and minimal physical effort. State employment with its security, high salaries, opportunities for business contacts, and short work hours which allow for the pursuit of private business activities is particularly attractive.

The former predominance of domestically organized labor in agriculture, crafts, and to an extent trade continues in the present in the many small-scale individualistically organized enterprises. However, the prevalence today of paid employment has led to the emergence of hierarchical employment structures based on contractual relationships rather than personal ones. When working in the private sector, almost all local people opt for ownership/management positions and avoid employment in enterprises owned and managed by others from ʿUnayzah. They largely avoid such jobs because of their low pay, a phenomenon directly related to the present labor market, which includes expatriates who do not demand high wages or salaries. In addition, local people are influenced by social factors and, unless no other alternative exists, avoid such employment so as not to come under the supervisory control of other people from ʿUnayzah who are perceived to be social equals or inferiors. In the past, supervisory relations were present, but they often were in the context of a social tie and had the nature of an apprenticeship. In state employment, people are under the supervisory control of other Saudi Arabians, but this is in the context of the contractual and impersonal nature of the bureaucracy. The same considerations, along with relatively good pay, explain the occasional employment of Saudi Arabians in large companies owned by other Saudi Arabians.

The new work ethic is shared by members of both the *qabili* and *khadiri* descent categories of the old sedentary population of ʿUnayzah, as they both respond to economic opportunities in similar ways. Occupations that were disdained in the past by the *qabili* have been reclassified as they have been modernized. Such occupations as goldsmithery and butchery are now engaged in by the *qabili,* who, however, always hire expatriates to do the work. It can be argued that the owner of a small workshop which produces gold jewelry is not a goldsmith; but it is still true that his enterprise involves an occupation which the *qabili* disdain and in which they did not invest in the past. By the same logic, few local *qabili* youth enroll in the technical training institute in ʿUnayzah, although the occupations taught there do not carry any stigma according to the old classification of work. Their lack of involvement in such technical occupations is largely determined by economic conditions and not by the value system.

The *khadiri* segment of the population, in theory, was not barred from any occupation in the past (with the exception of that of amir), although they tended to predominate in occupations that the *qabili* refused. At present, the *khadiri* have mainly moved into the same kind of jobs as the rest of the local population. Like the *qabili,* they have come to prefer salaried employment in the bureaucracy, education, and private sector managerial/ownership positions.

It is correct that work values among many of the youth and adults constitute barriers to their deployment in some sectors of the work force. That they prefer state employment, trade, and managerial positions in general and, if possible, avoid manual work and semiskilled occupations involving long hours of laborious and tedious work is not attributable to "tradition," for in the parental generation such work was common. The interpretation of the present work ethic must be sought in the nature of the economic system that marginalizes production, increases the service sector, and imports cheap expatriate labor to maximize profits. Consequently, local people prefer the more profitable work in trade or the secure and well-paid state employment to the low-paid and hard manual work of production. It is such individual rationality rather than "traditional values" which has led to a new work ethic that makes manual work disdainful. This interpretation is consistent with observations and analyses made by Arab social scientists concerned with other oil-based economies in the Arabian Gulf (cf. ʿAbd al-Muʿti 1982; al-Khatib 1982; Rumaihi 1981; ʿAbd al-Jawad 1981; Fergani 1983). The present work ethic, we argue, will change according to economic imperatives.

From this perspective, the present work ethic should not be considered so much as a barrier to development but as a result of the particular course that economic change took during the boom. It is unlikely that descent considerations will affect occupational choices when both *khadiri* and *qabili* face unemployment in their preferred occupations in ʿUnayzah. If they choose to remain in ʿUnayzah, they will have to take on skilled and semiskilled technical occupations as well as employment in private sector commercial enterprises.

The Changing Social Order

Transformation in ʿUnayzah is marked by a change from domestically organized work to wage labor and now to salaried employment for most of the local people. Trade and entrepreneurship have existed throughout; but trade changed from being regional and export-oriented to local distribution of products imported from abroad by firms in other cities. Local financing of entrepreneurs has been replaced predominantly by state financing and subsidization. A transformed agriculture continues, but local crafts have disappeared and have not been replaced by significant industrialization. Most of the local population now works in service sector occupations. Transformation in ʿUnayzah also includes a change from no expatriates to the inclusion of a few as salaried employees in professional work and now to a very large number predominantly engaged as unskilled and semi-skilled wage laborers.

Concomitant with this transformation are changes in the social order. As Vasiliev (1986) argues, class divisions are emergent in Saudi Arabia. However, class divisions continue to be crosscut by loyalties to family and kinship groups. Moreover, the presence of expatriates temporarily resident as individuals and divided among themselves on the basis of national origin adds a special and complicating dimension to the social order. As a category, the expatriates largely occupy the position of a working class. However, because they are not *of* the society, they do not perform the political and social functions one might expect of an indigenous proletariat.

Given the transformation that has occurred, most local people in ʿUnayzah are middle class. The foundations for the emergence of this component were laid down in the period before the boom. However, the expansion of state employment and the mushrooming of business enterprises during the boom led to an acceleration in its growth.

Our analysis indicates that future growth of the middle class is unlikely. Figures and observation from ʿUnayzah indicate that the number of people employed both in the bureaucracy and in teaching often exceeds the number needed to perform the required tasks. Moreover, most of those with such positions are young and thus likely to block employment opportunities for others for the next fifteen to twenty years. Educated young women have already been faced with serious unemployment. Young men, being more mobile than women, now face the choice of migration to other job markets in the country or unemployment in ʿUnayzah unless the job market in private sector establishments opens up to include local people. Remaining in ʿUnayzah is likely to lead to downward mobility for the young in terms of type of occupation, employment status, and income.

The boom disproportionately benefited a small segment of the local population composed of some members of old prominent trading and landowning families and some individuals from other backgrounds. The major avenues for obtaining substantial wealth during the boom were land speculation, construction, and other business enterprises related to new housing and new agricultural development.

Also, increased sales in the market—especially of gold jewelry—provided some merchants with opportunities for considerable wealth. With the end of the boom, such avenues are now blocked. Moreover, many are faced with a major decline in the market value of property owned and are burdened with debts.

Also existing within the local population is a component referred to as *ad-dakhl al-mahdud,* "those of limited income." Many of these are former Bedouin and others who did not benefit from modern education. They mainly work in low skilled jobs when employed or in small-scale trade in the *suq.* Sometimes they may even own a small piece of old agricultural land, which generates a limited income. The children of these people are now receiving a modern education and are beginning the process of upward mobility. Whether this process will be fully realized depends on economic forces affecting employment in the future.

People of limited income in ʿUnayzah include, of course, most of the expatriates. As a category, their presence in the community is directly tied to the economy and dependent on the deployment of local manpower. Expatriates in administrative and most professional occupations have been replaced by local people. Construction workers disappeared with the end of the construction boom. Those most likely to be replaced in the not too distant future are sales workers and higher-level employees in private sector enterprises. Agricultural and menial laborers are likely to remain as a category indefinitely.

Present Directions of Change

The presence of new houses, newly paved streets and highways filled with automobiles, and new wheat fields would seem to belie our bleak evaluation of present conditions. Another apparent contradiction is the continuation of conspicuous and wasteful consumption patterns in striking contrast to the past. Although less pronounced in ʿUnayzah than in larger cities, the consumerism seen in Saudi Arabia in recent years is part of a pervasive pattern of conspicuous consumption that has been documented for other oil-producing states in the peninsula (Rumaihi 1981; ʿAbd al-Mutʿi 1982; an-Najjar 1982). People have become accustomed to the new, higher levels of consumption. As affluence has declined, some attempt has been made to maintain previous levels of consumption through drawing on savings or through borrowing. It is clear, however, that such practices cannot continue indefinitely.

The following two cases support our evaluation of the present circumstances. They also provide reflections on the wider process of change that has relegated ʿUnayzah to the status of a provincial city with limited job opportunities and few possibilities for career advancement. The first case is that of Abu Yusif, who is sixty-eight years old and retired.

> ʿUnayzah is like a chicken hatchery. It produces a lot, but it throws them out. The people it produces do not stay here. This has been for two main reasons. One is trade and the other is education. Trade pushes a man to go to other places where the market is better and where there is more opportunity to make money. Education also is a gate that leads to migration out of the city because those who become educated seek government employment, and the best positions are in Riyadh and other big cities. Those who are successful in their careers seldom return except perhaps to retire.
>
> I decided to retire here. I took a loan from the Real Estate Development Fund and built a house. I do not do any work or have a farm. My money is in the bank and is invested in foreign exchange and that brings me an income which is enough to live on. ʿUnayzah is a nice place for an old man. It is quiet and there are old friends and relatives around. But it is not a place for a young man who is ambitious and wants to achieve something in his life. Such a man will leave. If he is successful, he will not come back except maybe to retire.

Another man who left ʿUnayzah about forty years ago as a laborer and who advanced to become a high official in the oil industry expressed a similar point of view. According to Abu ʿAbd al-Muhsin,

> I plan to retire here in a few years. The children of those of us who left and were successful and did not return are now getting excellent university educations. Many of them are working in highly technical jobs, especially in the computerized aspects of the oil industry. Other youth from ʿUnayzah now sign up with ARAMCO or PETROMIN upon completing their secondary education. If they are good, they get advanced university training. They will not come back here. I love ʿUnayzah, but unfortunately I do not believe there is a future for the young here.

As both cases show, education has the potential for overqualifying people for the kinds of jobs and careers available in ʿUnayzah. Numerous cases exist of ʿUnayzah youth who have received university education both in the country and abroad. A few have returned to ʿUnayzah, but many have taken employment in large cities where there have been more opportunities for them to work in careers related to their specialized training. Such has especially been the case for those with degrees in engineering, medicine, or other advanced technical and scientific training.

We can only speculate about continued job opportunities in other parts of the country. The new industrial complexes of Jubayl and Yanbuʿ, which aim at contributing to diversification of the national economy (Khawajkiyah 1986), have the potential for providing employment opportunities for skilled technical labor. Some youth from ʿUnayzah are reported to have taken jobs in Jubayl. However, full participation in these new complexes will not happen unless more technical training of the local labor force takes place. Given the history of work-related internal migration and of employment in modern technical work since the establishment of the oil industry, lack of specialized training is the only major barrier confronting the participation of at least some of ʿUnayzah's youth in that sector at present.

Migration is obviously not a feasible alternative for all. Because state employment is no longer available, a few of the youth in ʿUnayzah have already taken jobs in private sector employment despite relatively low pay. We believe such employment will continue to increase and that they will increasingly take on technical work. The motivations for this change are purely economic. This process is already underway in the case of recently settled Bedouin in ʿUnayzah.

Due to their recent full sedentarization, the Bedouin (all of whom are *qabili*) had less access to modern education and thus to employment in the bureaucracy than has been the case for the old sedentary population of ʿUnayzah. Their participation in ʿUnayzah's economic life, therefore, has been limited to small-scale involvement in the *suq*, to transport, and more recently to agriculture and skilled and semi-skilled technical work.

The first of these occupations can be seen as a continuation of an activity the Bedouin always engaged in, albeit to a lesser degree in the past. Work in modern transport is analogous to their previous involvement in caravan transport. Both agriculture and technical work were formerly disdained. While they do not engage in regular agricultural labor, they now own and manage new agricultural holdings made available to them largely by state loans. The growing number of Bedouin youth enrolled in the technical training institute in ʿUnayzah and their reported work in modern technical occupations must be seen as a consequence of their need for employment and an indication of their greater integration into the modern economy in the city.

As the case of the Bedouin and our earlier discussion of the new work ethic show, the relationship of descent to occupation has been modified as new occupations have been introduced and as the attributes of old ones have been modified. The major barrier to work in technical fields and in private sector employment in general has been lack of economic need coupled with artificially low wages and salaries due to competition by expatriates. Private entrepreneurs, many of whom are closely allied with the state, are likely to combat the replacement of cheap expatriates with local people who demand higher wages and salaries and who can defend their rights as workers and employees. However, the specter of increasingly large numbers of unemployed and dissatisfied local youth is one that neither local entrepreneurs nor the state can confront indefinitely.

The state has a major role to play in preparing the youth to work in modern technical fields. Achievements have already been made in basic, general education. Scientific and technical training have recently received greater state support and are being encouraged by various private voluntary organizations. Continued support of these fields and their introduction throughout the educational system are essential.

In conclusion, the old ʿUnayzah did not survive. A continuous series of changes occurred in the city throughout the twentieth century. Most of the changes emanated from beyond the community and, taken together, can be classified as development or modernization. Local political autonomy ended. The locally centered self-sustaining economy based on production and trade was undermined.

ʿUnayzah was transformed into a Third World community—a provincial city in a new national political unit economically dependent on the sale of a single, primary product. The boom brought affluence and a standard of living similar to those of the First World. The boom, however, did not solve the underlying problem of economic development—the creation of a modern productive economy capable of sustaining a high standard of living.

Most likely, expatriates will continue to be phased out, with the exception of agricultural and other menial laborers. The local people will continue to be faced with less income and a deteriorating standard of living. Political and social turmoil may break out. It is remarkable, however, that a strong identity with and loyalty to the community have prevailed throughout. Moreover, many of the foundations of development established prior to the boom have persisted. People in ʿUnayzah thus face an uncertain future.

GLOSSARY OF ARABIC TERMS

ʿabayah. Cloak worn by women that covers the head and body.

ʿabd. Slave; a social category of people of slave descent.

abu. Father.

akhawi. Tribal retainers/companions of an amir.

ʿalim. Man of religious learning.

ʾaʿmal hurrah. Free work; self-employment.

amir. Commander; ruler; prince.

ʿardah. A group dance performed by men and traditional to Najd.

ʾard baydah. Literally, white land; undeveloped land.

asakir. Soldiers; policemen.

ʾathal. Tamarisk.

ʿayb. Shame; shameful (also spelled *ʿaib*).

badiyah. Desert; desert dwellers; Bedouin.

balawt. A card game.

barhi. A type of date of excellent quality.

barr. Wilderness; refers to the uninhabited environs of the city.

basatin. Plural of *bustan*.

birkah. Basin; pool.

bisht. Cloak worn by men.

budaʿah. Merchandise. Also a process of trade where one partner provides goods or capital and the other provides labor and both share any profits according to an agreed-upon formula.

bustan. Garden.

dabbabir. Leather processors; tanners.

daʾirah. A regular rotation of social visitations and participating members.

dakakin. Plural of *dukan*.

dakhl al-mahdud. Limited income.

dallal. Broker; auctioneer.

dallalin. Plural of *dallal.*

dawa'ir. Plural of *da'irah.*

dirah. Communal territory or area.

diwan al-malaki. Royal court.

diyah. Bloodwealth paid for injuries or death by the person or group responsible to the kindred of the person injured or killed.

dukan. Shop.

fallah. Tiller of the soil; peasant.

fallalih. Plural of *fallah.*

farrash. Messenger; coffee and tea maker and server.

farrasha. Feminine of *farrash.*

farrashat. Feminine plural of *farrash.*

farrashin. Plural of *farrash.*

hadar. Sedentary.

hammarah. Porters who transport goods by donkey.

hasu. Well and sitting area where women gathered in old homes.

hima. Preserve.

hudu'. Inner calm; serenity; quietness.

hudud. Limits; boundaries. Refers especially to the limits of acceptable behavior.

'id. Feast. Refers to either of two annual Islamic feasts. One follows the end of the Islamic lunar month of Ramadan during which Muslims fast between dawn and sunset. The other commemorates Ibrahim's covenant with Allah and is celebrated beginning on the tenth day of the Islamic month Dhu al-Hajjah.

ihya'. To endow with life; Islamic process of obtaining private ownership of land.

Ikhwan. Brotherhood; religio-politico-military movement active in the creation of the present Saudi Arabian state.

'iqta'. Land grant.

jammal. Cameleer; caravanner.

jammamil. Plural of *jammal.*

jarad. Locusts.

jusah. Storage compartment for dates inside a house.

kafil. Guarantor; sponsor; legal guardian.

kamar. Traditional hearth and associated shelves located in the reception room of a house and used in the preparation of coffee and tea.

karantina. Quarantine.

katatib. Plural of *kuttab.*

katib. Clerk; scribe.

khadiri. A social category of freeborn people who are not of recognized Arab tribal descent.

khilwah. Privacy; seclusion. Refers especially to a male and female being alone together. This is forbidden unless they are married to each other or barred by incest taboos from marrying each other.

khuwah. Tribute paid by client villagers or nomads to a tribe in return for protection.

klayjah. A dish, traditional to the Qasim, made of dates, wheat, and ghee.

kuttab. Traditional Islamic school.

madafiʿ. Plural of *madfaʿ.*

madfaʿ. Cannon; stationary irrigation mechanism.

maʾdhun. Official authorized by a *qadi* to perform marriages. He also assists in writing the marriage contract.

madinah. City.

mahr. Dower.

majalis. Plural of *majlis.*

majlis. Sitting; also the name of an area in ʿUnayzah where the amir held his court; also reception area for men in private homes.

muʾadhdhin. Caller for prayer.

mub halal. Impure; not righteous (colloquial usage).

mulk hurr. Freehold.

muwatan. Citizen.

muzaraʿ. Farmer; agriculturalist.

nizam. System; routine, especially of a bureaucracy.

qabili. Tribal; a social category of people of recognized Arab tribal descent.

qadi. Judge who administers the Shariʿah (Islamic law).

rafiq. Bedouin companion; guarantor of safe passage through a tribally controlled territory.

rashshash. Sprinkler; machine gun; central pivot irrigation mechanism.

rashshashat. Plural of *rashshash.*

riba. Interest; usury.

rizq. Bounty; luck.

sagh. Bushel.

sammari. Folk songs and folk dances traditional to ʿUnayzah.

samn. Ghee.

sanadiq. Trunks; boxes; shacks.

saniʿ. Craftsworker; artisan.

sawani. A mechanism for and a system of irrigation traditional to the Qasim.

saʿy. Commission.

shawk. Thorn; thorny plant.

simum. Hot wind from the southwest that sometimes blows in the autumn and spring.

subi. Youth; apprentice.

subiyan. Plural of *subi.*

subrah. A type of (long-term) leasing arrangement.

sukkari. A type of date of excellent quality.

sultah. Authority; sovereignty.

sunna‘. Plural of *sani‘*.

suq. Market; marketplace.

suq al-harim. Women's market.

tajir. Merchant; trader.

tufrah. Boom.

tuftar. Booklet; notebook.

tujjar. Plural of *tajir*.

tzat. Alfalfa.

‘ulama’. Plural of *‘alim*.

umara’. Plural of *amir*.

umm. Mother.

‘uqaylat. Plural of *‘uqayli*.

‘uqayli. Long-distance trader; paid soldier; in the past, labor migrant.

‘ushb. A type of desert grass highly valued by the Bedouin and collected by people of ‘Unayzah for fodder.

ustadh. Master craftsman.

wahah. Oasis.

wajh. Literally, face; a complex pattern involving honor, protection, and safe passage granted by an amir or other shaykhs of a tribe.

wali. Governor, especially of a province of the Ottoman Empire.

waqf. Islamic trust.

watan. Homeland; nation.

waznah. A weight measure.

zaffah. Procession.

zakat. Religious tax; tithe.

zira‘ah al-qadimah. Old agriculture.

zira‘ah at-taqilidiyah. Traditional agriculture.

BIBLIOGRAPHY

ʿAbd al-Jawad, Inʿam
> 1981 "Al-ʿAwamil al-Binaʾiyah al-Muhadiddah lil Musharakah al-ʾIjtima-ʿiyah lil Marʾah al-Khalijiyah" (Structural factors constraining the Gulf woman's social participation). In *Al-Marʾah wal-Tanmiyah fil Thamaniyat* (Women and development in the eighties). Proceedings of the Second Regional Conference on Women in the Gulf and Arabian Peninsula 1:147–169.

ʿAbd al-Mutʿi, ʿAbd al-Basit
> 1981 "Fi al-Waʿi az-Zaʾif lil-Marʾah al-Khalijiyah" (On the Gulf woman's false consciousness). In *Al-Marʾah wal-Tanmiyah fil Thamaniyat* (Women and development in the eighties). Proceedings of the Second Regional Conference on Women in the Gulf and Arabian Peninsula 2:723–734.
> 1982 "Fi at-Taklifah al-ʾIjtimaʿiyah lil-ʿAmalah al-Asyawiyah fil Khalij" (On the social cost of Asian labor in the Gulf). *al-Mustaqbal al-ʿArabi* 37:40–52.

Abdel-Fadil, Mahmoud
> 1987 "The Macro-behaviour of Oil-Rentier States in the Arab Region." In *The Rentier State,* ed. Hazem Beblawi and Giacomo Luciani, 83–107. London: Croom Helm.

Abu-Lughod, Janet L.
> 1971 *Cairo: 1001 Years of the City Victorious.* Princeton: Princeton University Press.

Adams, Richard N.
> 1975 *Energy and Structure, A Theory of Social Power.* Austin: University of Texas Press.
> 1982 *Paradoxical Harvest: Energy and Explanation in British History, 1870–1914.* New York: Cambridge University Press.

1988   *The Eighth Day: Social Evolution as the Self-Organization of Energy.*
       Austin: University of Texas Press.

Almana, Mohammed

1980   *Arabia Unified: A Portrait of Ibn Saud.* London: Hutchinson Benham.

Altorki, Soraya

1973   "Religion and Social Organization of Elite Families in Urban Saudi
       Arabia." Ph.D. dissertation, University of California, Berkeley.

1977   "Family Organization and Women's Power in Urban Saudi Ara-
       bian Society." *Journal of Anthropological Research* 33(3):277–287.

1980   "Milk Kinship in Arab Society: An Unexplored Problem in the
       Ethnography of Marriage." *Ethnology* 19(2):233–244.

1982   "The Anthropologist in the Field: A Case of 'Indigenous Anthro-
       pology' from Saudi Arabia." In *Indigenous Anthropology in Non-
       Western Countries,* ed. Hussein Fahim. Chapel Hill: Carolina Aca-
       demic Press.

1986   *Women in Saudi Arabia: Ideology and Behavior among the Elite.* New
       York: Columbia University Press.

1987a "The Ideology and Praxis of Female Employment in Saudi Ara-
       bia." *Journal of South Asian and Middle East Studies* 10(4):51–76.

1987b "Tafawut al-Qiyam fi al-Mujtamaʿ al-ʿArabi as-Saʿudi" (Ideologi-
       cal lag between the generations in the changing society of Saudi
       Arabia). *al-Mustaqbal al-ʿArabi* 97(3):76–90.

1987c "Dawr at-Tawhid al-Thaqafi fi Nushuʾ al-Mujtamaʿ as-Saʿudi"
       (The role of cultural homogeneity in the rise of Saʿudi society). *al-
       Yaqazah al-ʿArabiyah* 3:107–130.

Amin, Samir

1973   *Le Développement inégal.* Paris: Les Editions de Minuit.

1982   *The Arab Economy Today.* London: Zed Press.

Barsalou, Judith Marie

1985   "Foreign Labor in Saʿudi Arabia: The Creation of a Plural So-
       ciety." Ph.D. dissertation, Columbia University.

Barth, Fredrik

1983   *Sohar: Culture and Society in an Omani Town.* Baltimore: Johns
       Hopkins University Press.

Beblawi, Hazem

1987   "The Rentier State in the Arab World." In *The Rentier State,* ed.
       Hazem Beblawi and Giacomo Luciani, 49–62. London: Croom
       Helm.

Bindaji, Hussein Hamza

1978   *Atlas of Saudi Arabia.* Oxford: Oxford University Press.

Birks, J. S., and C. A. Sinclair

1980   *International Migration and Development in the Arab Region.* Geneva:
       ILO.

Bujra, Abdalla S.
1971   *The Politics of Stratification: A Study of Political Change in a South Arabian Town.* Oxford: Clarendon Press.

Cardoso, Fernando Enrique, and Enzo Faletto
1969   *Dependencia y desarrollo en América Latina.* Mexico City: Siglo XXI Editores.

Chatelus, Michel
1987   "Policies for Development: Attitudes towards Industry and Services." In *The Rentier State,* ed. Hazem Beblawi and Giacomo Luciani, 108–137. London: Croom Helm.

Cole, Donald P.
1971   "The Social and Economic Structure of the Al Murrah: A Saʿudi Arabian Bedouin Tribe." Ph.D. dissertation, University of California, Berkeley.
1973   "The Enmeshment of Nomads in Saudi Arabian Society: The Case of the Al Murrah." In *The Desert and the Sown: Nomads in the Wider Society,* ed. Cynthia Nelson, 113–128. Berkeley: University of California, Institute of International Studies, Research Series, no. 21.
1975   *Nomads of the Nomads: The Al Murrah Bedouin of the Empty Quarter.* Chicago: Aldine Publishing Company.
1981   "The Bedouin and Social Change in Saudi Arabia." *Journal of Asian and African Affairs* 16:128–149.
1982   "Tribal and Non-Tribal Structures among the Bedouin of Saʿudi Arabia." *al-Abhath* 30:77–93.
1984   "Alliance and Descent in the Middle East and the 'Problem' of Patrilateral Parallel Cousin Marriage." In *Islam in Tribal Societies: From the Atlas to the Indus,* ed. Akbar Ahmad and David Hart, 169–186. London: Routledge and Kegan Paul.

Coon, Carleton S.
1965   *Caravan: The Story of the Middle East.* New York: Holt, Rinehart and Winston.

Doughty, Charles M.
1979   *Travels in Arabia Deserta.* New York: Dover Publications. (First published 1888.)

Eickelman, Christine
1984   *Women and Community in Oman.* New York: New York University Press.

Fergani, Nader
1983   *Al-Hijrah ila an-Naft: ʾAbʿad al-Hijrah lil ʿAmal fil Buldan an-Naftiyyah wa Atharuha ʿala at-Tanmiyah fil Watan al-ʿArabi* (Migration to the oil: Dimensions of migration for work in oil countries

and its effect on development in the Arab homeland). Beirut: Markaz Dirasat al-Wahdah al-ᶜArabiyah.

Fernea, Elizabeth Warnock, and Robert A. Fernea

1985 *The Arab World: Personal Encounters.* Garden City: Anchor Press/ Doubleday.

Fernea, Robert A.

1970 *Shaykh and Effendi: Changing Patterns of Authority among the El Shabana of Southern Iraq.* Cambridge: Harvard University Press.

1987 "Technological Innovation and Class Development among the Beduwin of Hail, Saudi Arabia." In *Terroirs et sociétés au Maghreb et au Moyen Orient,* ed. Byron Cannon, 389–405. Paris: Maison de l'Orient.

First, Ruth

1975 *Libya: The Elusive Revolution.* New York: Africana Publishing Company.

Frank, André Gunder

1979 *Dependent Accumulation and Underdevelopment.* New York: Monthly Review Press.

Gerholm, Thomas

1977 *Market, Mosque, and Mafraj: Social Inequality in a Yemeni Town.* Stockholm: Studies in Anthropology, no. 5.

Habib, John S.

1978 *Ibn Saᶜud's Warriors of Islam: The Ikhwan of Najd and Their Role in the Creation of the Saᶜudi Kingdom, 1910–1930.* Leiden: E. J. Brill.

Hajrah, Hassan Hamza

1982 *Public Land Distribution in Saudi Arabia.* London: Longman.

al-Hamad, Turki

1986 "Tawhid al-Jazirah al-ᶜArabiyah: Dawr al-ʾIdyulujiyah wa al-Tanzim fi Tahtim al-Bunyah al-ʾIjtimaᶜiyah al-ʾIqtisadiyah al-Muᶜayyiqah lil-Wahdah" (The unification of the Arabian Peninsula: The role of ideology and organization in destroying the socioeconomic structure which hinders unity). *al-Mustaqbal al-ᶜArabi* 93:27–40.

Harik, Iliya

1987 "The Origins of the Arab State System." In *The Foundations of the Arab State,* ed. Ghassan Salamé, 19–46. London: Croom Helm.

Helms, Christine Moss

1981 *The Cohesion of Saudi Arabia.* London: Croom Helm.

Ibrahim, Saad Eddin

1982 *The New Arab Social Order: A Study of the Social Impact of Oil Wealth.* Boulder: Westview.

al-ᶜIsa, Juhayrah

1983 "al-Taʾthirat al-ʾIjtimaᶜiyah lil Murabiyah al-Ajnabiyah ᶜala al-

Usrah" (The social effects of foreign nannies on the family). In *al-ʿAmalah al-Ajnabiyah fi ʾAqtar al-Khalij al-ʿArabi* (Foreign workers in the Arabian Gulf), ed. Nader Fergani. Beirut: Markaz Dirasat al-Wahdah al-ʿArabiyah.

Katakura, Motoko
1977   *Bedouin Village: A Study of a Saudi Arabian People in Transition.* Tokyo: University of Tokyo Press.

Khan, Joel S., and Josep R. Llobera, eds.
1981   *The Anthropology of Pre-Capitalist Societies.* Atlantic Highlands, N.J.: Humanities Press.

al-Khatib, ʿUmr Ibrahim
1982   "at-Tanmiyah wal-Musharakah fi ʾAqtar al-Khalij al-ʿArabi" (Development and participation in the Arab Gulf region). *al-Mustaqbal al-ʿArabi* 40:4–26.

Khawajkiyah, Muhammad Hisham
1986   "Tajribat at-Tanmiyah al-ʾIqtisadiyah min Muntalaq al-ʾIstiqlal wa at-Tabʿiyah fi al-Mamlakah al-ʿArabiyah as-Saʿudiyah" (The experiment of economic development from the perspective of autonomy and dependence in Saudi Arabia). *al-Mustaqbal al-ʿArabi* 92:107–147.

Khouri, Faud
1980   *Tribe and State in Bahrain: The Transformation of Social and Political Authority in an Arab State.* Chicago: University of Chicago Press.

Kingdom of Saudi Arabia
1984   *Achievements of the Development Plans 1390–1404 (1970–1984): Facts and Figures.* Riyadh: Ministry of Planning.
1987   *Annual Report 1406 (1986).* Riyadh: Saudi Arabian Monetary Agency.

Kishk, Muhammad Jalal
1981   *As-Saʿudiyun wa al-Hal al-Islami: Masdar Sharʿiyah lil Nizam as-Saʿudi* (The Saudis and the Islamic solution: A source of legitimacy for the Saʿudi regime). Cairo: al-Matbaʿah al-Fanniyah (1984 edition).

Lapidus, Ira
1967   *Muslim Cities in the Later Middle Ages.* Berkeley and Los Angeles: University of California Press.

Lawrence, T. E.
1935   *Seven Pillars of Wisdom, A Triumph.* Garden City: Doubleday, Doran and Company.

Mabro, Robert
1969   "La Libye, un état rentier?" *Projet* 39: 1090–1101.

Mahdavy, H.
1970   "The Patterns and Problems of Economic Development in Rentier

States: The Case of Iran." In *Studies in the Economic History of the Middle East,* ed. M. A. Cook. London: Oxford University Press.

Meillassoux, Claude

1981   *Maidens, Meal, and Money: Capitalism and the Domestic Community.* Cambridge: Cambridge University Press.

al-Misallam, Ibrahim

1985   *al-ᶜUqaylat* (The *ᶜuqaylat*). Riyadh: Dar al-Asasalah lil Thaqafah wa al-Nashr wa al-ᵓAᶜlam.

Mynthi, Cynthia

1979   *Women and Development in Yemen Arab Republic.* Eschborn: German Agency for Technical Cooperation.

an-Najjar, Baqir

1985   "Athar li-ᶜAmalah Wafidah am ᶜAwaqib li-Maᵓzaq Tanmawi: Halat al-ᵓAqtar al-ᶜArabiyah al-Khalijiyah al-Musadirah lil-Naft" (Effects of expatriate labor or consequences of development bottlenecks: Conditions of Arab Gulf oil-exporting regions). *al-Mustaqbal al-ᶜArabi* 82:114–129.

Nowshirvani, Vahid

1987   "The Yellow Brick Road: Self-Sufficiency or Self-Enrichment in Saudi Agriculture?" *Middle East Report* 17(2):7–13.

Palerm, Angel

1976   *Modos de producción y formaciones socioeconómicas.* Mexico City: Editorial Edicól.

Palmer, Monte, Ibrahim Fahad Alghofaily, and Saud Mohammed Alnimir

1984   "The Behavioral Correlates of Rentier Economies: A Case Study of Saudi Arabia." In *The Arabian Peninsula: Zone of Ferment,* ed. Robert W. Stookey, 17–36. Stanford: Hoover Institution Press.

Philby, Harry St. John

1928   *Arabia of the Wahhabis.* London: Constable and Company.

Rihani, Amin

1976   *Muluk al-ᶜArab* (Kings of the Arabs). Beirut: Dar al-Rihani lil Tibaᶜah wal Nashr. (First published 1924.)

Rosenfeld, Henry

1965   "The Social Composition of the Military in the Process of State Formation in the Arabian Desert." *Journal of the Royal Anthropological Institute* 95:75–86, 174–194.

Rumaihi, Muhammad Ghanim

1975   *al-Pitrul wa at-Taghayyur al-ᵓIjtimaᶜi fi al-Khalij al-ᶜArabi* (Oil and social change in the Arab Gulf). Cairo: Dar ash-Shaᶜb.

1981   "ᵓAthr an-Naft ᶜala Wadᶜ al-Marᵓah al-ᶜArabiyah fi al-Khalij" (The effects of oil on the status of the Arab woman in the Gulf). *al-Mustaqbal al-ᶜArabi* 34:99–116.

1984   *Muᶜawiqat at-Tanmiyah al-ᵓIjtimaᶜiyah wa al-ᵓIqtisadiyah fi Mujtamaᶜat al-Khalij al-ʿArabi al-Muʿasirah* (Obstacles to social and economic development in the contemporary societies of the Arabian Gulf). Kuwait: Sharikat Kazimah lil Nashr wa at-Tarjamah wa at-Tawziʿ.

Saʿd ad-Din, Ibrahim, and Mahmoud Abdel-Fadil

　1983　*Intiqal al-ʿAmalah al-ʿArabiyah: Al-Mashakil wa al-Athar al-Siyasiyah* (Transfer of Arab labor: Problems and political effects). Beirut: Markaz Dirasat al-Wahdah al-ʿArabiyah.

Safran, Nadav

　1985　*Saudi Arabia: The Ceaseless Quest for Security.* Cambridge: Harvard University Press.

Sahlins, Marshall

　1972　*Stone Age Economics.* Chicago: Aldine Publishing Company.

Said, Edward W.

　1978　*Orientalism.* New York: Pantheon.

Salamé, Ghassan

　1980　*As-Siyasah al-Kharijiyah as-Saʿudiyah Mundhu ʿAmm 1945* (Saʿudi foreign policy since 1945). Beirut: Maʿhad al-Inmaʾ al-ʿArabi.

Sharif, ʿAbd ar-Rahman Sadiq

　1970　*Mantiqat ʿUnayzah: Dirasah ʾIqlimiyah* (ʿUnayzah district: A regional study). Cairo: Matbaʿat an-Nahdah al-ʿArabiyah.

Sirageldin, Ismail A., Naiem A. Sherbiny, and M. Ismail Serageldin

　1984　*Saudis in Transition: The Challenges of a Changing Labor Market.* Oxford: Oxford University Press.

Sjoberg, Gideon

　1960　*The Preindustrial City, Past and Present.* Glencoe: The Free Press.

Sowayan, Saad Abdullah

　1985　*Nabati Poetry: The Oral Poetry of Arabia.* Berkeley and Los Angeles: University of California Press.

Sweet, Louise E.

　1965　"Camel Raiding of North Arabian Bedouin: A Mechanism of Ecological Adaptation." *American Anthropologist* 67:1132–1150.

　1971　*The Central Middle East: A Handbook of Anthropology and Published Research on the Nile Valley, the Arab Levant, Southern Mesopotamia, the Arabian Peninsula, and Israel.* New Haven: HRAF Press.

Tidrick, Kathryn

　1981　*Heart-beguiling Araby.* Cambridge: Cambridge University Press.

Vasiliev, Aleksei Mikhaïlovich

　1986　*Tarikh al-ʿArabiyah as-Saʿudiyah* (History of Saudi Arabia). Moscow: Dar al-Taqaddum. (First published in Russian, 1982.)

Vidal, F. S.

　1955　*The Oasis of Al-Hasa.* Dhahran: Arabian American Oil Company.

Wallerstein, Immanuel

　1974　*The Modern World System: Capitalist Agriculture and the Origin of the*

European World Economy in the Sixteenth Century. New York: Academic Press.

al-Wasil, ʿAbd ar-Rahman bin ʿAbd Allah

1986   "al-ʿUmran ar-Rifi fi Mantiqat ʿUnayzah" (Rural settlement in ʿUnayzah district). M.A. thesis, Imam Muhammad Ibn Saʿud University, Saudi Arabia.

Waterbury, John

1972   *North for the Trade: The Life and Times of a Berber Merchant.* Berkeley and Los Angeles: University of California Press.

Wikan, Unni

1982   *Behind the Veil in Arabia: Women in Oman.* Baltimore: Johns Hopkins University Press.

Winder, R. Bayly

1965   *Saudi Arabia in the Nineteenth Century.* New York: St. Martin's Press.

Wolf, Eric R.

1982   *Europe and the People without History.* Berkeley and Los Angeles: University of California Press.

INDEX